THE WORLD IN STAMPS

LAURENT LEMERLE

THE WORLD IN STAMPS

TRANSLATED FROM THE FRENCH BY ALAYNE PULLEN

ABRAMS, NEW YORK

CONTENTS

SOCIETY

COMPETITIVE SPORTS

NATURE

APPENDIX

DISTRIBUTION OF STAMPS BY COUNTRY

This book contains 3,581 stamps from 208 different issuing countries, listed here in order of the number of stamps chosen. This selection is the result of personal choice to illustrate the 113 different themes of this book, with as broad a range of countries as possible, and comes from my personal collection.

United States: 261 stamps; France: 228; Great Britain: 210; Russia: 156 (187 including the new independent republics); Germany: 142; China: 132; Japan: 113; Italy: 85; Spain: 75; Austria: 64; Brazil: 59; Poland: 55; Turkey: 51; Vietnam: 50; Belgium: 49; Canada: 46; Hungary and New Caledonia: 45; Greece: 43; India: 42; Australia and French Polynesia: 41; Mexico: 38; Laos: 35; Portugal: 34; Korea (North and South) and Czechoslovakia: 33; Taiwan: 30; Egypt and Switzerland: 27; Argentina: 26; French Southern and Antarctic Lands, Chile, Morocco, and Norway: 25; Algeria and Republic of Ireland: 24; Senegal, Sweden, and Tunisia: 23; Iran, Mongolia, and Romania: 22; South Africa: 21; Cuba: 20; Netherlands and Wallis & Futuna: 19; Denmark: 18; Cambodia and Niger: 17; Congo: 16; Benin, Indonesia, Mali, French Equatorial and West Africa: 15; United Arab Emirates, Ivory Coast, Mayotte, New Zealand, Sri Lanka, St. Pierre & Miquelon, and Thailand: 14; Burkina, Central African Republic, Colombia, Israel, Monaco, Peru, Togo, and the Vatican: 13; Somali coast (Afars and Issas), Bulgaria, Finland, Madagascar, and Chad: 12; Angola, Bolivia, Iceland, Mauritania, and Syria: 11; Bosnia, Comoros Islands, Lebanon, Singapore, and Ukraine: 10.

The remaining 10 percent of stamps represent 120 more countries:

Gabon, Mauritius, Pakistan, Philippines, Vanuatu, and Yugoslavia: 9; Cameroon, Estonia, Hong Kong, Kenya, Liechtenstein, and Uruguay: 8; Faeroe Islands, Guinea, Luxembourg, Malaysia, Malta, Namibia, and Slovakia: 7; Croatia, British territories (Jersey, Guernsey, Isle of Man, Gibraltar), Kazakhstan, Macao, Nicaragua, and Rwanda: 6; Afghanistan, Bhutan, Djibouti, Slovenia, Tanzania, and Venezuela: 5; Cyprus, Ecuador, Ghana, Grenada, Jordan, Libya, Lithuania, Micronesia, Nepal, Paraguay, San Marino, Swaziland, Tajikistan, and Zimbabwe: 4; Aland, British Antarctic Territory, Dutch Antilles, Bahamas, Bahrain, Belarus, Burundi, Ethiopia, Fiji Islands, Greenland, Guinea-Bissau, Haiti, Iraq, Jamaica, Lesotho, Montserrat, Mozambique, Nigeria, Transkei, the United Nations, Uzbekistan, and Zaire: 3; Albania, Andorra, Antigua, Saudi Arabia, Azerbaijan, Bangladesh, Guyana, Panama, Spanish Sahara, Sierra Leone, St. Vincent, St. Helena and Union Island: 2; and finally 1 stamp from each of the following issuing countries: Aitutaki, Anguilla, French Antilles, Armenia, Ascension Island, Barbados, Bermuda, Biafra, Botswana, Burma, Cape Verde, Cayman Islands, Christmas Island, Ciskei, Cocos Islands, Cook Island, Falkland Islands (Malvinas), Equatorial Guinea, French Guyana, Kuwait, Kyrgyzstan, Latvia, Liberia, Macedonia, Maldives, Nauru, Palestine, Papua, Pitcairn Island, Rio Muni, El Salvador, Sealand, Seychelles, St. Kitts, St. Lucia, Surinam, Trinidad, Tristan da Cunha, Turkmenistan, Turks and Caicos Islands, Virgin Islands, and Zambia.

In total, Africa and the Middle East are represented by 614 stamps, Europe by 1,553, Asia and the Pacific by 816, and the Americas by 598 stamps.

ACKNOWLEDGMENTS

To my wife Brigitte for her unfailing support and her judicious corrections;
To my daughter Vanessa for her decisive help in rewriting the history of the world;
To Biche and Paul, without whom this work would never have seen the light of day.

Thanks to Gauthier Toulemonde and Michel Melot, of *Timbres Magazine*, for their enlightened advice on philately.
Thanks equally to all those who brought me stamps from distant countries to enrich this book: my daughter Virginie, Paul and Jacqueline, Annie and Philippe, Alain, Renée, Corinne, Pierre, and Christiane.
Finally, thanks to Mrs Xiao-Qing Pellemele for her luminous explanations of Chinese stamps, and to Mrs Weber and Mrs Ashley for their help in the United States.

I should also like to pay tribute to Willy, Stéphane, Pierre-Marie, and Nathalie for their outstanding teamwork at Éditions de La Martinière in the Herculean task that was the final selection of stamps.

The author and publisher must also thank Anne Grunenwald for her assistance, as well as those individuals, artists, and rights holders who have given their permission to reproduce the works that appear in this book, in particular Pierre Albuisson, Louis Briat, François Bruère, Francine Deroudille, Christophe Drochon, Mrs Renée Forget, Roxane Jubert, Jean-Claude Mézières, and Plantu.

PREFACE

Invented in 1840 by Rowland Hill, stamps were originally simply a means of indicating that delivery of a letter had been prepaid. However, they soon attracted collectors interested in the envelopes and different postmarks used, which were often evocative of distant destinations.

In the 20th century, "commemorative" stamps began to appear: these were no longer restricted simply to certain official figures but celebrated famous events, places, and individuals through images on hundreds of thousands of letters — the "illustrated stamp" was born. The obvious promotional advantages for countries meant that numbers increased rapidly to the point where now, at the beginning of the 21st century, as many different images are issued each week as appeared during the entire first century of the stamp's existence. Many small countries take advantage of this lucrative source of currency from collectors of theme-based stamps with an annual philately program as extensive as that of much larger nations and run for commercial rather than postal purposes.

There are some 500,000 different stamps in the world. Many of these provide fascinating evidence of the image that postal authorities wish to give of their country, year by year. They reveal the cultural continuity of many nations while also reflecting the evolution of their political "propaganda" or their vision of different aspects of society. In addition, stamps are an exceptional tool for raising awareness and for educating people, and are used in international campaigns in support of major humanitarian causes such as "the fight against racism" and "world hunger." Many stamps are also aesthetic objects in their own right, reproducing beautiful works of art from cultures all over the world, the wonders of nature, the power and commitment of Olympic athletes, and major industrial and architectural achievements. If we compare the images presented by countries geographically remote from us, we can gain a better understanding of how different cultures may see the same subject.

With such a wealth of raw material to draw on, finding a way of conveying this diversity in what is necessarily a limited number of examples proved far from easy.

At the outset I had decided to select "the world's most beautiful stamps," but discovered that the criteria for judging the "beauty" of a stamp are far too subjective. Moreover, this type of selection would have resulted in the elimination of stamps considered ordinary aesthetically speaking, but which may be of great importance in a country's cultural heritage. Out of the many subjects addressed on a global scale, rather than choose the most "beautiful" stamp on a particular subject, I have opted to apply the criterion of legitimacy — that is to say, selecting according to a subject's country of origin (for example, German stamps to reflect German cars, and Japanese stamps to illustrate Kabuki, the traditional form of Japanese theater). This also means that where a number of choices are possible the criteria of aesthetics or originality can still come into play, the simple criterion being: "That's a stamp I'd like to have in my collection."

To ensure a sense of balance, I have endeavored to include as many countries or regions of the globe as possible for each theme. However, to avoid the volume becoming prohibitively large, and thus losing clarity, the number of stamps had to be limited, which led to some agonizing decisions.

In the end, the book nevertheless contains over 3,500 stamps, issued by more than 200 countries.

The choice of themes also stems from a desire to reflect the great variety of stamps in existence. However, the subjects most often addressed in philately are not necessarily always the same as those found in history books or volumes on art, the sciences, and animals. Historically, it is dogs, cats, and dinosaurs, and images of Lenin and Princess Diana that are over-represented on postage stamps.

Conversely, there may be those who object that a certain subject has not been included. Given the immensity of stamp production, it is quite possible that some particular type of stamp has eluded me, but often there is simply no stamp on a particular subject. For example, there are no images of Mohammed as this is forbidden by the Koran; there is no commemoration of genocides such as those in Cambodia or Rwanda, whereas the Jewish Holocaust has been the subject of numerous issues from various countries.

Philatelists may be surprised, or even shocked, to find their stamps either enlarged or made smaller. This is deliberate: no stamp is shown true to size as legislation in most countries prohibits the reproduction of stamps at their actual size.

I hope that through my endeavors the reader will find in this volume what I wished it to be: a reflection on the stamp as a tool for "reading" the world of the past and the present, and the aesthetic satisfaction of discovering many beautiful or highly original stamps, often designed by internationally renowned artists.

If I succeed in persuading readers to start collections of their own on a theme of their choice I will consider my aim accomplished.

A HISTORY OF MANKIND

PREHISTORIC MAN

Countries in Africa, Europe, and Asia have used stamps to celebrate the evolution of prehistoric man, from his earliest origins to the dawn of the great civilizations. Today, Africa is considered the cradle of mankind, with the appearance of the genus *Australopithecus* some 3 to 6 million years ago. The first hominids evolved to walk upright, created tools, discovered fire, and moved into the Eurasian continent 1.8 million years ago. It was only much later that they began to spread across the continent of America, crossing the Bering Strait 30,000 to 50,000 years ago.
In Europe, archaeologists have taken an interest in our prehistoric past since the 19th century, focusing on such celebrated sites as the Lascaux caves in France and Altamira in Spain.

The countries of north and sub-Saharan Africa have also issued stamps commemorating the prehistoric heritage of their region, where rock paintings have been discovered showing that 10,000 years ago the desert of today was a verdant land abounding in game.
This panoramic view of our origins also extends from the first towns created in the 6th millennium BCE by the sedentary farmers of Asia Minor to the megalithic civilization, dating from 4,000 years BCE in Europe and Africa — that is to say 1,000 years before the first pyramids of Egypt.

CHAD 1966
Skull of 2 million year old *Tchad anthropus* (excavated by Yves Coppens in Chad). It was also in Chad that another of our ancestors, known as Toumai and dating back over 6 million years, was found.

CAMBODIA 2001
The evolution of prehistoric man.
• Australopithecus *anamensis* (Africa, 4 million years ago) stood upright and walked.
• *Homo erectus* (1 million years ago) walked upright and used tools.
• Neanderthal man (300,000 years ago) buried his dead. Competed with *Homo sapiens* (our common ancestor), who appeared 80,000 years ago.

FRENCH TERRITORY OF THE AFARS AND ISSAS 1973
Stone tools.
• Shaped disk and axe.

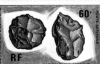

CHINA 1991
Homo sinensis (500,000 years ago).

FRANCE 1992
Tautavel man (450,000 years ago): used fire and hunting weapons.

CROATIA 1999
Kaprina woman (300,000 years ago): facial reconstruction.

SRI LANKA 1994
Year of Indigenous Peoples (prehistoric man with bow).

UNITED STATES 1991
The first Asians cross the frozen Bering Strait to America.

ITALY 1988
Isernia man (736,000 years ago): carving stone tools.

FRANCE 1968
Paintings of horses and bison in the Lascaux Caves (15,000 years BCE).

SPAIN 1967
Painting of a bison in the Altamira Caves (from 16,000 to 9,000 years BCE) during a glacial period.

SPAIN 1967
Negative handprint in the El Castillo Cave.

FRANCE 1976
Brassempouy Venus, a 1¼-inch-high (3cm) ivory figurine (20,000 years BCE).

LESOTHO 1983
Rock painting: bushmen (1500 BCE).

FRENCH TERRITORY OF THE AFARS AND ISSAS 1974
Rock carving in Balho.

CHAD 1998
Prehistoric man and rock carvings in a valley in the Tibesti mountains.

ALGERIA 1967
Rock painting in the Tassili mountains: archers.

MAURITANIA 1975
Rock painting in Zemmour: elephant.

CHAD 1968
Bailloud expedition to Ennedi.
• Courtly scene: woman and harp player.
• Quarrel scene.

MAURITANIA 1966
Rock painting from Adrar: hunter and antelope.

CHAD 1966
Buta Kebira excavations: Sao art figurine.

LAOS 1991
Plain of jars, Xieng Khuang province.

TURKEY 1992
Fertility goddess (6000 BCE) at Catal Höyük, one of the earliest Neolithic villages.

NORWAY 1966
Rock painting of a skier, 4,000 years old.

Megaliths

FRANCE 1965
The menhirs at Carnac (3200 BCE), purpose unknown (perhaps worship of the dead or astronomical observatory).

DENMARK 1966
Dolmen.

SENEGAL 1967
Megalithic lyre stone in Kaffrine.

GUERNSEY 1977
Sculpted menhir: "La Gran'mere du Chimquiere" (The Old Lady of Chimquiere).

ANCIENT EGYPT AND PERSIA

Among the earliest organized civilizations, it was that of Ancient Egypt that lasted for the longest period of time: almost three millennia (from 3100 to 332 BCE), thanks to a centralized structure dominated by the sacred figure of the pharaoh and supported by a strong, structured administrative system composed of scribes and priests.

Rediscovered in 1798 by scholars accompanying Napoleon Bonaparte on his military expedition, and rendered comprehensible by Champollion's deciphering of hieroglyphics in 1822, Ancient Egypt set the western mind alight. The colossal task that was the construction of the pyramids, the mystery of the civilization's sacred rights, and the discovery of the tomb of Tutankhamun by Howard Carter in 1922 and the fabulous riches it revealed, all contributed to perpetuating this fascination with Ancient Egypt throughout the 20th century. Today, stamps relating to Ancient Egypt are much sought after.

The Nile, Egypt's "source of life," is also present as a theme: the construction of a massive dam on the river in 1970 inspired UNESCO to take decisive action to safeguard the Nubian monuments; this rescue operation was supported by many countries which raised funds through a campaign of coordinated stamp issues.

Yet philately has done little to commemorate other powers that struggled for supremacy in Asia Minor in ancient times (the Hittites, Assyrians, Babylonians, and Philistines, for example), with the exception of Persia, which is remembered in a fine series of Iranian stamps dedicated to Cyrus the Great (c. 500 BCE).

The principal countries to issue stamps on Egypt are those whose archaeologists have contributed most to bringing its treasures to light: France, Great Britain, Germany, and, of course, Egypt itself.

EGYPT 2003
The golden mask of Tutankhamun (1350–1342 BCE); this pharaoh, who restored the religious order overthrown by his father Akhenaton, died at the age of 20. His tomb remained undisturbed by robbers until its rediscovery.

FRANCE 1972
Scholars on Napoleon Bonaparte's expedition to Egypt.

EGYPT 2003
The Sphinx at Giza – a protective monster with the head of a pharaoh and the body of a lion.

GREAT BRITAIN 2003
Sarcophagus dating from 900 BCE.

EGYPT 1988
The Great Pyramids at Giza: the Cheops (2590 BCE), Chephren, and Mykerinos Pyramids.

EGYPT 2003, GERMANY (GFR) 1988
Nefertiti, wife of Akhenaton and follower of the cult of Aton. Her bust is currently in the Berlin Museum.

GREAT BRITAIN 1972
Discovery of the fabulous tomb of Tutankhamun by Howard Carter and Lord Carnarvon in 1922.

FRANCE 1972
Champollion's deciphering of hieroglyphics in 1822.

EGYPT 2003
The Rosetta Stone. The same text is inscribed on the stone in hieroglyphs, and Greek and Aramaic script, making it possible to decipher the hieroglyphs.

EGYPT 1985
Akhenaton (reigned 1370–1350 BCE); the pharaoh who introduced the cult of Aton, and revolutionized the arts by encouraging distorted representations of the human form.

FRANCE 1976
Rameses II (reigned 1298–1232 BCE), one of the most illustrious of the pharaohs known for his conquests and building projects.

EGYPT 2003
The sacred eye of Horus or Eye of the Pharaohs.

EGYPT 2003
A scribe, an administrative servant, seated cross-legged.

EGYPT 1967
Anubis, god of the dead, with the head of a jackal.

EGYPT 2002
The library at Alexandria, the largest in antiquity, in the city founded by Alexander the Great in 332 BCE.

EGYPT POST بريد مصر ٢٠٠٢
125PT ١٢٥ق مكتبة الإسكندرية القديمة

EGYPT 1994
Performance of Aïda, the Egyptian heroine of Verdi's opera, in Luxor.

EGYPT مصر بريد
1994 اوبرا عايدة 15P ١٥ق OPÉRA AIDA

IVORY COAST 1964
Rameses II and Nefertari at Abu Simbel.

REPUBLIQUE DE COTE D'IVOIRE
60F UNESCO
POSTE AERIENNE
SAUVEGARDE DES MONUMENTS DE NUBIE

EGYPT 1972
Rising waters in the Temple at Philæ.

فيله ١٩٧٢ ٥٥
UNESCO PHILAE 1972
POSTAGE
55M AR EGYPT جمهورية مصر العربية

DDR
DETAIL VOM ISCHTARTOR VON BABYLON UM 580 V U Z
VORDERASIATISCHES MUSEUM ZU BERLIN
20

GERMANY (GDR) 1966
Detail of the Ishtar Gate, Babylon.

LIBAN ٣٠ق لبنان
LE LIBAN INVENTEUR DE L'ALPHABET
30P
POSTE AERIENNE

LEBANON 1966
The Phoenicians invent the first alphabetic form of writing in the 16th century BCE.

الجمهورية الجزائرية الديمقراطية الشعبية
UNESCO ALGERIE
0.30 POSTES

ALGERIA 1964
Statues submerged under the waves.

الملكة المغربية
SAUVEGARDE DES MONUMENTS NUBIE
0.30
ROYAUME DU MAROC
UNESCO
ZAVOD ZA IZRADU NOVĆANICA · BEOGRAD · JUGOSLAVIJA

MOROCCO 1963
The goddess Isis.

Stone head of a bull, Achemenidian period.

Golden winged lion with horns, Achemenidian period.

Parthian prince.

Persian archer.

CÉLÉBRATION DU 2500ème ANNIVERSAIRE DE LA FONDATION DE L'EMPIRE PERSE PAR CYRUS-LE-GRAND
4 R.
TÊTE D'UN TAUREAU EN PIERRE, ÉPOQUE ACHÉMÉNIDE.
IRAN 1971-1350 ایران

CÉLÉBRATION DU 2500ème ANNIVERSAIRE DE LA FONDATION DE L'EMPIRE PERSE PAR CYRUS-LE-GRAND
5 R.
LION AILÉ ET CORNU, EN OR, ÉPOQUE ACHÉMÉNIDE.
IRAN 1971-1350 ایران

FONDATION DE L'EMPIRE PERSE PAR CYRUS-LE-GRAND CÉLÉBRATION DU 2500ème ANNIVERSAIRE DE LA
1971 1350
IRAN
PRINCE PARTHE.
10 R.

CÉLÉBRATION DU 2500ème ANNIVERSAIRE DE LA FONDATION DE L'EMPIRE PERSE PAR CYRUS-LE-GRAND 1971-1350
IRAN
6 R.
ARCHER PERSE

Iran 1971: 2,500th anniversary of the foundation of the Persian Empire by Cyrus the Great

THE GRECO-ROMAN WORLD

Between 1400 and 1200 BCE, the Mycenaean civilization, discovered by the German archaeologist Heinrich Schliemann in 1876, reached its pinnacle. Unlike Egypt, which was a centralized state, Greece was composed of independent city-states unified by Philip of Macedon and then by his son Alexander the Great during the 4th century BCE.

Today, Greece celebrates with its stamps the figures and exploits of this ancient time that still persist in western culture — its philosophers, the founders of modern democracy, the mythology of the gods of Olympus, the epic tales of heroes such as Herakles (Hercules), and the Olympic Games.

In 332 BCE, Alexander's Greek Empire extended as far as Egypt and Mesopotamia. In the 1st century BCE, it was annexed by Rome, a city built on military organization and exemplary politics, which would go on to create the first Mediterranean-European Empire by assimilating into its system the nations it conquered: Africa, Iberia, Gaul, Britannia. At the height of the Roman Empire, in the 2nd century, a Roman citizen could move freely from the Middle East to England without changing either his language or currency. Unlike Greece, which has issued many stamps on the theme of Ancient Greece, modern-day Italy has been relatively slow to produce stamps on the Roman Empire. Paradoxically, the finest stamps on this period are to be found in the countries conquered by Rome: France, Spain, Tunisia, and England.

Following the division in two of the Roman Empire, in 476 the western empire collapsed under the onslaught of the Barbars, while the eastern, Byzantine Empire continued until 1453.

GREECE 1968
The Winged Victory of Samothrace: marble statue dating from the 3rd century BCE. The statue, its wings swept back, commemorates a naval victory.

GREAT BRITAIN 2003, GREECE 1968
Alexander the Great, Greek conqueror of Asia Minor and Egypt.

FRANCE 1982
Statue of Greek ephebe, discovered in Agde (Languedoc).

GERMANY (GDR) 1990
The Lion Gate: in 1876 archaeologist Schliemann began his excavations on Mycenae.

GREECE 1998
Greek philosophers: Sophocles and Plato.

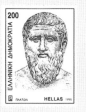

FRANCE 1999
Statue of Venus discovered on the Isle of Milo.

GREECE 1965
Citadel of the Acropolis, overlooking Athens: fortress and religious center from the 2nd millennium BCE.

GREECE 1984
Head of a horse on a frieze from the Parthenon (Acropolis). The frieze is in the British Museum in London.

GREECE 1958
Zeus, king of the gods of Olympus.

GREECE 1968
The city of Athens is named after Athena, goddess of war and wisdom (bronze, 2nd century BCE).

GREECE 1970, GREECE 1966
Greek vase decorations.
• The labors of Herakles (Hercules) on an ochre background: the Erymanthian boar and the centaur Nessus.
• Dionysus, god of wine and drunkenness, dancing (on a black background).

SAN MARINO 1971
Sarcophagus of the spouses (Etruscan sarcophagus sculpture).

ITALY 1981
Etruscan warrior (bronze statue).

ITALY 1944
The Founding of Rome (753 BCE): Roman she-wolf suckling Romulus and Remus.

TUNISIA 1976
Mosaic from a Roman villa in Africa showing the poet Virgil.

ITALY 1979
Aeneas, hero of Virgil's epic, the Aeneid, which recounts the origins of Rome.

UNITED STATES 2004
Athlete of the Athens Olympic Games in 2004, recalling the 1st Olympiad of 776 BCE.

GREECE 1991
The Muses.

ITALY 1957
Cicero, lawyer and politician, brilliant orator and author of the Catiline Oration.

TUNISIA 1995
Hannibal, Carthaginian general who fought against Rome (2nd Punic War, 218–201 BCE); crossed the Alps with his elephants.

SYRIA 1969
Roman amphitheater at Palmira.

SPAIN 1974
The Emperor Trajan (53–117), born in the Roman province of Spain.

FRANCE 1966
Vercingetorix, leader of the Gaul insurgents.

GREECE 1965
Performance in the ancient theater of Epidaurus.

GREECE 1969
Chorus of an ancient Greek tragedy.

SPAIN 1968
Iberian (Spanish) soldier of the 7th Roman Legion.

GREAT BRITAIN 1993
Roman emperors.

GERMANY (GFR) 1977
Bronze head of a centaur (Schwartzenacker, Germania).

GREECE 1961
Emperor of the Eastern Roman Empire, liberator of Crete in 961.

FRANCE 2002
The Nîmes Arena (Roman province of Gallia Narbonensis).

TUNISIA 1976
Mosaic of a lioness. Wild animals were much valued for their ferocity in the arena.

• Claudius, conqueror of the province of Britannia (England) in 43 CE.

• Hadrian, who built the defensive wall between England and the barbarians of Scotland.

ANCIENT CHINA

Far away in the Orient, a remarkable civilization developed in northern China from the 2nd millennium BCE to the 2nd century BCE. Many inventions such as the compass and paper originated in China. With calligraphy, writing had become a major art form, conferring even greater prestige on imperial mandarins (scholarly officials) than on soldiers or merchants, with erudition being the most highly respected moral value.

The rules of good conduct for the honest man laid down by Confucius around 500 BCE became legally binding for more than a millennium and competed with existing religions.

In the 5th century BCE, to protect themselves from Barbar invasions, the Chinese had begun to build a vast wall almost 4,000 miles (6,000km) long: the largest construction ever made by man. The wall and its fortifications were completed in 220 BCE by the Qin dynasty emperor, whose tomb contained the spectacular terracotta army of 7,000 life-size soldiers and horses that were buried with him.

Another way of protecting against Barbar attacks was to enlist the support of Barbar chiefs by giving them Chinese princesses in marriage. After the fall of the Han dynasty in 220 CE, and a period of struggle between the three kingdoms (the Wei, Shu-Han, and Wu), imperial dynasties ruled one after another until the 12th-century Mongol invasion.

Modern Chinese stamps celebrate this rich historical heritage in a refined and easily recognizable style of art that derives from ancient paintings.

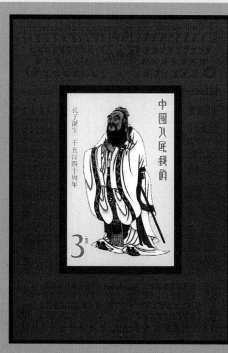

CHINA 1989
Confucius (555–479 BCE), Chinese functionary who founded a philosophy based on individual wisdom and respect for tradition that enabled society to live together in harmony.

CHINA 1962
The inventor of the paper manufacturing process (1st century) and a paper works.

CHINA 1953
Chinese inventions of the 1st millennium.
• The compass (300 BCE).
• Seismograph for detecting earthquakes (2nd century BCE).
• Drum cart for measuring distances (300 BCE).

CHINA 1979
The Great Wall (3rd century BCE) seen in different seasons. It was modernized under the Ming dynasty (1368–1644).

CHINA 1990
Chariot driver and horse (220 BCE).

CHINA 1984
Imperial seal in red ink.

CHINA 1984
Example of the art of calligraphy.

CHINA 1989
The teachings of Confucius influenced China for 2,500 years.

CHINA 1983
Terracotta army found in the tomb of the Qin emperor who unified the empire in 221 BCE.

CHINA 1989

Chinese literary masterpiece *Outlaws of the Marsh*.
• Qin Ming on horseback pursued by a flight of arrows.
• Single-handed combat on the water.

CHINA 1994

Marriage of a princess of the Han court with the barbarian king Ziongnu.
• The princess departs by camel.
• The marriage ceremony.

CHINA 1994

History of the late Han dynasty *Romance of Three Kingdoms* (battles c. 220 BCE).
• Passionate address.
• Warriors on horseback with lances.

CHINA 1953

Wall paintings in the Tun Huang caves.
• Battle scene (between 581 and 617).
• Ox-drawn palanquin (between 618 and 906).
• Messenger with horse (between 386 and 580).
• Offerings.

REPUBLIC OF CHINA

TAIWAN 1992

Imperial dignitaries: general and prime minister.

CHINA 1995

Shaolin Temple (Henan province) c. 495: 13 monks come to the aid of the Qin prince.

TAIWAN 1962

Chinese emperor of the Song dynasty (960–1279).

TAIWAN 1962

Chinese emperor of the Tang dynasty (618–907).

CHINA 1981

Vase with tiger, Song dynasty (960–1279).

CHINA 1961

Tang dynasty pottery (618–907): donkey and horse.

INVADERS AND SETTLERS

For the Greeks and then the Romans, people from outside the empire were considered "barbarians," as they knew nothing of writing. The absence of written records of the many tribes ruled by the oral tradition makes it impossible today to discover their view of history. However, the abundance and beauty of the objects found in their tombs indicates an advanced civilization, and their skill in working bronze and later iron was sufficient to reverse the balance of power with the Romans.

During the 1st millennium, there were impressive barbarian migrations towards the west: the Huns, who came from the confines of Northern China, invaded central Europe and laid waste the land as far as Gaul in 451; the Goths and the Vandals from central Europe founded kingdoms as far away as Spain and North Africa (431); the Angles and Saxons besieged England from the 5th to 9th centuries, driving the Celts westward; the Germanic Franks

subjugated Gaul (480) and in 800 Charlemagne founded the first European Empire, encompassing France, Germany, Austria, and Northern Italy.

The Vikings, who were exceptional navigators, left Scandinavia in the 9th century to pillage the monasteries of western Europe. They also colonized Normandy, and discovered Iceland, Greenland and North America. Although stamps from most European countries on this "barbarian" period of Europe's history are relatively scarce, Viking epics and mythology have been abundantly commemorated in stamps issued by Nordic countries.

In the 11th century, when the christianization of Europe was complete, the end of slave trafficking brought the Vikings' principal activity to a halt.

In 1066, the Normans successfully invaded England — the last successful invasion of the country in history — and displayed their talent as administrators with the *Domesday Book* census.

ROMANIA 1973
Treasure of the Daces of Pietroasa: gold fibulas.

Barbarian invasions

FRANCE 1966
The Vix Crater (Burgundy), a gigantic, Greek bronze vase, providing evidence of trade between the Greeks and Celts.

UKRAINE 1999
Art of the Steppes (4th century BCE): animal figurines (Scythian gold from the nomadic Scythes tribe).

SWEDEN 1995
• Bronze cult figurines.
• Gold necklace with imaginary animals and masks.

FRANCE 1966
Clovis, leader of the Franks, baptized in Rheims in 492.

GREAT BRITAIN 1999
5th-century migration of the Scots from Ireland to Caledonia, which later became Scotland.

GREAT BRITAIN 1997
St. Columbus, the Irish monk who founded the Caledonian monasteries in the 6th century.

GREAT BRITAIN 1997
St. Augustine, sent by the Pope in 546 to evangelize the Anglo-Saxons; founded Canterbury.

TURKEY 1984
Raids by Attila (395–453) and the Huns (descendants of the Xiongnu Chinese barbarians).

GERMANY (GDR) 1987
Roland, nephew of Charlemagne, killed in the Saracen ambush at Roncesvalles in the Pyrenees.

BULGARIA 2001
Creation of the first Bulgarian state from the merger of Turko–Mongol tribes with the Slavs (7th century).

HUNGARY 1995
Finno–Hungarian tribes from the north arrive in the Carpathian Basin.

FRANCE 1966
Charlemagne, emperor of the west in 800, visiting the schools he founded in the empire.

UNITED STATES 1968
Leif Erikson lands in America (1001).

DENMARK 1976
Drakkar braving the Atlantic on route to America.

FAEROE ISLANDS (DENMARK) 2002
The Viking crossing of the Atlantic: Shetland Isles, Faeroe Islands, Iceland, Greenland, and America.

ISLE OF MAN 1998
The Vikings pillage a castle.

AUSTRIA 1972
The christianization of Europe: creation of the diocese of Gurk in 1072.

HUNGARY 1970
Stephen I, saint and founder of the first Hungarian state, in the year 1000.

POLAND 1988
Casimir I, the Restorer (1016–1058), brought order to Poland.

The Normans

GREAT BRITAIN 1986
Domesday Book 1086: census made by the Normans of the property and population of England.

FRANCE 1958, GREAT BRITAIN 1966
The Battle of Hastings (1066), which marked the start of the Norman conquest of England, has been commemorated by both France and Britain with stamps showing scenes from the Bayeux Tapestry (11th century), embroidered by Queen Matilda, wife of William the Conqueror: Norman horsemen and English infantry.

KNIGHTS

Almost every country in Europe has produced stamps on the theme of chivalry, showing battle scenes and tournaments. However, the Samurai, the Japanese equivalent of knights, are only represented on Japanese stamps in the form of theatrical performances.

Chivalry arose with the raising of moral standards by the Church during the 10th century and the feudal system in force in Europe in the Middle Ages: the knight was bound by oath to his suzerain, and owed him loyalty and support in war, while the suzerain lord was bound to protect his vassal and provide him with the means to live.

A knight was a man of great physical strength who knew how to fight. His horse and his weapons, which were very costly, were given to him by his suzerain lord at the dubbing ceremony, where he swore allegiance to his

lord. Wars and tournaments provided an opportunity for the knight to profit from the spoils and from ransoms paid by the vanquished. Tournaments were also occasions on which a knight could demonstrate his bravery and prowess in front of other knights and ladies.

In the 11th century, the art of "courtliness" began to emerge in the seigniorial courts of southern France and during the following century spread to northern Europe. Courtliness described a new attitude of respect toward women: the knight had to earn the love of his lady through the exploits he executed on her behalf. The ideal knight was valiant, faithful to his word, generous to the weak and magnanimous to his adversaries. He traveled far and wide in search of adventure and glory as typified in the tales of King Arthur and the Knights of the Round Table.

FRANCE 1967
Philip Augustus, King of France, at the Battle of Bouvines (1214).

UKRAINE 2001
Daniel Romanov (1201–1264), son of the founder of the state of Kiev, at the head of his troops.

FRANCE 1964
12th-century Limousin knight.

GREAT BRITAIN 1985
The Knights of the Round Table.
• Sir Lancelot on horseback with Guinevere, wife of King Arthur.
• Sir Galahad and the quest for the Holy Grail.

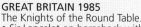

UKRAINE 1999
12th-century knight with sword and shield, astride a golden lion, the emblem of Ukraine.

BOSNIA-HERZOGOVINA 2003
King Stephen I Kotromanic, in his castle (12th century).

USSR 1967
Alexander Nevski (1220–1263), crushing the Teutonic knights in 1242 (at the "Battle on the Ice" fought on a frozen lake). He governed as a vassal of the Mongols.

FRANCE 2004
Eleanor of Aquitaine (1122–1204), daughter of the Duke of Aquitaine; later Queen of France, and then Queen of England; mother of Richard the Lionheart, and John Lackland.

UKRAINE 1998
Princess Anne of Kiev, married Henry I, King of France, in 1049.

FRANCE 1946
Joan of Arc (1412–1431). Exceptional in the history of chivalry, this young woman took arms at the age of 16 to "drive the English out of France." As a consequence of her exploits, she was burned alive in Rouen for witchcraft.

GREAT BRITAIN 1974
Knights of the Hundred Years' War.
• The Black Prince (1330–1376), son of Edward III, triumphed at the Battle of Poitiers.
• Henry V (1387–1422), won the Battle of Agincourt where the English archers demonstrated the superiority of their arrows over the armor of the French knights.

SLOVENIA 2003
Knight wounded at a tournament. The aim was to break one's own lance on the adversary's armor, not to kill him.

AUSTRIA 1969
Armor worn by Maximilian I of Hapsburg (16th century). After this period armor was rendered ineffective by the advent of firearms and was no longer ceremonial dress.

BELGIUM 2002
Battle of the Spurs at Courtrai (1302).

GERMANY (GFR) 1970
Knights preparing for combat.

POLAND 1972
Knight charging with lance (15th century).

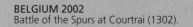

AUSTRIA 1978
Two knights fighting in a tournament (13th century).

GERMANY (GFR) 1975
Tournament in 1475.

SPAIN 1973
Knight of the Old Guard of Castile (1493).

THE SILK ROUTE

In 1206, Genghis Khan was crowned "universal chief" by the nomadic tribes of the Mongolian Desert. He unified the peoples of Asia in the largest empire ever to exist. In 1368, this empire was conquered by Tamburlane. In the 16th century, the Mongols were driven back from the Indian peninsula by Sher Khan. The height of his empire coincided with that of the Silk Route between East and West.

Silk fabric formed part of the rich gifts exchanged by the Chinese. Gradually it captivated the Parthians and then western Europe. The Silk Route, opened before the 2nd century, remained active for more than a thousand years. With its starting point in Xi'ang in the Shanxi province of China, it stretched as far as the ports of Antioch and Alexandria, crossing almost 4,000 miles (6,000km) of plains, deserts, marshes, and high mountains, and passing through China, central Asia, Afghanistan, Iran, Iraq, and Syria.

In addition to silk, other consumer goods passed along this strategic route and have been celebrated in images on stamps reminding us of this fact: items such as porcelain, and Chinese inventions like powder and paper traveled westward while products such as glass, as well as new religions (including Nestorianism and Islam), traveled eastward to China.
In the West, trade with the Orient was dominated by the Venetian and Genoese merchants, who, at this period, controlled the Mediterranean: Marco Polo's journeys to China and the court of the Great Khan date from 1279.
In the 14th century, the Silk Route was gradually abandoned due to the decline in Mongol power and the rise of the Turks, but also because of epidemics of the Black Plague in Europe. The abandonment of the Silk Route encouraged Europeans to search for a sea route to replace it, and led to the discovery of the New World (pages 28 and 29).

MONGOLIA 1997
Genghis Khan (1162–1227), founder of the Mongol Empire.

MONGOLIA 1997
Kubla Khan (1215–1294), founded the Yuan dynasty of China and opened up Peking to foreigners.

MONGOLIA 1997
Soldiers of Genghis Khan.

MONACO 2004
Marco Polo's travels in China (1254–1324).

SAN MARINO 1971
The Republic of Venice:
St. Mark's Square, by Canaletto.

TURKEY 1987
Tamburlane (or Timur Lang), 1336–1405, conquered a great empire in central Asia.

TURKEY 1989
Silkworm eating a mulberry leaf. The export of silkworms was punishable by death in China.

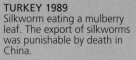

USSR 1969
Monuments of Samarkand, Tamburlane's capital city in the 14th century.

CHINA 1952
Wall paintings in the Tun-Huang cave, the final staging post in China of the Silk Route to the west.
• Mystical allegory of Buddha.
• Dragon.

TURKEY 2003
Ceremonial silk gown.

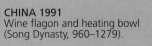

CHINA 1991
Wine flagon and heating bowl
(Song Dynasty, 960–1279).

CHINA 1981
Jar with phoenix (Yuang
Dynasty, 1280–1368).

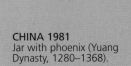

CHINA 1991
Blue and white porcelain vase,
Yuan period.

CZECHOSLOVAKIA 1985
Glass flagon with blue
handles (4th century).

CHINA 1991
Mount Hengshan under snow (Shanxi province).

Traded goods

TURKEY 2004
Caravan stop at a caravanserai.
These were built at intervals
of one day's travel along the
Silk Route.

AFGHANISTAN 1985
Caravan under the archway of
the citadel of Bost.

AFGHANISTAN 1984
Crossing the mountains on
oxen.

TURKEY 1973
Colossal heads at the
Mausoleum of Antiochus I
(69–34 BCE).

USSR 1978
Bronze statue at Erebuni in
Armenia (8th century).

PAKISTAN 1991
The emperor Sher Shah Suri, or Sher Khan (1472–1545), drove the
Mongols out of the Indian peninsula. The tiger in *The Jungle Book* is
named after him.

THE GOLDEN AGE OF ISLAM

During the 7th and 8th centuries, Islam underwent expansion which included, in 762, the removal of the caliphate of the Commander of the Believers from Damascus to Baghdad, and, in 756, the independence of the emirate of Córdoba. In the period from the 9th to the 11th centuries, Islamic intellectual ideas flourished and enjoyed widespread influence.

During this golden age, the refined splendors of the caliphate of Baghdad reached their pinnacle with Harun al-Rachid, a contemporary of Charlemagne. Andalusia had been conquered in 711 by Berber Arab armies, and in the city of Córdoba scholars and craftsmen of different religions — Muslim, Jewish, and Christian — lived and worked side by side. This period, in which philosophers, doctors, astronomers, and poets flourished, has been commemorated in stamps issued by Spain, the countries of North Africa, and the Middle East.

In the 11th century, the Seljuk Turks conquered the Byzantine Empire (at the Battle of Malazgirt), and took control of Baghdad and Jerusalem. This provoked a reaction among the Christians, and gave rise to the Crusades to liberate the tomb of Christ. Although triumphant in Jerusalem, the crusaders were defeated by Saladin in 1187, and were eventually driven out of the Middle East after a number of unsuccessful crusades. As a result, the Crusades have been commemorated on various stamps issued by Muslim countries in the Near East but rarely, if at all, by European countries. Between the 11th and 15th centuries, the rising power of the Ottoman Empire, which was to play a major role in central Europe and the Mediterranean after the capture of Constantinople in 1453, followed by the Catholic Reconquest of Spain, which was completed in 1492, marked the end of the Arab golden age.

SPAIN 1967
- Averroes (1126–1198), Arab scholar born in Cordoba, wrote commentaries on Aristotle.
- Maimonides (1135–1204), Jewish philosopher born in Cordoba, physician to the sultan of Egypt.

TURKEY 1957
Koca Sinan, architect of the Great Mosque of Soliman (1557).

TUNISIA 1984
Ibn el-Jazzar (878–980), doctor and philosopher, author of *The Traveler's Viaticum*.

TURKEY 1971
The poet Yunus Emre, died in 1321.

MOROCCO 1963
Ibn Khaldun (1332–1406), Arab historian and philosopher.

MOROCCO 1963
Ibn Battuta (1304–1378), great Arab traveler (visited Spain, China, and Russia).

TUNISIA 1987
Ibn Mandur (1233–1312), linguist and author of a monumental Arabic dictionary.

SYRIA 1994
Al-Kinsi, philosopher (1190).

TUNISIA 1980
Arab contribution to science (astronomy and introduction of the figure zero to the West).

SPAIN 1986
The astronomer Al-Zarqali (1029–1087), with astrolabe.

TUNISIA 1998
Doctors Ibn el-Jazzar, Ibn Suleiman, and Constantine the African (Latin translation).

COMOROS ISLANDS (FR) 1966
Avicenna (980–1037), Iranian doctor, philosopher, and mystic, author of *The Canon of Medicine*, forming the basis of medical study in the East and the West.

Doctors, philosophers, and scholars

SYRIA 1969
The Omeyyades Mosque in Damascus, founded in the 7th century.

AJMAN 1972
The Book of the *Thousand and One Nights* evokes the splendor of 9th-century Baghdad.

MOROCCO 1980
Europe and Africa linked by the Strait of Gibraltar.

SPAIN 1986
Sultan Abd al-Rahman II (792–852) and the arcades of the Cordoba Mosque.

TURKEY 1971
The Turkish victory at Malazgirt (1071) in central Anatolia.

Muslim achievements

SYRIA 1925
The Aleppo Fortress at the time of the Crusades.

SYRIA 1987, JORDAN 1974
Saladin triumphs against the crusaders at the Battle of Hattin (1187).

FRANCE 1959
Geoffrey of Villehardouin (1151–1213), one of the leaders and chronicler of the 4th Crusade.

The Crusades

EGYPT 1993
Saladin and the Dome of the Rock, the mosque constructed on the site of the Jerusalem Temple.

Battle of Constantinople

SPAIN 1999
El Cid Campeador (1043–1099), a great figure of the Spanish Reconquest.

PORTUGAL 1947
Reconquest of Lisbon from the Moors in 1147.

PORTUGAL 1999
Reconquest of the Algarve from the Moors in 1249.

TURKEY 1981
Sultan Mehmet, who conquered Constantinople in 1453.

GREECE 1968
Constantine the Paleologist (1404–1453), last Byzantine emperor.

SPAIN 1985
Battle between the Moors and Christians at Alcoy.

TURKEY 1992
Welcoming the Jews expelled from Spain in 1492.

The Spanish and Portuguese Reconquest

SPAIN 1988
Spanish soldiers of the Reconquest.

THE RENAISSANCE AND THE WARS OF RELIGION

The strong population growth in 15th-century Europe, the rejection of feudal values, the thirst for discovery and new ventures, and the wider diffusion of ideas as a result of the newly developed printing process made the Renaissance a pivotal period in which Europe, from the 16th century onward, gained ascendancy over the other continents — a fact it has chosen to commemorate in numerous stamps.

With Spain, the Low Countries, Germany, and the Spanish colonies under his scepter, Charles V ruled an empire "on which the sun never set," stretching from Europe as far as the Pacific Ocean.

In England, Henry VIII juggled his alliances between Charles V and Francis I, but when the Pope refused him permission to divorce his first wife, Henry created his own church, the Anglican Church, which was independent of the Vatican. During the 16th century, this in turn provoked conflicts and persecutions, and would eventually lead Spain to intervene and suffer the loss of its fleet, the Armada, in 1588.

In Italy, despite internal struggles between the city-states, there was a flowering of the arts with the Renaissance. When Francis I of France embarked, unsuccessfully, on war with Italy, he discovered the new art being produced there and promoted it by inviting Italian artists to visit his country.

The proliferation of new ideas also produced schisms between Christian faiths, with some speaking out in favor of the "Reformation" of the Catholic Church. These theological disputes, which were underpinned by political motives, culminated in veritable wars of religion between Catholics, Lutheran Protestants, and Calvinists. Eventually, most of northern Europe ended up in the Protestant camp in the 16th century. On Europe's eastern borders, where the Ottoman Empire had replaced the Byzantine Empire, Turkish civilization reached its pinnacle under Soliman the Magnificent, who ruled an empire stretching from Hungary to Iraq, and from the Black Sea to Algeria.

England

GREAT BRITAIN 1973
Sir Francis Drake (1541–1596), explorer and admiral, triumphed over the invincible Armada.

GREAT BRITAIN 1988
The invincible Spanish Armada harried by the English fleet, and finally destroyed in a storm.

BELGIUM 2000
Charles V (1500–1558), Germanic emperor, King of Spain and Sicily, prince of the Netherlands.

GERMANY (GFR) 1954
Gutenberg and the first bible, printed in 1454.

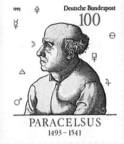

GERMANY 1993
Paracelsus (1493–1541), doctor and alchemist.

BELGIUM 1979
Till Eulenspiegel: legend about a hero who played tricks on the nobility and clergy, published in 1515.

GERMANY 1995
Emperor Maximilian I and the Diet of Worms, 1495.

Henry VIII and his six wives

GREAT BRITAIN 1997
Henry VIII (1491–1547), King of England.

GREAT BRITAIN 1997
The six wives of Henry VIII:
Catherine of Aragon, divorced;
Anne Boleyn, executed;
Jane Seymour, died in childbirth;
Anne of Cleves, divorced;
Catherine Howard, executed;
Catherine Parr, survived the king.

FRANCE 1998
The Edict of Nantes, by which
Henry IV established religious
tolerance in France (1598).

GERMANY 1998
The Treaty of Westphalia (1648)
put an end to the war between
Protestants and Catholics in
Germany.

GERMANY 1999
Katharina von Bora
(1499–1552), Martin Luther's
politically active wife.

GERMANY (GFR) 1983
Martin Luther (1483–1546),
Protestant reformer.

FRANCE 1964
John Calvin (1509–1564),
Protestant reformer.

Wars of religion

FRANCE 1967
Francis I (1494–1547), King of France.

FRANCE 1952
Leonardo da Vinci (1452–1519),
painter, architect, sculptor,
engineer.

ITALY 1952
Savonarola (1452–1498),
intransigent Catholic preacher,
instigator of a dictatorship of virtue,
excommunicated by the Pope and
put to death by the Florentines.

USSR 1978
Modern version of Leonardo da
Vinci's "Vitruvian Man," reflecting
the universal reach of his work.

Turkey

ALGERIA 1966
Barbarossa (1476–1546), Turkish
privateer, regent of Algiers.

ITALY 1949
Lorenzo de' Medici, Florentine prince and powerful
banker (Catherine de' Medici, his great-granddaughter,
would later become Queen of France).

SPAIN 1984
The perfect proportions of Leonardo
da Vinci's "Vitruvian Man."

TURKEY 1968
Miniature: receiving an
ambassador.

TURKEY 1969
Sultana Hafsa, mother of
Soliman.

TURKEY 2003
Soliman the Magnificent
(1494–1566), Ottoman
sultan.

ALGERIA 1981
Algerian pirate galley.

SPAIN 1971
The Battle of Lepanto (1571):
victory over the Turkish force.

OCEANIC DISCOVERY

During the 15th century, with the gradual decline in popularity of the Silk Route, intrepid navigators set sail to discover new oceans, driven by the need to find a sea route linking Europe with China and India in order to facilitate the trade in spices and other rare commodities. Their endeavors were made possible by the development of navigational instruments such as the compass for direction, and vessels like the caravel which could withstand high seas. The maps produced on these early explorations became jealously guarded secrets.

While the Chinese explored the seas to the west, the Portuguese, under Henry the Navigator, discovered Madeira, the Azores, the Cape Verde Islands, and the coasts of Africa. They rounded the south of Africa by the Cape of Good Hope, and in 1497 Vasco da Gama reached the East Indies and later became viceroy of India.

The Spanish headed west and discovered America in 1492. In 1494, with the Pope as arbiter, Portugal and Spain reached an agreement about sharing the new worlds waiting to be discovered. As a result, coastal areas of Africa, India, and Brazil became Portuguese territories, while the Pacific and the rest of the Americas became Spanish possessions. Portugal and its former colonies have commemorated this period rich in adventure through their stamps.

PORTUGAL 1998
King Manuel I visits the naval shipyards.

PORTUGAL 1990
Zarco and Teixeira discover Madeira in 1419.

PORTUGAL 1990
Silves discovers the Azores in 1432.

PORTUGAL AZORES 1997
The legend of the seven cities.

PORTUGAL 1994
Henry the Navigator (1394–1460), Portuguese prince who began the exploration of the African coast.

SENEGAL 1994
First contact between the Senegalese and the Portuguese in 1444.

SOUTH AFRICA 1988
Bartolomeo Diaz, the first European to round the Cape of Good Hope, in 1488.

CHINA 1985
The mariner Zheng (1405–1433), discovered the Indian Ocean and the South Pacific aboard a 425-ft (130m) junk (five times the size of a caravel).

PORTUGAL 1969
Vasco da Gama (1469–1524), founded trading posts in Mozambique and discovered the route to the East Indies in 1497. He was appointed viceroy of the Portuguese East Indies.

PORTUGAL 1998
Rounding the Cape of Good Hope.

PORTUGAL 1994
The Treaty of Tordesillas (1494), dividing the world between the Spanish and the Portuguese.

PORTUGAL 1993

Ferdinand Magellan (1480–1521), entered the service of Spain, and discovered the strait linking the Atlantic and Pacific (the Magellan Strait) in 1520, thus completing the first circumnavigation of the globe.

PORTUGAL 1998

Being received by the King of Malindi (on the east coast of Africa).

PORTUGAL 1997

Portuguese mariners put in at Natal (South Africa) in 1497.

The Lusiads (1572), an epic poem by Camoëns.
• Founding a mission in Angola.
• The island of Mozambique.

Património Classificado - Ilhas da Taipa e Coloane

MACAO 2003

The islands of Taipa and Colane, designated heritage sites.

BRAZIL 1968

Pedro Alvarez Cabral (1460–1526), discovers Brazil in 1500.

BRAZIL 1987

Gabriel de Sousa, wrote a *Descriptive Treatise on Brazil* in 1587.

TURKEY 2004

The Turkish admiral Piri Reis, produced the first map of the world showing the Americas (1513).

THE SPANISH CONQUEST OF THE NEW WORLD

Christopher Columbus, by royal appointment to Isabel the Catholic, Queen of Castile, sailed forth into uncharted waters with three caravels in the hope of discovering a western route to the Indies. On October 12, 1492 he touched land, probably the island of San Salvador in the Greater Antilles, and named the inhabitants "Indians," believing he had reached the Indies. In fact, Columbus had discovered the Americas, one of the largest continents on the planet. This key date in the history of mankind has been commemorated on stamps from all over the world, particularly in 1992, the 500th anniversary. In the 16th century, the courageous but brutal Spanish conquistadors were drawn to the New World by its supposed gold and other riches. They conquered vast territories with only a few hundred men – the natives were a thousand times greater in number, but less well armed and often peace-loving. Furthermore, epidemics of diseases inadvertently imported with the

Europeans led to the collapse of entire civilizations: the Incas in Peru, and the Aztecs and Mayas in Mexico. The richness of these pre-Hispanic civilizations is known to us through the many temples, sculptures, and manuscripts that have survived and which have been abundantly celebrated in the stamps of South American countries.

The Vatican, aware of what was at stake with the discovery of the New World, sent Catholic missionaries to evangelize the indigenous population. These missionaries were often forced to protect the native people from mistreatment by the colonists.

The Spanish colonization of Florida and California, eclipsed for many years by the Anglo-Saxon domination of North America, now occupies center stage due to the strong population growth that has made Hispanics the largest minority population in the United States of America.

ITALY 1992
The Genoese navigator Columbus, in the service of Spain, claims discovery of the Americas in 1492.

FRENCH POLYNESIA 1992
Commemorating the 500th anniversary of the discovery of the Americas: humorously, a native explains to the Spanish that they are not in the East Indies.

BRAZIL 1952
Isabel the Catholic, Queen of Castile, who appointed Columbus.

MEXICO 1971
The Dresden Codex (deerskin parchment).

PERU 1989
Low-relief from the Chan Chan temple.

PERU 1972
Head of an Inca warrior (Mochica civilization).

MEXICO 1980
Pre-Hispanic monuments: seated divinity.

GREAT BRITAIN 2003
15th-century Aztec mask.

COLOMBIA 2004
Gold Muisca raft. Gold fever was one of the conquistadors' prime motivations.

SPAIN 1963
Vasco Nuñez de Balboa: in 1513 he became the first man to reach the Pacific, leading an expedition of 90 men. Falsely accused of treason, he was beheaded in 1519.

SPAIN 1964
Francisco Pizarro (1471–1541), conquered Panama and Ecuador in 1529, then Cuzco in Peru with 250 men. Founded the city of Lima in 1535.

SPAIN 1968
Diego de Losada (1511–1569), conquered Venezuela in 1567.

SPAIN 1964
Francisco de Toledo (1520–1583), viceroy of Peru in 1569; abolished the forced labor used among the Incas.

SPAIN 1964
Archbishop Toribio de Mogrovejo (1538–1606), Grand Inquisitor of Spain, sent to Peru in 1581, peacefully converted the native people, built schools, hospitals, and chapels. Canonized in 1726.

VATICAN 1992
Discovery and evangelization of the Americas.

UNITED STATES 1982
Ponce de León (1460–1521), founded Porto Rico in 1511 and discovered Florida on April 2, 1513 (celebrated as *Pascua florida* day (Floral Easter). He faced up to the native warriors with 200 men.

UNITED STATES 1985
Brother Junípero Serra (1713–1784), founder of the Franciscan missions in California in 1769.

PERU 1970
Altar of the church of Las Nazarenas, Lima.

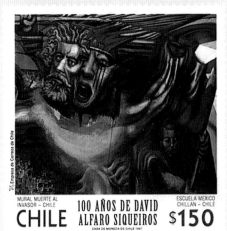

CHILE 1990
16th-century Inca figure and Spanish infantry soldier.

UNITED STATES 1984
The proud heritage of Hispanic Americans.

SPAIN 1969
Spanish mission in San Diego in 1769.

CHILE 1997
Mural "Death to the invader" (Mexican–Chilean school).

THE COLONIES OF NORTH AMERICA AND THE CARIBBEAN

In the 16th century, the English, French, and Dutch each set off to discover the New World, the northern part of which had been neglected by the Spanish and Portuguese. In Canada, John Cabot and Jacques Cartier searched for a sea passage to the Indies (1534), and Walter Raleigh explored Virginia.

The immensity of the North American continent, its harsh but healthy climate, and the richness of its lands attracted adventurers and colonists who strove with great fervor to explore and exploit it. In the early 17th century, a few hundred English people settled in Virginia, and a similar number in Quebec.

Two centuries later, as a result of massive immigration, there were 1.5 million English people in the new territories but only 60,000 French.

Fighting between English and French colonists, and between these same colonists and the native tribes (English against Iroquoi and French against Hurons), ended in 1783 with the Anglo-Saxon domination of North America. In the Caribbean, where they found the climate hard to bear, the Europeans, like the Portuguese in South America, turned to slave labor imported from Africa to work their sugar cane plantations, thus perpetuating the practice of slavery still current in the 17th century.

The West Indies were also a staging post for Spanish galleons laden with gold, and attracted pirates of all nationalities. Their pillaging and violence did not come to an end until the 18th century, and left behind a strong image in the popular imagination – piracy is a theme much sought after by philatelists.

CANADA 1934
In 1534, Jacques Cartier, sent by the King of France, discovered the St. Lawrence. He forged links with the Iroquois, but failed to find the passage to China that he was seeking.

GREAT BRITAIN 1973
Sir Walter Raleigh (1552–1618), poet, historian, and soldier, explored the coast of America to set up colonies. In 1585, he christened Virginia in honor of Queen Elizabeth I, the "Virgin Queen."

GREAT BRITAIN 1971
Martin Frobisher (1552–1618), searched unsuccessfully from 1576 to 1585 for a route to the Indies via the north of America.

CANADA 1958
In 1743, the French Canadian La Vérendrye (1685–1749) was the first person to reach the Rocky Mountains in the west.

CANADA 1972
Frontenac (1622–1698), governor of New France (Quebec).

CANADA 1973
The expulsion of the Acadians ("the Great Upheaval") and arrival of Scottish colonists in Acadia, renamed Nova Scotia.

BELGIUM 1962
The discoveries of the 16th century made it possible for Mercator to create a new map of the world (1578).

GREAT BRITAIN 1971
In 1610, Henry Hudson (1560–1611) reached Hudson Bay when the ice thawed, but was abandoned at sea by his crew.

FRANCE/CANADA 2004
In 1604, Pierre Dugua de Mons, at his own expense, founded the first colony in North America, in present-day Maine, with 80 French colonists.

CANADA 1991
The legend of the "chasse-galerie," or witch canoe.

CANADA 1975
Marguerite Bourgeoys (1620–1700), founded a Catholic congregation that cared for destitute children.

CANADA 1986
Molly Brant (1736–1774), a Mohawk, devoted to her people and to the British crown.

Canada

JERSEY 1976
Sir John Carteret, governor of Jersey and founder of the colony of New Jersey (1664).

UNITED STATES 1964
The founding of New Jersey, from the American viewpoint.

UNITED STATES 1987
Jean-Baptiste Pointe du Sable, a mestizo from the French colony of Haiti, founded Chicago in 1779.

UNITED STATES 1968
Father Marquette and French Canadians, explored the Mississippi in 1672.

FRANCE 1982
Cavelier de La Salle (1645–1687), discovered the mouth of the Mississippi in 1682 and founded the colony of Louisiana in honor of King Louis XIV.

UNITED STATES 1970
The Puritans of the *Mayflower*, fleeing religious persecution in England, landed in America in 1620.

GREAT BRITAIN 1999
The Pilgrim Fathers, from the English viewpoint.

The Americas

The West Indies

Pirates

GREAT BRITAIN 2003
The pirate flag the "Jolly Roger."

TURKS AND CAICOS ISLANDS 1971
Pirates burying their plundered booty on an island.

SAINT KITTS AND NEVIS 1973
The arrival of Sir Thomas Warner's English colonists in 1623.

DUTCH WEST INDIES 1959
Colonial buildings in Curaçao.

NETHERLANDS 1976
Michiel de Ruyter (1607–1676), admiral of the Dutch fleet, in the West Indies in 1674.

BAHAMAS 1997
Pirates of the Caribbean.
- Captain Edward Teach, known as Blackbeard (1680–1718). His fearsome reputation encouraged the boats he attacked to surrender quickly. He died from 20 wounds inflicted after being boarded by the Royal Navy.
- John Rackam, known as Calico Jack, sailed the Caribbean with his wife, Anne Bonny, disguised as a man. Boarded in 1720 without a fight, he was tried and hanged.
- Anne Bonny, together with Mary Read, was a member of Calico Jack's crew. Both women disguised themselves as men and were even fiercer in battle than some of the men. They were spared at the 1720 trial, as both claimed to be pregnant.

ANTIGUA 1970
Caribbean native and war canoe.

VIRGIN ISLANDS 1972
British sailor, c. 1800.

MARTINIQUE 1935
Belain d'Esnambuc, colonized Guadeloupe and Martinique in 1635.

GUYANA 1929
17th-century French colonization: natives in a canoe on the Oyapok river.

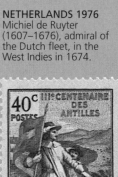

ST. VINCENT 1973
Slaves on a sugar cane plantation in the 18th century.

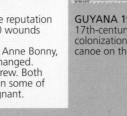

HAITI 1968
In 1804, Haiti became the first colony to gain independence, after the slaves revolted (the Bois Caiman ceremony, 1791).

TRINIDAD AND TOBAGO 1984
Toussaint Louverture, a former slave, led the fight against the colonists. He died in captivity in France, but his successors won independence.

THE INDIAN AND PACIFIC OCEANS

The first missions to evangelize the Far East were, in China, those of the Jesuits. In the 17th century, with the decline of Portuguese power, the English, French, and Dutch embarked on a battle for maritime trade with the East Indies. They, too, established trading posts along the African coast and on the islands of the Indian Ocean and, taking advantage of dissension over the decline of the Indian Empire, they fought one another to seize territorial concessions from the maharajahs.

In the 18th century, the British were finally victorious in the battle for India and began the systematic colonization of what would become the "pearl of the British Empire," while the Dutch colonized Indonesia, and French privateers used islands in the Indian Ocean as bases from which to attack and hold ransom foreign ships laden with goods.

In the Pacific, the Polynesians, using only their primitive dugout canoes, succeeded in colonizing myriad islands scattered across the largest stretch of water on the planet.

In the 18th century (the Age of the Enlightenment), navigators from Britain and Europe, including Cook and Bougainville, set out on scientific expeditions to explore these virtually uncharted, vast expanses of sea and land. Australia, a continent in its own right, was discovered by the Dutch and the east coast was colonized by the British, as was New Zealand.

In the 19th century, navigators pushed exploration as far as the icy wastes of Antarctica, finally conquering the frozen continent in 1840 (Dumont d'Urville on the Adélie Coast).

WALLIS AND FUTUNA 1986
Shouten and Lemaire, the first navigators to round Cape Horn, which they named after their home town in the Netherlands; they discovered the Horn (or Futuna) Islands in 1616.

FRENCH OCEANIA 1955
Tahitian girl combing her hair.

FRENCH POLYNESIA 1968
Antoine de Bougainville, discovered Tahiti in 1768 and vaunted its beauty.

FRENCH POLYNESIA 1976
Pirogue canoes with sails, used by Polynesian navigators.

PHILIPPINES 1984
Pirogue. The first Polynesians set out from south-east Asia and colonized all the islands of the Pacific by the 15th century.

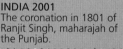

FRENCH ESTABLISHMENTS IN THE INDIES 1948
Temple of Chidambaram, at the height of Aurangzeb's rule (17th century).

FRANCE 1965
The French East India Company populated Bourbon Island (Reunion Island) in 1665.

FRANCE 1951
Robert Surcouf (1773–1827), privateer ennobled by Napoleon, plundered English and Dutch vessels.

MAURITIUS 1972
The French pirate Lememe and his brig, the *Hirondelle*.

MAURITIUS 1968
The novel *Paul and Virginia*, a tragic and moving tale of love between two colonist children, enjoyed worldwide popularity.

INDIA 2001
The coronation in 1801 of Ranjit Singh, maharajah of the Punjab.

JAPAN 1989
Dutch East Indiaman, the only vessel allowed in Japan in the 17th century.

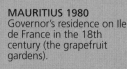

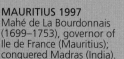

TAIWAN 1966
Adam Schall von Bell (1592–1666), German astronomer and Jesuit missionary in China.

INDIA 2004
Western vessels in Madras in the 18th century.

MAURITIUS 1997
Mahé de La Bourdonnais (1699–1753), governor of Ile de France (Mauritius); conquered Madras (India).

MAURITIUS 1980
Governor's residence on Ile de France in the 18th century (the grapefruit gardens).

SEYCHELLES 1969
Privateers preparing to board. In the 18th century, with the suppression of piracy in the Caribbean, pirates moved into the Indian Ocean.

AUSTRALIA 1988
The first colonization of Australia, in 1788.

GREAT BRITAIN 1999
Cook and indigenous Maori.

NEW HEBRIDES 1974
Cook's voyage of 1774: scientific study.

NEW ZEALAND 1994
Maori mythology: encounter with a monster from the deep.

COOK ISLANDS 1979
Death of Cook in Hawaii, 1779.

AUSTRALIA 1982
Aborigines and British immigrants living side by side.

FRENCH SOUTHERN AND ANTARCTIC LANDS 1981
Adèle Dumont d'Urville died with her husband in the first railway accident in history, near Paris in 1842.

FRENCH SOUTHERN AND ANTARCTIC LANDS 2000
Dumont d'Urville discovered the remains of the La Pérouse expedition and was the first person to set foot in Antarctica (1840). He named the place Adélie after his wife Adèle.

FRENCH POLYNESIA 1989
The Mutiny on the *Bounty*, 1789. The mutineers set their captain adrift at sea.

USSR 1991
Russian trading post in America (Pacific coast) in 1804.

ESTONIA 2003
Adam von Krusenstern, led the first Russian expedition to circumnavigate the globe in 1803.

NEW CALEDONIA 1988
The *Boussole* and the *Astrolabe*, ships on La Pérouse's round-the-world scientific expedition of 1787, authorized by King Louis XIV in 1787.

NEW CALEDONIA 1988
La Pérouse encountered the English fleet in Botany Bay (Australia) in 1788. His expedition, men and goods, disappeared shortly after in the Pacific. Note the French flag: white with three fleur de lys. The tricolor dates from the French Revolution, two years later (1790).

THE BIRTH OF THE UNITED STATES OF AMERICA

Having driven the French and Dutch from the 13 founding colonies on America's coast during the 18th century, the descendants of the British immigrants formed states and claimed independence, finding the tax burden and power of the English too onerous.

The Declaration of Independence, drawn up by Jefferson in 1776, is the document that marks the birth of the United States. Impassioned by the "Spirit of 76," Europeans, including La Fayette and Kosciuszkco, went to fight for the American cause. The War of Independence that followed ended in victory for the Americans, who were helped by the soldiers and gold provided by France. In 1976, many countries all over the world commemorated the bicentenary of American Independence through their stamps.

The expansion of the United States during the 19th century was remarkable: Louisiana was purchased from France in 1803 (constituting a third of the territory of the United States at that period); Florida was purchased from Spain in 1819; Texas defeated Mexico in 1845; and new states were created in the west in 1848.

Many Europeans (German, Irish, British, etc.) emigrated to the United States, fleeing famine and harsh living conditions in their countries of birth, or attracted by the prospect of owning and farming new lands. This "stampede to the west" has been amply celebrated by American cinema, highlighting the struggle between the colonists and Native Americans, as well as by numerous stamps dedicated to the brief but turbulent history of the United States.

The bloody years of the American Civil War (1861–1865), between the industrial north and the agricultural south, which used black slaves, ended in victory for the north and the abolition of slavery in the United States in 1865, following the examples of Great Britain in 1836 and France in 1848.

UNITED STATES 1973
The "Boston Tea Party" marked the start of rebellion by the American colonists who threw English merchandise overboard.

UNITED STATES 1977
George Washington (1732–1799), leader of the insurgents, praying at Valley Forge.

POLAND 1975
Tadeusz Kosciuszko (1746–1817), Polish officer who went to America to support the cause of independence.

MEXICO 1976
The cracked Liberty Bell in Independence Hall, Philadelphia. American Independence has been commemorated in many countries of the world.

DUTCH WEST INDIES 1961
The arrival in St. Eustache of the first American ship in 1776 was greeted with a gun salute.

FRANCE 1980
Rochambeau arrives in Newport in 1780 with 6,000 French soldiers and gold to help the American cause.

UNITED STATES 1977
English surrender at Saratoga in 1777.

UNITED STATES 1987
Drafting of the United States Constitution in 1787.

UNITED STATES 1973
The rise of the spirit of independence.
• Printing a patriotic pamphlet.
• Posting up public notices.
• Galloping messenger.
• Drummer.

GREAT BRITAIN 1976
Benjamin Franklin (1706–1790), physician, ambassador of the colonies in Great Britain, unified the first American states and was one of the principal architects of independence.

Lafayette

UNITED STATES 1977
Lafayette (1757–1834), a fervent partisan, was appointed major general in the army of independence at the age of 20.

UNITED STATES 1975
American sailor.

UNITED STATES 1976
"Spirit of 76": American volunteers set off to do battle in 1776.

UNITED STATES 2003
The "Louisiana Purchase": Louisiana purchased from France in the largest property sale of all time, anywhere: nine states, from the Great Lakes to the Gulf of Mexico.

UNITED STATES 1996
The creation of Iowa in 1846.

UNITED STATES 1947
The creation of Utah in 1847.

REPUBLIC OF IRELAND 1981
The agrarian law of 1881 reduced the rights of large landowners to some extent, after the famine of 1845 led to massive emigration by the rural population.

GERMANY (GFR) 1983
German immigration in 1683 on board the *Concord*.

REPUBLIC OF IRELAND 1988
Irish immigration from Cork to New York in 1838.

UNITED STATES 1999
The California Gold Rush (1849).

UNITED STATES 1993
The Cherokee Strip Land Run of 1893 saw towns rise from nothing along this 226-mile (362km) stretch of land.

UNITED STATES 1994
Figures from the "Legend of the West."
• Buffalo Bill: hunter, guide, Native American fighter, and flamboyant showman of the West.
• Annie Oakley, known as "Little Miss Sureshot": sharpshooter and star of Buffalo Bill's show.
• Chief Joseph, known as "Pierced Nose": eloquent war leader and tactician, drove back the American army.
• Bat Masterson: lawman and gambler who died slumped over his typewriter.
• Wyatt Earp: gunslinger, gambler, and stagecoach robber who fought at the OK Corral.

UNITED STATES 1995
American Civil War figures (1863–1865).
• Robert E. Lee, southern general.
• Ulysses S. Grant, northern general.
• Abraham Lincoln, President of the United States; abolished slavery in 1863, assassinated in 1865.
• Harriet Tubman, fought for the abolition of slavery.

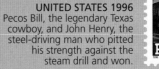

UNITED STATES 1964
The Battle of Wilderness, 1864.

UNITED STATES 1961
The Battle of Gettysburg, 1863.

UNITED STATES 1996
Pecos Bill, the legendary Texas cowboy, and John Henry, the steel-driving man who pitted his strength against the steam drill and won.

THE FRENCH REVOLUTION AND THE NAPOLEONIC WARS

In 1789, the French people (the Third Estate) challenged the absolute power of the monarchy and the privileges enjoyed by the nobility. The storming of the Bastille on July 14, 1789 was greeted in Europe as crucial, symbolizing the triumph of the modern ideas of the Enlightenment over the Ancien Régime. The impact of the French Revolution went well beyond the national boundaries of France and was emulated in other parts of the world. European monarchies were deeply disturbed by the Terror that held sway in France, initiated by Robespierre, who used the guillotine to execute nobles, clergy, and other opponents of the new regime.

In 1989, the bicentenary of the French Revolution was commemorated on stamps from all over the world.

The Declaration of the Rights of Man and of the Citizen of 1789 forms the basis of the modern Universal Declaration of Human Rights, adopted by the majority of the world's countries in 1948.

The Napoleonic Wars that followed the French Revolution, from 1799 to 1815, were fought only in Europe. Today, each of the countries involved has reflected its view of these events, in which gallantry and horror lived side by side, with some interesting stamps. It is an episode of history still talked about today and attracts many experts among collectors.

These wars also had other consequences: the wider diffusion of the ideas of the Revolution and the adoption of the remarkable Napoleonic Code by a number of countries.

FRANCE 1950
Danton, lawyer and revolutionary orator, guillotined during the Terror.

FRANCE 1950
Robespierre, leader of the revolutionaries, instigator of the death of the King and the Terror in 1793.

FRANCE 1936
Rouget de Lisle, composer of *La Marseillaise*, which became the French national anthem.

FRANCE 1988
Assembly of the Three Orders (nobility, clergy, third estate) in 1788.

BULGARIA 1989
Marat, doctor and revolutionary journalist, supported the massacres of September 1792.

USSR 1989
The *Marseillaise*, sculpture by François Rude at the Arc de Triomphe in Paris.

FRANCE 1989
Madame Roland, schoolteacher and founder of the Republican Women's Club.

FRANCE 1989
Kellerman, revolutionary general, saved the Republic at Valmy (1792).

FRANCE 1991
Planting "liberty trees" in 1791.

GERMANY (GDR) 1989
The storming of the state prison, the Bastille, in July 1789.

COLOMBIA 1989
"Liberty, Equality, Fraternity" (motto of the French Revolution).

POLAND 1989
The figure of Liberty in a Phrygian cap with a tricolor rosette.

UNITED STATES 1989
The French Revolution.

JAPAN 1998
Liberty Leading the People, painting by Delacroix to commemorate the July revolution of 1830.

REPUBLIC OF IRELAND 1979
Padraig Mac Piarais, Irish revolutionary in 1916, inspired by Delacroix's *Liberty*.

FRANCE 1972
Bonaparte at Arcole Bridge: feat of bravery by Napoleon Bonaparte at the age of 25.

FRANCE 1973
The coronation of Napoleon. Impatient, the new emperor himself crowns his wife Josephine.

SAAR 1947
Marshal Ney, victor at Elchingen, Friedland, "bravest of the brave" in Russia and at Waterloo.

ITALY 2000
Cavalry charge at the Battle of Marengo (1800), a victory for Bonaparte over the Austrians.

FRANCE 1973
Drawing up the Napoleonic Civil Code, still in force in France and in a number of other countries.

FRANCE 1962
Officer of the Imperial Guard (painting by Géricault, 1812).

HUNGARY 1978
Hussar of 1809. The Hungarian hussars were an elite corps that provided the inspiration for Napoleon's hussars.

POLAND 1992
Prince Poniatowski, Marshal of the Empire.

GERMANY (GFR) 1981
Karl von Clausewitz, Prussian general and theoretician of modern warfare.

GERMANY 1992
Gebhard von Blücher, Prussian marshal. His arrival was decisive for the allies at Waterloo.

FRANCE 1951
Emperor Napoleon. He made family members and close allies heads of European countries.

RUSSIA 1993
Kutusov, Russian marshal, forced Napoleon to retreat from Russia in 1812.

USSR 1987
The Battle of Borodino, 1812.

FRANCE 1989
Declaration of the Rights of Man and of the Citizen (1789), abolishing the privileges of the nobles.

GREAT BRITAIN 1982
Admiral Nelson, victor of the Battle of Trafalgar, 1805.

BELGIUM 1990
Waterloo, the Belgian plain where Napoleon was defeated in 1815.

ST. HELENA 1971
Wellington, victor of the Battle of Waterloo, painting by Goya.

ST. HELENA 1971
The death of Napoleon (1821): Napoleon on horseback (painting by David) and his tomb on the island.

39

THE NATION STATES OF EUROPE

Following Napoleon's defeat in 1815, his conquests in Europe were divided up by England, Russia, Austria-Hungary, and Prussia, with careful consideration for the balance of power; this was based on royal legitimacy but failed to take into account the growing nationalist sentiments of the people. Worsened by the economic crisis of the time, a revolutionary, nationalist movement swept across Europe, starting with uprisings in Paris and Vienna in 1848, and leading to the dismantling of the great empires: Austria and Hungary separated in 1867, but the Prague revolt was suppressed and the creation of the future Czechoslovakia (from Bohemia, Moravia, and Slovakia) had to wait until 1918. The Ottoman Empire gradually lost its European possessions: after Greece won its independence in 1821, Bosnia and Herzogovina freed itself from the yoke of Turkey in 1875, and Bulgaria and Serbia followed in 1878. Romania was created in 1859, after the Crimean War, uniting the once-Turkish areas of Wallachia and Moldavia, with further territories ceded by Russia. It became free from the Ottoman Empire in 1877. While Great Britain, Austria-Hungary, and France were already established powers, nationalist feeling drove more divided countries to seek unity: Italy between 1859 and 1870; Germany in relation to Prussia through the war against Austria in 1866 and against France in 1870. Poland was the major absentee from this new division of Europe: with each new insurrection the country lost a little more of its territory, which was divided between Russia, Prussia, and Austria, and disappeared from the map of Europe from 1795 to 1918.

The problem of the extreme nationalism of the Balkan countries had not been resolved and the region was a veritable powder keg in 1914, on the eve of the First World War. For philatelists it is interesting to explore the different ways in which countries have addressed the complex history of 19th-century Europe.

GREECE 1968
Greece on the Ruins of Missolonghi, by Delacroix: the legendary defense against the Turks from 1821 to 1826.

ROMANIA 1977
Romanian soldier of the war of independence against Turkey (1877).

GREECE 1971
The death of the Bishop of Salona at the Battle of Alamana (1821).

YUGOSLAVIA 1975
War of independence between Bosnia-Herzogovina and the Turks (1875).

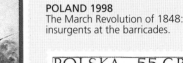

POLAND 1998
The March Revolution of 1848: insurgents at the barricades.

GREECE 1969
Greek ships in the fight for independence (1821).

GREECE 1977
The naval battle of Navarino (1827).

BULGARIA 1988
The Chiprovsko rebellion against the Ottoman Empire (1688): infantry charge.

HUNGARY 1950
General Jozsef Bem (1794–1850); expelled from the Imperial army, he led battles in the Hungarian and Polish revolutions before siding with the Turks.

HUNGARY 1944
Lajos Kossuth (1802–1894), one of the instigators of the 1848 revolution and the split with Austria.

BULGARIA 1978
Cossack and young Bulgarian girl (war of independence, 1878).

BULGARIA 1978
Bugler and liberation from the yoke of Turkey (1878).

SLOVAKIA 1998
The 1848 uprising.

BULGARIA 2003
Delchev (1872–1903), Macedonian apostle of the struggle for liberation against the Turks.

USSR 1987
Admiral Nakhimov and the Russian fleet at the defense of Sebastopol (1855).

RUSSIA 2003
Naval battle on the Black Sea (Crimean War 1854–1855).

ITALY 1982
Giuseppe Garibaldi and his Red Shirts: the Expedition of a Thousand to Sicily (1860).

ITALY 1959
The architects of independence (1859): Victor Emmanuel II, Garibaldi, Cavour, and Mazzini.

ITALY 1987
The Battle of Mentana (1867): French and papal forces defeat Garibaldi.

ITALY 1970
Garibaldi at Dijon in 1870, with the French against the Prussians.

GERMANY (GFR) 1986
King Louis II of Bavaria (1845–1886), a Romantic and depressive, he accepted Prussian protection.

GREAT BRITAIN 1987
Victoria (1819–1901), became Queen of England at 18 and Empress of India in 1876.

GERMANY (GFR) 1965
Bismarck (1815–1898), the architect of German unity.

FRANCE 1970
Colonel Denfert-Rochereau at the Prussian siege of Belfort (war of 1870–1871).

FRANCE 1966
Ambulance woman tending a wounded man at the Battle of Solferino, 1859.

AUSTRIA 2004
Marriage of Emperor Franz-Joseph to Elisabeth, known as Sisi (1854).

GREAT BRITAIN 1990
The world's first stamp (the Victoria one penny) and allegory of British power during the Victorian era.

SOUTH AMERICAN INDEPENDENCE

After three centuries of colonization by the Spanish and Portuguese, a wind of revolt blew across South America, fanned by the example of the French Revolution and American Independence. The uprising began in Uruguay in 1811 with the so-called "grito de Asencio."

In the space of ten years, two officers of Spanish origin liberated the majority of South America after a series of battles against loyalist forces. Simón Bolívar liberated what was then Colombia (present-day Venezuela, Colombia, Ecuador, and Panama), and José de San Martín liberated Argentina and the vice-kingdom of Peru (present-day Chile, Peru, and Bolivia).

San Martín left the presidency of Chile in the hands of a Chilean officer, O'Higgins, and that of Peru to Bolívar, while General Sucre, Bolívar's deputy, was elected president of the newly constituted Bolivia. Following the departure of San Martín in 1824 – who retired to France once his work was done – the new republics tore each other apart in fratricidal wars.

The principal liberators have been commemorated in stamps issued both by Spain and by the South American countries that were liberated.

Mexico was liberated from Spanish protection in 1821 through the action of rebel priests (Hidalgo and Morelos), and insurgent officers (Guerrero and Iturbide), but the country fell into the hands of creole landowners. After a troubled period, marked in 1845 by the loss of Texas and California to the United States, a second Mexican revolution took place between 1910 and 1920, led by peasant militants (Zapata and Pancho Villa), and was successful in bringing the disadvantaged classes into power.

Lastly, Brazil gained its independence without a struggle when the son of the King of Portugal decided to grant the country independence in 1822 and become constitutional emperor. The emancipation of slaves in 1888 caused unrest in Brazil and led many to favor a republic. After a military revolt in 1889, a republic was proclaimed.

VENEZUELA 1969
Bolívar's marriage in Madrid in 1802.

URUGUAY 1961
The "grito de Asencio" of February 28, 1811 marked the start of the insurrection against the Spanish.

ARGENTINA 1963
The Battle of San Lorenzo (1813).

ARGENTINA 2003
General San Martín's regiment of mounted grenadiers.

PERU 1982
Pedro Vilcapaza, organized the first insurrection by native peasants in Peru in 1781.

VENEZUELA 1969
Simón Bolívar, a wealthy young heir, rallied the Venezuelan independence movement in 1810.

SPAIN 1978
The officers of Spanish origin who liberated South America.
- José de San Martín (1778–1850), liberated Argentina, Chile, and Peru.
- Simón Bolívar (1783–1830), liberated Colombia, Venezuela, Ecuador, Panama, and Bolivia.

BOLIVIA 1974
The Battle of Ayacucho (1824), symbol of South American independence.

ARGENTINA 1972
The meeting at Guyaquil (1822), at which San Martín voluntarily handed over power to Bolívar.

CHILE 1980
Bueras charging in battle, April 5, 1818.

CHILE 1971
José Carrera, Chilean aristocrat and principal leader in the early fight for Chilean independence, shot in 1821.

CHILE 1978
General Bernardo O'Higgins, liberated Chile with San Martín (1818). Elected supreme dictator and later overthrown (1823).

ARGENTINA 2003
San Martín, founded the Buenos Aires masonic lodge in 1812.

VENEZUELA 1960
General Sucre, Bolívar's deputy, elected president of Bolivia in 1826, assassinated in 1830.

MEXICO 1965
Morelos, a mestizo Mexican priest, led the 1811 revolt and proclaimed independence, but was defeated by the Spanish and shot in 1815.

MEXICO 1982
General Vicente Guerrero, revolutionary and later president (1829). Shot in 1831.

CHILE 1979
Naval battle of Iquique (1879), between Chile and Peru.

UNITED STATES 1995
The United States defeats Mexico and wins Texas (1845).

MEXICO 1971
Mariano Matamoros, second-in-command to Morelos, captured and shot in 1814.

MEXICO 1982
Museum of the Mexican Revolution, Chihuahua: a century of revolts, 1811 to 1914.

MEXICO 1962
The French expeditionary force that came to support the conservatives is defeated at Puebla (1862).

MEXICO 1978
Francisco (Pancho) Villa (1878–1923), peasant revolutionary and leader, formed an army that occupied Mexico in 1914 but finally surrendered in 1920.

MEXICO 1979
Emiliano Zapata (1879–1919), led the peasant revolt of 1911 against the big landowners.

BRAZIL 1985
The Brazilian people rise up in popular revolt at Cabanagem (1835).

Brazil

BRAZIL 1982
Brazil gains independence in 1822: "Liberty, order, and progress."

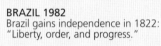

MEXICO 1979
Doña Josefa Ortiz de Dominguez (1768–1829), used her wealth to support the revolution.

VENEZUELA 1960
Doña Luisa Caceres, heroine of Venezuelan independence, married Colonel Arismendi in 1814 and joined the resistance.

BOLIVIA 1980
General Juana Azurduy de Padrilla, heroine of South American independence.

BRAZIL 1971
Anita Garibaldi, gaucho-Brazilian fighter, wife of the Italian revolutionary Garibaldi.

Women in the fight for independence

19TH-CENTURY COLONIAL EMPIRES

During the 19th century, European political, economic, and technical supremacy gathered strength worldwide. Substantial population growth played a decisive role in Europe, resulting in mass migration to other continents. Moreover, with the industrial revolution, Europe experienced a growing need for raw materials that it had to search for further and further afield.

Added to this was the desire to evangelize the populations of less-developed countries and a genuine wish to bring them the "benefits" of civilization. This was true of the islands of the Pacific, where Catholic and Protestant missionaries competed throughout the century.

Two main powers battled over the world: Great Britain, the foremost colonial power at the end of the 18th century (counting India, Canada, and Australia among its colonies), and France, driven by a desire to regain territory after the almost total loss of its colonies (Canada, Louisiana, etc.).

Africa was the first territory under dispute: France claimed North Africa and western and equatorial Africa, while Great Britain claimed East Africa and the south. To ensure its control of the latter, Britain needed to get rid of the Boers, the descendants of Dutch colonists, but this came at a cost, after bitter fighting that forced entire populations into exile.

In Asia, India was in the firm grip of the British crown (which repressed the sepoy revolt of 1857), and it was not until Gandhi's peaceful resistance in the 20th century that the country finally gained its independence – but at the cost of religious partition between India and Pakistan.

Indochina became a French territory in 1881, and its fate was not finally decided until after 1945 and two successive wars, while Indonesia was not freed from Dutch control until 1949.

In 1868, with the Meiji period, Japan awoke to the world beyond its borders with expansionist aims: war against China in 1894, against Russia in 1905, and the annexation of Korea in 1910.

Many stamps have been produced showing the history of the colonies, both by the colonial powers themselves, and by the countries colonized, after they gained independence.

MALAYSIA 1957
Image of the Sultan of Perak, one of the 13 Malay states, and tiger.

SOUTHERN RHODESIA 1937
The British monarchs, Victoria Falls, and the railroad.

ST. LUCIA 1936
Image of King George V and Columbus Square.

UGANDA, TANGANYIKA, KENYA 1954
Image of Queen Elizabeth II, and giraffe on the savannah.

SIERRA LEONE 1938
Rice harvest.

SOUTH AFRICA 1952
Wife of a Dutch colonist; they emigrated in 1652.

SOUTH AFRICA 1982
Lord Baden Powell, English army scout officer, founded the Boy Scouts in 1907.

British colonies

SOUTH AFRICA 1999
Boer and British cavalry preparing for the Second Boer War (1899–1902).

AUSTRALIA 1985
British colonial troops: the Sudan Contingent and the Royal Victoria Volunteer Artillery.

SOUTH AFRICA 1988
The Great Trek (1837–1840), exodus of the Boers, driven out by British occupation.

SOUTH AFRICA 1980
Joubert, Kruger, and Pretorius, the triumvirate of the Boer government (1880).

SOUTH AFRICA 1981
First Boer victory over the British, at Amajuba (1881).

South Africa

INDIA 1998
Leader Nahar Singh, died during the Sikh revolt of 1848.

SRI LANKA 1991
Sir Muthu Coomaraswamy, Tamil leader, appointed member of the legislative council of Ceylon in 1865.

BANGLADESH 1994
Nawab Faizunnessa (1834–1903), advocate of women's education.

JAPAN 1999
Transport of the wounded during the Russian–Japanese war (1905).

MALI 1979
Explorer René Caillié, the first European to reach Timbuktu, in 1829.

ALGERIA (FR) 1950
Bugeaud and Abd-el-Kader, adversaries during the conquest of Algeria (1830–1844).

ALGERIA 1983
Resistance led by Abd-el-Kader.

ALGERIA (FR) 1952
French Muslim Saharan Meharist Companies (1902).

FRANCE 1958
Charles de Foucauld, former military officer, became a hermit at Tamanrasset (Sahara), killed in 1916.

ALGERIA 1967
Tuareg of the Tassili Desert, mounted on a dromedary.

CENTRAL AFRICAN REPUBLIC 1989
Founding of the town of Bangui by Dolisie in 1889.

INDOCHINA 1943
Lieutenant Doudart de Lagrée, led the French expedition up the Mekong river (1866).

FRENCH EQUATORIAL AFRICA 1938
Admiral Willaumez, boarded an illegal slave ship in 1849. The slaves he freed founded the town of Libreville (Gabon).

MAYOTTE (FR) 1941
Purchase of the Mayotte (Comoros) Islands and Nossi-Bé (Madagascar) in 1841 by Admiral Hell.

FRENCH EQUATORIAL AFRICA 1952
Savorgnan de Brazza and the peaceful conquest of the Congo (1852).

INDOCHINA 1944
Auguste Pavie makes Laos a French protectorate (1888).

BENIN 1978
El-Hadj Omar, Muslim fundamentalist, triggered the war against the Bambarans and then against the French advance into the Sudan (1857).

IVORY COAST 1962
French post at Assinie (1862).

FRENCH WEST AFRICA 1957
General Faidherbe and African colonial troops (1857).

FRENCH EQUATORIAL AFRICA 1952
Monsignor Augouard and the evangelization of the Central African Republic (1852).

CAMBODIA 1995
Phnom Penh colonial post office building in 1895.

French colonies

THE FIRST WORLD WAR AND THE RISE OF FASCISM

In 1914, Europe lay at the center of the world, but the balance of power was threatened by the rise of nationalism, which led to the formation of two antagonistic blocs: the Triple Entente (France, England, and Russia), strengthened by Japan, and the Triple Alliance (Germany, Austria-Hungary, and Italy), which were joined by Turkey.

The powder keg that was the Balkans unleashed a war in Europe that would spread throughout the world. In 1915, Italy changed allegiance, in 1917 Russia withdrew due to the revolution taking place within its own borders, and the United States entered the war.

After a frantic arms race it was out-and-out war with hitherto unseen weapons of destruction (huge cannons, submarines, tanks, airplanes, poison gas, and flamethrowers in the trenches). At the end of the war, with 8 million dead and 6 million invalids, Europe's population was severely depleted. France, more than any other country, has commemorated the First World War most through its stamps.

The treaties of 1919–1920 were very one-sided and carried within them the seeds of revenge: Austria–Hungary and the Ottoman Empire were dismantled, while the creation of Czechoslovakia and reconstruction of Poland took place at Germany's expense.

The humiliation resulting from the peace treaties, the colossal war debt, the occupation of the Saar region by France, and galloping inflation (cf. the 1923 series of German stamps) paved the way for Hitler's rise to power in Germany, while Italy and Spain toppled into fascism, and the Soviet Union dug itself into a repressive communism. All the ingredients for the Second World War were in place.

In 1939, after the annexation of Czechoslovakia, Germany, allied with the USSR, invaded Poland, triggering France and Great Britain's entry into the war. In May 1940, France capitulated with 1 million prisoners-of-war and the rest of western Europe was invaded — only Great Britain held out with its allies Australia, New Zealand, and the United States.

CZECHOSLOVAKIA 1938
Creation of Czechoslovakia, independence from Austria (1918).

TURKEY 1955
Turkish soldier holding a shell (Battle of the Dardanelles, 1915).

GERMANY 1935
German soldier of the First World War.

FRANCE 1964
Battle of the Marne (1914), won by France thanks to requisitioned Paris taxis.

NEW ZEALAND 1936
Troops from Australia and New Zealand (ANZACs) land in the Dardanelles (1915).

FRANCE 1956
The trenches at the Battle of Verdun (1916), the bloodiest battle of the war.

ITALY 1967
Italian resistance against Austria in 1917, at Piave in the Alps.

UNITED STATES 1985
First World War combatants (1917): tribute to the veterans.

CZECHOSLOVAKIA 1938
Czech soldiers at the Battle of Vouziers (1918).

FRANCE 1918
Stamp in aid of war orphans: woman plowing (absent husband).

GREECE 1968
Evzone (Greek light infantry soldier) in combat.

FRANCE 1988
Armistice of November 11, 1918 (soldiers leaving the trenches).

GERMANY 1994
German military cemetery.

FRANCE 1940
Marshal Foch, commander-in-chief of the allied armies in 1918.

GREAT BRITAIN 1986
Lord Trenchard and English biplane.

FRANCE 1940
Guynemer, the only pilot to have brought down four planes on the same day. Killed in 1917.

UNITED STATES 1999
Billy Mitchell, the best American pilot of the First World War.

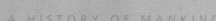

GERMANY 1923
Inflation in Germany: stamps – 5 marks in January 1923, 125,000 marks in July, 2 million marks in August, 200 million marks in September 1923.

GERMANY 1941
Adolf Hitler is brought to power (1933) and the symbol of the National Socialist Party (swastika).

SAAR 1922
Stamp issued in Francs: Saar is annexed to France (coal mines and heavy industry).

GERMANY 1935
Saar returned to Germany by referendum (mother and child reunited).

GERMANY 1944
The introduction of the German National Work Service in 1934 providing plentiful labor for the German war effort.

GERMANY 1935, GERMANY 1943
Creation of the Hitler Youth (1935) and young bugler (1944).

ITALY 1941
Alliance between Hitler and Mussolini.

Hitler's rise to power

SPAIN 1948
General Franco takes power in 1937.

GERMANY 1938
Return of the Sudetenland to Germany (annexation of Czechoslovakia in 1938).

HUNGARY 1944
Hungarian soldier and nurse.

CROATIA 1944
The foundation of the Black Legion of Croatian volunteers by Major Francetic in 1941.

POLAND 1989
Invasion by Germany and the USSR, 1939: Polish general and the Battle of Lvov.

TURKEY 1952
Mustapha Kemal (Ataturk) rejects the Turkish defeat treaty and overthrows the sultan (1922).

FRANCE 1941
French prisoners-of-war in a camp.

GERMANY 1943
Germany attacks Europe (1939): airplanes, armored vehicles, submarines, motorized infantry.

ROMANIA 1942
Romanian troops at the liberation of Bessarabia in 1941.

THE SECOND WORLD WAR

Many countries became embroiled in the Second World War and all those who finished on the winning side have commemorated their victory abundantly in their stamps, each in their own way, right up to the present day.

Britain has focused on its victorious battle against the Germans for air superiority, whereas the USSR – which in 1941 changed to the Allied side and halted the German advance at Stalingrad – has celebrated its combatants, diverting attention away from its communist dictatorship over the countries of central Europe by recalling its victory over fascism.

The occupied countries of Europe have focused on their resistance movements against German occupation and, in the case of France, have chosen to highlight the important role played by the country's colonial forces. The United States has taken a didactic approach to its decisive intervention in the war between 1941 and 1945, both in the Pacific against Japan, and in Europe with the Normandy landings. The landings and the jubilation of those that were liberated have also been celebrated in the stamps of other participant countries.

The racist atrocities of Nazism and the liberation of the concentration camps – where more than 6 million Jews, gypsies, and European resistance fighters perished – have also been extensively remembered in stamps, and tribute paid to the 20 million who died in the war.

On the losing side, there has been a fitting sobriety in their post-war commemorations; Japan has waited more than 50 years to commemorate the massacre of the atomic bomb at Hiroshima, evoking the event with a simple child's drawing.

ST. PIERRE AND MIQUELON (FR) 1990
General De Gaulle's appeal for resistance (June 18, 1940) was heard throughout France and in all the French colonies.

BELGIUM 1964
Belgian resistance fighter.

GREECE 1982
Greek resistance fighters.

POLAND 1994
The heroic struggle of the Polish forces at Monte Cassino (Italy campaign, 1944).

FRANCE 1943
Propaganda stamp under the Vichy regime against Allied bombardment in France.

POLAND 1995
In remembrance of the "Katyn Massacre" (1945): 15,000 army officers and members of the Polish police force were deliberately murdered by the Soviets, who claimed the Germans were responsible.

FRENCH EQUATORIAL AFRICA 1946
Leclerc's Free French Forces leave Chad for the Rhine.

The Battle of Britain

GREAT BRITAIN 1974
Winston Churchill, Prime Minister and inspiration to British resistance in 1940.

GREAT BRITAIN 1986
Lord Dowding, victorious at the Battle of Britain, and Hurricane aircraft.

GREAT BRITAIN 1965
The Battle of Britain (1940): German aircraft in a dive.

USSR 1965
Heroic Soviet sailor.

USSR 1967
The Arctic Convoys, which provided supplies for the Soviet resistance at Stalingrad (1941–1942).

RUSSIA 2004
Soviet operational strategy in 1944.

CANADA 1994
Canadian forces at the Allied landings in Normandy.

1941: A World at War

UNITED STATES 1999
The Normandy landings, June 6, 1944.

UNITED STATES 1991
1941: A World at War. This explanatory plate is the first in a series of five commemorating the war year by year.

UNITED STATES 1945
The capture of Iwo Jima island in February 1945, a great feat of arms by the US marines.

JAPAN 1999
Japanese bomber and kamikaze pilot on board the suicide plane known as the Zero.

JAPAN 1995
The first Japanese stamp commemorating the atomic bomb dropped on Hiroshima in 1945: the dome, the only building that remained standing in the city (child's drawing).

ISRAEL 2003
The yellow star, the symbol the Jews were forced to wear from 1941 to the end of the war in 1945.

GERMANY (GFR) 1979
The Journal of Anne Frank, a young Jewish girl who died of typhus in a concentration camp at the age of 15.

NETHERLANDS 1975
The liberation of the concentration camps by the Allies in 1945.

GREAT BRITAIN 1995
The British Army welcomed by the liberated people of France (photo).

HUNGARY 1950
The Soviet Army welcomed by the liberated people of Hungary in 1945 (painting).

AUSTRIA 1947
Austrian soldier, prisoner-of-war.

THE SOVIET REVOLUTION

Tsar Nicolas II, his power weakened by the discontent of the exploited peasant masses and by the famine caused by Russia's disorganization in the face of the First World War, was overthrown by the socialist revolution of February 1917.

In October 1917, the Bolsheviks took power: Lenin signed up for unconditional peace with Germany, abolished the large landholdings, and brought in the dictatorship of the proletariat. To safeguard the revolution, the Bolsheviks installed a regime of terror: the assassination of the Tsar and those who opposed them, the creation of political secret police (the Cheka), and the muzzling of the press.

The Red Army formed by Trotsky crushed the counter-revolutionary Whites in 1918, but Comintern (a worldwide association of communist parties) failed in its attempt to propagate communism to other countries in Europe. It then concentrated its efforts on undermining their authority over their colonies. With Stalin's arrival in power, the forced collectivization of the land led to a catastrophic famine in 1933, which he fostered in order to eliminate the recalcitrant peasant class.

After the Second World War, taking advantage of the standing of the Soviet Army after its decisive role in the victory against fascism, Stalin subjugated the countries of central Europe by force, and an "iron curtain" fell across Europe. Communist seizure of Moscow translated into the elimination of its opponents, the suppression of freedoms, the building of the Berlin Wall (1961) to prevent East Germans fleeing to the West, and the invasion of Budapest in 1956, and Prague in 1968.

Eventually, in 1989, the communist regime, rejected by the people, collapsed of its own accord after 72 years of dictatorship and tens of millions of people dead or transported to gulags – victims of Stalinist purges.

For today's collector, the main interest in the stamps issued during the period before 1989 lies in their use as propaganda tools, extolling the successes of the communist regime, both real (conquest of space) and imaginary (freedom of expression, economic success). This was supported by countless stamps produced by communist regimes all over the world showing Lenin, Marx, Engels, and the October Revolution, but intriguingly only rarely Stalin.

RUSSIA 1998
Tsar Nicolas II and his family, before their execution (1918).

USSR 1968
50th anniversary of the Red Army (1918).

CUBA 1967
The October Revolution, 1917.

USSR 1977
The battleship *Potemkin* and the October Revolution of 1917.

The October Revolution

USSR 1958
Creation of the Comsomol (Soviet youth organization) in 1918: young soldier.

Application of Marxism

USSR 1980
Lenin (1870–1924), principal leader of the October Revolution and the policy of Sovietization. One example among countless images of Lenin on stamps.

USSR 1958
Bugler in the Young Pioneers (formed in 1922).

USSR 1958
Male and female workers.

UKRAINE 1993
60th anniversary of the great famine of 1933 and of the banishments, both orchestrated by Stalin.

USSR 1961
The 1936 Soviet Constitution.

USSR 1960
Lenin as a child, shown as an obedient little boy.

USSR 1962
Creation of *Pravda* ("Truth") in 1912, which became the single party newspaper.

USSR 1964
National Brigade militants.

GERMANY (GDR) 1971
Karl Marx (1818–1883), 19th-century communist theoretician.

A HISTORY OF MANKIND

USSR 1962
Youth solidarity against colonialism. Note: at this time (1962), almost all western colonies had become independent, whereas the countries of central Europe remained under the yoke of the Soviet Union.

CUBA 1962
The Bay of Pigs episode and Soviet missiles in Cuba marked the height of the cold war between East and West, with the Americans' failed attempt at invasion.

USSR 1985
Samantha Smith, an American schoolgirl, invited to visit the USSR by the Soviets as part of the thawing relationship between East and West, and the policy of transparency.

ROMANIA 1978
Combine harvesters belonging to an agricultural combine.

CZECHOSLOVAKIA 1981
16th Congress of the Communist Party of Czechoslovakia.

HUNGARY 1951
People's Army Day: 29 September.

BULGARIA 1953
Soldier, and industrial and agricultural activities.

POLAND 1950
Celebrating the Six-Year Plan.

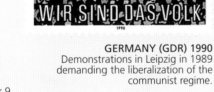

SLOVAKIA 1999
The fall of communism with the Velvet Revolution of November 1989.

GERMANY (GDR) 1986
25th anniversary of the Berlin Wall (1961): soldiers and young woman with flowers.

Satellite countries

GERMANY (GDR) 1990
Demonstrations in Leipzig in 1989 demanding the liberalization of the communist regime.

POLAND 1990
10th anniversary of the free trade union Solidarnosc (Solidarity).

GERMANY (GFR) 1989
The fall of the Berlin Wall, November 9, 1989, and liberation of East Germany.

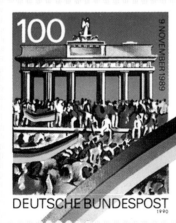

CROATIA 1994
Centenary of cooperation between Croatia and the United States.

51

COMMUNISM IN ASIA

Initiated by Sun Yat-sen in 1912, in 1927 the Chinese Revolution brought the nationalists of Chiang Kai-shek into conflict with the communists of Mao Zedong, who were forced to retreat to Shanxi after the Long March of 1934–1935. United for a time with the communists against Japan, which had set its sights on control over China, the nationalists were eventually forced to take refuge in Taiwan in 1949, when Mao founded the People's Republic of China introducing a totalitarian communist regime adapted to suit a rural country where public and private capital existed side by side.

Nevertheless, the implementation of the Great Leap Forward (1958–1959) led to an unprecedented famine, while the Cultural Revolution (1965–1969) brought ideological repression, exposing people to the violence, murders, and mass deportations perpetrated by the Red Guard, with some 20 million either dead or deported.

From 1989, apart from the suppression of demonstrations (1,000 died in Tiananmen Square), the regime wavered between maintaining communism and opening up the most populated country on the planet to a market economy. As in the Soviet Union, stamps were used as propaganda tools by Beijing. There is a striking contrast between the satisfied smiles of the workers, peasants, intellectuals, and sportspeople of popular China, and the distress of the refugees from the communist regime, visible on two stamps from Taiwan. The Korean War (1950–1953) and the Vietnam War (1950–1975) are, of course, illustrated differently: with a few, rare examples from the West but abundantly commemorated in stamps issued by communist countries all over the world.

The genocide in Cambodia, perpetrated by the communist Khmer Rouge from 1975 to 1979, deserves special mention: of a total population of 8 million Cambodians, 2 million died. Exceptionally in the history of philately, no stamps were issued by Cambodia during these four years. Even today, many years after these events – the perpetrators of which remain unpunished – no stamp has ever been issued to commemorate the victims.

CHINA 1993
Mao Zedong (1893–1976), the "great helmsman," posing in front of the Great Wall of China. Dressed in casual clothes, he tries to present a reassuring image.

TAIWAN 1958
Chiang Kai-shek (1886–1975), leader of nationalist China after the death of Sun Yat-sen (1925), forced to take refuge in Taiwan in 1949 after the civil war against the communists.

TAIWAN 1985
Sun Yat-sen (1866–1925), father of the Chinese Revolution against the Qing dynasty (1912).

CHINA 1965
The People's Liberation Army during the Cultural Revolution.

CHINA 1982
Jiang Qing, radical-thinking wife of Mao, staged an unsuccessful coup after Mao's death with the Gang of Four.

Propaganda stamps
•Communist viewpoint

CHINA 1974
Happy peasants.

CHINA 1974
Happy worker.

CHINA 1975
Happy sportspeople.

CHINA 1984
35th anniversary of the People's Republic of China: triumphant soldier and physicist.

CHINA 1966
Cultural Revolution: Red Guards and portrait of Mao.

• Nationalist viewpoint

CHINA 1954
The new Constitution.

CHINA 1955
Stalin and Mao: Chinese–Soviet friendship treaty.

CHINA 1970
Chinese soldiers in 1969 during the Chinese–Soviet conflict.

TAIWAN 1963
The other side of the coin: the pain and humiliation of Chinese refugees from communism.

CHINA 1965
Arms aid for North Vietnam.

GERMANY (GDR) 1968
Aid for North Vietnam: mother carrying her child and a rifle.

NORTH VIETNAM 1972
Air defense (4,000th aircraft shot down).

CUBA 1966
Support for North Vietnam: "genocide" gassing by the United States of America.

• Vietnam

NORTH KOREA 1975
Monument to the glory of communism.

NORTH KOREA 1975
30th anniversary of the victory over fascism. Strangely, the defeated side is marked "US" on this stamp.

NORTH KOREA 1976
The dictator Kim Il Sung in a scene of everyday life: "Dear leader, lying before you is the first line of the front."

CHINA 1952
Chinese troops fighting in Korea.

FRANCE 2004
French soldiers at Dien Bien Phu.

• Korea, Cambodia

KAMPUCHEA (CAMBODIA) 1984
National liberation, January 7, 1979: by invading Cambodia, the Vietnamese put an end to the genocide perpetrated by the Khmer Rouge against the Cambodian people.

UNITED STATES 2003
American soldiers in the Korean War.

NORTH VIETNAM 1967
American pilot taken prisoner (2,000th aircraft shot down).

NORTH VIETNAM 1954
Vietminh artillery in position at the Battle of Dien Bien Phu.

SOUTH VIETNAM 1964
Liberation by the November 1963 revolution.

UNITED STATES 1999
American marines landing by helicopter.

UNITED STATES 1984
Memorial to the American soldiers who died in Vietnam.

THE RISE OF ISLAM

After enjoying a golden age from the 8th to the 11th centuries, since the mid-1950s Islam has again become a powerful lever for nationalist movements. The creation of the state of Israel in 1948, imposed at the expense of the Palestinians, who were forced into refugee camps, created an endemic focus for wars with Arab countries right up to the present day. In 1979, the overthrow of the Shah of Iran and the imposition in Iran of an Islamic republic dependent on religious authority (the mullahs) gave a new impetus to political-religious forces which, from Africa to Asia, now demand a return to traditional Islam. Many countries, such as Afghanistan under the Taliban, rejected both materialist Marxism and the western values that are the legacy of the colonial period, and see Sharia law (derived from the Koran) as the model for the organization of society and one that should be imposed on all.

In the Middle East, this radicalization of Islam in what is a very important economic area because of its oil, and a very sensitive political area because of the conflict between Israel and the Arab countries, poses a serious danger to peace in the world.

Moreover, there are also conflicts between different Muslim tendencies — for example, Shiites against Sunni Muslims in Iran and Iraq. More moderate leaders, such as those of the United Arab Emirates, stand at odds with local dictators who exalt the nationalism of their people, using stamps as propaganda tools, often in an extreme fashion, as with Gaddafi in Libya, the religious authorities in Iran, and as Saddam Hussein once did in Iraq. Strong population growth in Muslim countries, combined with the gap between rich and poor, and a religious radicalization clearly opposed to western values, has contributed to the rise in international terrorism in recent years: the September 11 attack in the United States in 2001, the attack in Bali in October 2002, in Madrid in March 2004 and in London in July 2005, are the most remarkable examples but very few stamps have been produced by other western countries to condemn these atrocities.

Conflict between Israel and the Arab countries

ISRAEL 1964
Arrival of the first Israelis on board the *Exodus*, following the allocation by the UN of half the Palestinian territory (1947).

LEBANON 1965
Massacre of the Palestinian inhabitants of the village of Deir Yassin (April 9, 1948) by Zionist terrorists from Irgun. In May 1948, the state of Israel was created, and 750,000 Palestinians fled their villages.

ISRAEL 1955
Israeli colonists arrive in the new land of Israel.

ISRAEL 1994
Murder of Israeli athletes at the Olympic Games in Munich (1972) by Palestinian terrorists.

SYRIA 1983
Massacre of Palestinians in the Sabra and Shatilla refugee camps.

IRAN 1989
Mosque of the Dome of the Rock in Jerusalem, represented symbolically as imprisoned behind Israeli barbed wire.

Iran

IRAN 1988
"Tragic bombing of Iranian schools by the Zionist regime of Iraq."

IRAN 1968
The Shah of Iran leads an ambitious program for the social and economic transformation of his country.

IRAN 1968
Farah Diba, a young student in Paris, marries the Shah and becomes Empress of Iran (1959).

IRAN 1991
The Shah is overthrown by revolution in 1979: Ayatollah Khomeini takes power and introduces strict Islamic law.

IRAN 1987
"The massacre of the Muslim pilgrims to holy Mecca," year 1407 of the Hirja calendar (1987 CE).

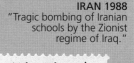

IRAN 1987
"The takeover of the US spy den (the American Embassy) in Teheran" (1979).

IRAN 1988
"Disastrous missile attack against Iranian airliner."

LIBYA 1998
"The Great Socialist People's Libyan Arab Jamahiriya": Gaddafi and fighter planes.

IRAQ
Propaganda bloc: Saddam and his missiles.

UNITED ARAB EMIRATES 1996
Sheikh Zayed and a desert cultivation program.

AFGHANISTAN 1975
Anniversary of the 1945 victory against fascism. The Soviet presence in Afghanistan explains the lightly clad female figure, which would have been unthinkable under the Taliban after independence.

AFGHANISTAN 1985
One of two statues of the Buddha of Bamyan, classified world heritage monuments but destroyed by the Taliban for reasons of religious ideology.

FRANCE 2003
Ahmed Shah Massoud, "the lion of Panshir," drove the Red Army out of Afghanistan (1991). Killed in 2001 during fratricidal inter-tribal fighting.

Terrorism

IRAQ
Propaganda bloc: the victors of the Crusades (Saladin and Saddam Hussein) with the Jerusalem mosque in the background.

AITUTAKI 2001
"United we stand."
All democratic countries express their support for the United States after the Islamist terrorist attack of September 11, 2001 on the stately twin towers of Manhattan.

UNITED STATES 2001
The heroic conduct of New York firemen on September 11.

SPAIN 2004
European day of mourning for the Islamist terrorist attack of March 11, 2004 in Madrid.

SERBIA AND MONTENEGRO 2004
A hood over the world: "Stop terrorism!"

IRAQ 1974
Nationalization of Iraqi oil in 1972.

EUROPA:
THE CONSTRUCTION OF EUROPE

Initiated by a small group of men determined that the horrors of two world wars should never be repeated, and convinced that union between the countries of Europe would be a factor for stability and peace in the world, the European Economic Community (EEC) came into being in 1957 with the Treaty of Rome, signed by the six founder members: Belgium, France, Germany, Italy, Luxembourg, and the Netherlands.

This central core grew as the years went by, becoming nine countries in 1973 (with the addition of Denmark, Great Britain, and the Republic of Ireland); ten in 1981 (with Greece); and 12 in 1986 (with Spain and Portugal). In 1993, the EEC was transformed into the European Union (EU) by the Maastricht Treaty. The process has continued with member countries reaching 15 in 1995 (with Austria, Finland, and Sweden) and 25 in 2004 (with the Baltic countries – Estonia, Latvia, and Lithuania, the Czech Republic, Hungary, Poland, Slovakia and Slovenia, plus the islands of Cyprus and Malta). Other countries are currently seeking membership, notably Bulgaria, Croatia, Romania, and Turkey.

The EU has become an area of 400 million inhabitants sharing common values and rules, and 12 of these countries also share a single currency. The initial objective of peace has been achieved at present, but questions remain on how to manage such a vast and diverse group of countries and people.

An example of success is the "Europa" philately program, the only coordinated program in the world on such a scale: since 1956, member countries of the European Conference of Postal and Telecommunications Administration issue stamps each year on a common theme. The first issues, from 1956 to 1973, may have given a very technocratic image with a single symbolic motif, but since 1974 each country has been free to choose its subject within the framework of a common annual theme. These issues have been so successful that every country in Europe, and more besides – whether official candidate countries or not – has joined the Europa program. The freedom each country enjoys of highlighting its own culture within an organized framework offers collectors a rich and magnificent kaleidoscope of culture.

GERMANY (GFR) 1956
Symbolic motif (European construction).

LUXEMBOURG 1956
Symbolic motif (European construction).

FRANCE 1958
Symbolic motif (dove of peace over Europe).

REPUBLIC OF IRELAND 1980
Famous figures: Oscar Wilde.

GERMANY (GFR) 1977
Jean Monnet, economist, one of the founding fathers of Europe in 1957.

FRANCE 1988
Adenauer and De Gaulle sign the Franco-German Cooperation Treaty in 1963.

BELGIUM 1968
Symbolic motif (key).

NETHERLANDS 1968
Symbolic motif (key).

DENMARK 1987
Modern architecture: Hoje Tastrup High School.

GREECE 1981
National folk tradition: Macedonian dancers.

ITALY 1959
Symbolic motif (chain linking countries).

GREAT BRITAIN 1973
England joins the European jigsaw in 1973.

SWEDEN 1976
Crafts: Lapp spoon made from elk horn.

Founder members

SPAIN 1977
Countryside: Coto Doñana National Park.

PORTUGAL 1982
Historical facts: embassy of King Don Manuel to Pope Leo X in 1514.

REPUBLIC OF IRELAND 2004
European enlargement from 15 to 25 countries.

FINLAND 1990
Postal buildings: post office in Lapland.

AUSTRIA 1978
Monuments: Riegersburg Castle.

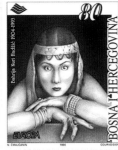

ROMANIA 1997
Tales and legends: Vlad Tepes, Count of Wallachia, 1448 (Dracula).

BULGARIA 1998
National holidays and festivals: young girls in traditional dress with flowers, going in procession to the river for their marriage prediction.

CROATIA 1998
National holidays and festivals: Dubrovnik summer festival.

TURKEY 1960
As this symbolic motif (wheel) from 1960 shows, Turkey has participated in the Europa program for many years.

BOSNIA-HERZOGOVINA 1996
Famous women: Bahrija Nuri Hadzic, actress.

USSR 1989
Dove, a vessel of peace between the Soviet Union and Europe.

MONACO 2003
Poster art: Monte Carlo, drawing by Doumergue (voted most beautiful stamp 2003).

POLAND 2001
Water, a natural resource: earth contained in a drop of water.

CZECH REPUBLIC 1994
Europe and discovery: the voyages of Marco Polo.

ESTONIA 1996
Famous women: the poet Marie Under (1883–1980).

LITHUANIA 1993
Contemporary art: painting of a ladle carver.

SLOVENIA 1999
Nature reserves and parks: Triglav National Park.

LIECHTENSTEIN 1967
Symbolic motif (countries shown as cogs in a machine).

HUNGARY 1991
Europe and space: the *Cassini* and *Huygens* space probes.

LATVIA 1995
Peace and liberty: 1918, and later 1991, the dates of Latvian independence.

SLOVAKIA 1998
National holidays and festivals: wedding (picture by Balaz).

MALTA 1983
Major buildings: the Sant'Anglu Fort.

CYPRUS 2004
Holidays: sea and archaeology.

Ten new member countries in 2004

THE EMERGENCE OF ALTERNATIVE POWERS

The Second World War turned the order that had existed among the world's leading powers upside down, signaling the weakening of Europe as it gradually bade farewell to its colonial empire, and bringing face to face the two superpowers – the United States and the USSR – which formed two blocs with their respective allies.

Decolonization began with India, which achieved independence peacefully in 1947, thanks to Gandhi. His successor, Nehru, followed by Indira Gandhi, succeeded in maintaining institutional stability in the country, but at the cost of scission between religious communities (India, Pakistan, and Bangladesh). In 1955, at the Bandung Conference in Indonesia, the non-aligned countries movement was born, with India as one of its leading lights, refusing to give allegiance to either of the two blocs. Population control was one of their major challenges.

Other countries and counter-powers also emerged: in the economic field, OPEC (the Organization of Petroleum Exporting Countries), ASEAN (Association of South East Asian Nations), and Mercosur (South American Common Market); in the social field the altermondialist movement, offering an alternative to the liberal model; in the cultural field, a French-speaking grouping, a platform offering an alternative to the dominant Anglo-Saxon culture, and Indian cinema, an Asian counterweight to western cinema.

In South America, while Brazil and Mexico may be following the altermondialist route, Argentina and Chile have seen periods of reformist power (under Perón and Allende) alternate with military dictatorships.

The economic and technological boom of the "four dragons" (South Korea, Hong Kong, Singapore, and Taiwan) illustrates the success of the emerging countries of Asia, whereas African countries, which ceased to be colonies in the 1960s, are still struggling to find the path to economic growth and political stability. Apartheid came to an end in South Africa, but the ethnic rivalry between African tribes continues in many African states and has led to many conflicts, and even to genocide in places such as Biafra and Rwanda.

INDIA 1937
George VI, the last British Emperor of India before independence (1947).

GREAT BRITAIN 1969
Mahatma Gandhi (1869–1948), apostle of independence through peaceful resistance.

INDIA 1954
Nehru (1889–1964), successor to Gandhi. Introduced the "Third Way" between capitalism and communism, and maintained stability in India.

INDIA 1985
Indira Gandhi, succeeded Nehru as Prime Minister of India. India had to fight two wars with Pakistan (1964 and 1970).

PAKISTAN 2000
Decorated Pakistani soldier. Kashmir remains a subject of discord between India and Pakistan.

BANGLADESH 1991
In remembrance of a demonstrator against autocracy, killed in 1987.

Oil

SAUDI ARABIA 1976
Oil-drilling platform. Saudi Arabia is the world's leading producer of "black gold," and plays a major role in OPEC regulating prices.

NIGERIA 1973
The oil industry. Nigeria is one of Africa's largest oil producers.

MEXICO 1983
Commemorating the anniversary of the International Maritime Trade Organization.

BRAZIL 1989
The tradition of Brazilian independence dates back to the *Inconfidencia mineira* movement in the Age of the Enlightenment.

INDONESIA 1969
Family planning and industrial production.

Non-aligned countries

Latin America

GERMANY (GDR) 1974
Pablo Neruda (1904–1973), Chilean poet and bard of communism.

CUBA 2003
Commemorating the birth of "Radio Rebelde," and Che Guevara's action in 1958.

CUBA 1999
Propaganda stamp on the triumph of the 1959 revolution.

ARGENTINA 2002
Eva Perón (1919–1952), wife of the dictator and reformer Juan Perón, venerated by the people, who called her Evita.

CHILE 1972
The Chilean military power pays tribute to its commander-in-chief.

FALKLAND ISLANDS 1987
In 1982, the Falklands War (as the British called it) was a conflict fought between two western nations, one within the American sphere of influence, the other within that of the developing nations.

HONG KONG 1988
One of the "four dragons" (Hong Kong, Singapore, Taiwan, and South Korea): Asian countries are undergoing dramatic development.

TAIWAN 1999
Another "dragon" country, battling for survival against its powerful enemy and brother, the People's Republic of China.

HONG KONG 1979
The electronics industry: integrated circuits.

SOUTH KOREA 1977
Industry and exports.

MALAYSIA 1992
ASEAN (Association of South East Asian Nations) celebrates its 25th anniversary: Malaysia, Singapore, the Philippines, Indonesia, and Thailand are joined by Brunei and Vietnam.

SINGAPORE 1986
Computer operators.

Decolonization

SWAZILAND 1977
Celebration of the jubilee of Queen Elizabeth II. Between 1947 and 1975, Great Britain granted independence to all its former colonies, the majority of which became members of the Commonwealth.

CONGO 1974
De Gaulle, "the decolonizer," fulfilling his commitments of 1944, gave the French colonies their independence between 1958 and 1962.

CONGO 1971
Anniversary of the Congolese revolution of 1963, with reference to *La Marseillaise* of the French Revolution of 1789.

USSR 1961
Lumumba, leader of the ex-Belgian Congo Independence Party, winner of the 1960 election, captured and killed by his African rival Mobutu in 1961.

"Dragon" countries of Asia and the countries of Africa

NIGER 1969
First Conference of French-speaking communities, platform for countries outside the Anglo-Saxon sphere of influence.

CANADA 1987
The British Commonwealth gives greater weight to the interests of member countries.

CENTRAL AFRICAN REPUBLIC 1977
Coronation of the self-proclaimed Emperor Bokassa I, and his wife.

RWANDA 1981
Disabled boy painting by mouth. In 1994, ethnic rivalries between the Hutus and Tutsis led to a civil war and the death of a million civilians.

NIGERIA 1981
The anti-apartheid movement. Denouncement of police brutality in South Africa.

SOUTH AFRICA 1989
President F. W. de Klerk puts an end to apartheid and organizes free elections.

SOUTH AFRICA 1994
Nelson Mandela, apostle of the struggle to end apartheid; elected president of South Africa in 1994.

BIAFRA 1968
The independence of the Nigerian province of Biafra, rich in important mineral and oil reserves, led to a war with Nigeria and the genocide of a million Biafrans in 1970.

MAN'S HABITAT

DESERT AND TROPICAL HABITATS

Whatever his way of life and however harsh the climate, man has always shown great imagination in constructing a habitat that would protect him from bad weather and predators, that would become a home, a place where his family could gather. In the mainly tropical countries where desert, steppe land, or virgin forest still exist, many stamps have been issued showing these habitats. Nomadic tribes and clans use light structures that can be dismantled and carried with them as they move around in search of new pastures or game, such as the yurts erected by Mongols on the steppes, the tents of desert Bedouins, and the animal skin tents built by Canadian trappers.

As man became more settled with the development of agriculture, tents became huts, the structure of these depending directly on the climate and local materials, with huts covered in leafy branches (palm or pandanus), or animal skins, to provide shelter from the tropical sun. These huts were grouped together to form villages, arranged in accordance with a complex system of organization linked to tribal traditions, and grain stores were built to hold the reserve supplies.

In virgin forests exposed to tropical rain, huts are built on piles to keep them safe from flooding, provide better ventilation against the heat and humidity, and better protection against reptiles and insects. The wood used is often rot-proof (teak, palm, or palmyra).

In the modern world, countries have developed programs for affordable housing that is healthier to live in than simple huts. On a more luxurious note, the traditional colonial houses of the tropics were built to last in stone or brick, with steeply pitched metal roofs, verandahs providing shade, air and protection against the rains, and windows with screened shutters allowing the air to circulate but keeping insects out.

In desert regions, houses are cubic in shape with very small openings to keep the interior shaded and cool; the roof is flat because of the lack of rain, and it is used for drying fruit or enjoying the cool evening air.

MONGOLIA 1974
Yurt.

CANADA 1950
Trapper's tent with animal skins drying.

NIGER 1964
Tuareg tent in the Azawak region.

TURKEY 2000
Nomads' tent on the plains of Turkey: women, children, and goats.

TANZANIA 1984
Traditional hut with circular structure.

UPPER VOLTA 1971
Fulani straw hut, simple semi-circular shape.

CANADA 1995
Inuit igloo. Round in shape, like the African hut on the left, an igloo is warmer than a tent and can be built in three to four hours anywhere on the ice floe.

TUNISIA 1954
Cave-style dwellings at Matmata, excavated below ground.

CHAD 1970
Scene of village life (painting by G. Narcisse).

UPPER VOLTA 1971
Gurunsi house: dwelling with elaborate architecture.

CAMEROON 1972
Traditional savannah dwelling, round structure with straw roof.

DAHOMEY 1960
Somba dwelling, a veritable castle with the upper rooms giving on to a terrace. The cylindrical towers serve as grain stores.

Tents

Dwellings and villages

AUSTRALIA 1975
Dwelling with a giant conch-shaped roof in Papua New Guinea. This shape may have been an inspiration for the roof of the Sydney Opera House.

VIETNAM 1986
House on piles with a steeply pitched roof.

MADAGASCAR 1969
Seaside village on the east coast of Madagascar (painting by A. Razafinjohany).

LAOS 1970
Dwelling on piles in a rice field in the rainy season (picture by M. Leguay).

Improvements in housing

DAHOMEY 1960
Ganvie lake village. Built on piles in a lake to provide greater protection against attacks and pillaging.

POLYNESIA 1996
House on piles in a lagoon (painting by T. Becaud).

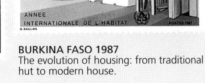

BURKINA FASO 1987
The evolution of housing: from traditional hut to modern house.

BURUNDI 1987
Homeless family living in a disused pipe.

BRAZIL 1975
Straw hut in Amazonia.

Houses in the tropics

FRANCE 1998
Colonial house in St. Pierre de la Réunion.

UNITED ARAB EMIRATES 2003
Rectangular house built of dry mud bricks.

NIGER 1987
House on the edge of the Sahara with mosaic decoration.

MEXICO 1981
"Casa de los Mascarones," originally the country residence of a Spanish nobleman in 1768.

NEW CALEDONIA 1979
Colonial house in Noumea old town (Artillery Point).

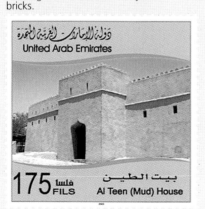

RURAL AND MOUNTAIN HABITATS

The architecture of rural habitats is essentially functional, adapted to suit the work to be carried out, to weather conditions and to locally available materials. Characteristically, no architects are involved, thus helping to maintain the local, traditional forms that come from years of experience. Most modern countries have sought to preserve and celebrate the heritage of their old rural buildings in stamps: depending on the region, traditional farmhouses are built in stone or wood, or constructed from a timber frame filled with cob; the roof can be thatched, covered in slates or tiles, sometimes with an overhang to provide extra protection against bad weather, snow, and rain.

Sometimes the main dwelling and the barn or shed, which are normally separate buildings, are joined together to conserve more heat. In mountain areas, the farms in the valleys are more solidly constructed than the shelters higher up used during the summer transhumance.

Although mills were imported into Europe from Asia Minor — water mills by the Romans in the 1st century and windmills by the crusaders in the 12th century — stamps showing them are mainly European. Once commonplace in the countryside of western Europe, mills were the precursors of industrial production: they made it possible to replace human or animal power with far more powerful mechanisms driven by free energy sources (wind, water courses, and tides), and were used to grind grain to make flour, to saw wood, to extract oil, to make paper, and to extract tannin. Far less common today, and replaced by modern wind turbines, they are still scattered across our countryside in groups on windy plateaus, or alone in valley bottoms.

The picturesque villages set up in the mountains that we still find today were originally built on these steep natural sites to protect them against invasion, or simply to keep out of the way of the local lord: their steep, narrow streets are much easier to defend.

UNITED STATES 1977
Farmhouses in El Pueblo, California.

NETHERLANDS 1975
Traditional Orvelte village, reconstruction (northern Netherlands).

NORWAY 1994
Wooden farmhouses under snow.

ICELAND 1986
Seydisfjordur village.

GERMANY (GDR) 1981
Half-timbered farmhouse.

Thatched houses

POLAND 1974
Cottage (Kurpic).

NORTH KOREA 1973
Shelter used by revolutionaries in 1932.

CUBA 1970
Farmhouse and tobacco plantation.

BRAZIL 1975
House in Santa Catarina province.

TURKEY 1972
Gebze village, Anatolia.

HONG KONG 1995
Rural dwelling.

Farmhouses

Mountain dwellings

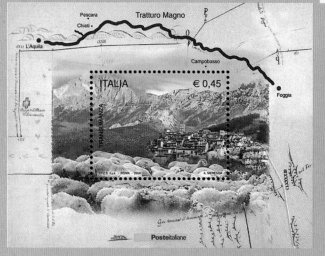

ITALY 2004
Summer transhumance, flocks of sheep are moved into the mountains.

SWITZERLAND 1973
Chalet in Simmental.

ANDORRA 1980
Mountain house in Cortinada.

AUSTRIA 1975
Farmhouse in Zillertal Valley in the Tyrol.

GREAT BRITAIN 1970
Country house near Oxford, made of the highly prized local Cotswold stone.

FRANCE 2003
Country house in the south of France, now much sought after for refurbishment.

Mills

FRANCE 1979
Windmill at Steenvorde. Mounted on a pivot, the mill can be turned to follow the wind direction.

LITHUANIA 1999
Brick-built windmill.

HUNGARY 1983
Watermill and lake at Tapolca.

POLAND 1986
Traditional watermill.

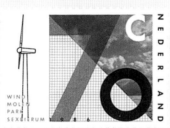

GREECE 1977
The last 24 windmills, restored and working on the Lasithi plateau in Crete.

NETHERLANDS 1986
Modern wind turbine, generating electricity.

SWEDEN 1971
Windmills on Oland Island.

YUGOSLAVIA 2002
Watermill on a fast-flowing river.

SPAIN 1998
The fortified town of Cuenca.

TUNISIA 1954
Ksar (fortified village) of Chenini, Tataouine.

Clifftop villages

GREECE 1977
Village on the island of Santorini.

FRANCE 2002
The village of Rocamadour, perched on a cliff (Lot) and pilgrims' chapel.

URBAN AND WATERSIDE HOUSES

Another universal theme of philately, house architecture became more organized with the appearance of towns, and the functionality of the building became less important than the desire for appearance felt by the owner. Furthermore, regulations began to increase (alignment of façades, taxes based on the width of the building or on the number of windows, etc.), and entire districts were torn down for reasons of health or to facilitate traffic circulation, which in turn led to a succession of different construction styles.

With the exception of "overnight structures" (such as the favelas of Rio de Janeiro, tolerated if built in one night) and lightweight buildings (such as those in Japan) adapted to cope with earthquakes, urban houses are normally built of stone or brick. They are also often embellished with ornamentation which, together with the size of the building, provides an opportunity not only for the owner to display his social standing, but also to follow fashions that extend beyond frontiers.

Different styles have succeeded one another over the course of the centuries; for example, the Renaissance style in the 16th century;

the classical or colonial style in the 17th century; the Georgian style in the 18th century, the neo-Greek, neo-Gothic, Second Empire, and Victorian styles in the 19th century; and international and post-modern in the 20th century – to mention just a few of the styles used in western architecture. Among the many schools of architecture, Bauhaus sought to create in the late 1920s a synthesis between aesthetics, the functional requirements of users, and the imperatives of industrial construction: this led to the widespread use of concrete and glass. Nevertheless, the dream of owning one's own "personalized" house remains universal.

As well as the general appearance of buildings, stamps also illustrate various architectural features that are interesting for their originality or which are characteristic of a particular style.

Various countries have used stamps to display their seaside or lakeside dwellings. Once the domain of fishermen, houses by the waterside have now become very attractive to the rest of the population, offering a more relaxed style of living, a more moderate climate, and the pleasure of being by the water.

JAPAN 1998
Traditional houses (former Baba House at Nagano, Naka House).

GREECE 1975
Private residence in Siatista.

TURKEY 2002
Rakoczi House (18th century).

ST. PIERRE AND MIQUELON (FR) 2001
Tambour porches.

NETHERLANDS 1975
Beguinage house in Amsterdam.

Urban houses

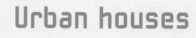

ST. PIERRE AND MIQUELON (FR) 1998
House in the town of St. Pierre, painted with leftover marine paint.

GERMANY 2003
Houses in the old town of Görlitz (Saxony).

CZECH REPUBLIC 1994
Baroque houses with arcades.

USSR 1972
House in Kiev.

MACEDONIA 2003
Family mansion.

GREAT BRITAIN 1975
Georgian houses in Charlotte Square, Edinburgh.

COLOMBIA 1960
The "Casa del Florero" (1810 revolution).

Architectural details

TUNISIA 1987
Arab Housing Day: Moorish house, mosaics, tools.

BURUNDI 1987
Homeless children looking longingly at a model house.

SRI LANKA 1993
Family moving into their new house.

Československo

CZECHOSLOVAKIA 1977
Historic window at the Bishop's Palace in Prague.

60h

The ideal of private houses

COLOMBIA 1978
The Carmen loggia, Bogotá.

GREAT BRITAIN 1995
Elizabethan window.

INDONESIA 1969
Family house, as envisaged by the five-year national plan.

UNITED STATES 1982
Gropius House (Walter Gropius was leader of the Bauhaus) in Lincoln, Massachusetts.

ITALY 1987
Villas at Pallanza on Lake Maggiore (Piedmont).

FRANCE 1987
1927 cubic-form functional housing by the architect Mallet-Stevens.

EGYPT 1989
Carved wooden balcony.

BELGIUM 1995
Art Nouveau: the "five continents" house in Antwerp.

TURKEY 1978
House in Istanbul, on the Bosphorus.

Waterside houses

GREECE 1986
Old houses and marina at the port of Chania, Crete.

NORWAY 1986
Port of Alesund during the polar night.

FAEROE ISLANDS (DENMARK) 1993
View of the village of Gjogv.

ITALY 1998
Marciana Marina, an old settlement on the island of Elba.

CASTLES AND MEDIEVAL TOWNS

Many stamps, mainly from Europe and the Middle East, have taken as their subject a typical image of the Middle Ages: the castle. A symbol of the power of the local lord, its purpose was essentially defensive, and this took priority over its function as a dwelling. Often uncomfortable, castles provided shelter to peasants of the fiefdom in the event of attack by bandits or the neighboring lord.

Originally a simple tower surrounded by a wooden palisade, the castle was gradually transformed into a veritable fortress in the 13th century, solid in appearance, protected by a moat, by a thick outer wall topped by a covered walkway, crenellations and machicolation, and dominated by a commanding keep capable of withstanding months of siege.

With the advent of artillery in the 15th century, defensive requirements changed completely and unsuitable castles were abandoned. In the 16th century, many were modified, enlarged, or rebuilt to bring them up to date.

Commemorated on stamps from various countries of the world, medieval towns were situated at the crossroads of trading routes or built around an imposing castle. By present-day standards they were not heavily populated:

10,000 inhabitants constituted a large town and the largest in Europe, such as Paris and Florence, remained below 200,000 inhabitants between the 11th and 16th centuries. Nevertheless, they swarmed with activity, with countless goods and tradesmen available in the streets during the day. In southern Africa, the mysterious site of Great Zimbabwe was home to between 20,000 and 40,000 people from the 12th to the 15th centuries, who lived in dwellings constructed around the fortifications of the temple and the mine. During the same period, the Khmer capital Angkor Thom in Cambodia had almost a million inhabitants living around the temples and the vast reservoirs that provided irrigation for farming, but the city was abandoned in the 15th century and invaded by the jungle.

Of the many medieval cities and towns in existence, only a few have managed to preserve their architectural heritage — mainly those that have not "benefited" from the kind of economic expansion that leads to the demolition of city walls, or where development has been halted, preserving the architectural unity that now gives them their charm. Today, such towns often benefit from the protection of UNESCO, and enjoy the status of World Heritage Sites.

ESTONIA 1993
The Monks' Tower at Kiiu Castle (1517). The stairway, providing access to the four floors, is built into the outer wall.

BELARUS 1992
Mir Castle (16th century).

USSR 1972
Kamenec Fortress (Ukraine).

POLAND 1971
Bedzin Castle (13th century).

CZECHOSLOVAKIA 1982
Krivoklat Castle, built in 1348 to safeguard the crown jewels of Bohemia.

SPAIN 1968
Sobroso Castle.

ROMANIA 1978
Bran Castle (15th century) at Brasov, residence of Vlad Tepes (Dracula).

SWITZERLAND 1978
Chillon Castle (13th century), on Lake Geneva (Vaud canton).

FRANCE 2001
Nogent-le-Rotrou Castle (11th–16th centuries) with its impressive keep.

GREAT BRITAIN 1978
Hampton Court (1514), built during the Tudor period for the Archbishop of York. Elizabeth I is believed to have entertained her lovers here in privacy.

ITALY 1977
Castel del Monte, octagonal structure built between 1229 and 1249.

FRANCE 2000
The medieval city of Carcassonne (13th century), with its city walls.

ZIMBABWE 1986
Great Zimbabwe, city with a 33-ft-high (10m) stone wall (12th century), protecting a temple and mine foundry.

Medieval cities

BELGIUM 1977
Bailiff's House, Gembloux (16th century).

FRANCE 1976
Rue du Gros-Horloge, Rouen.

JORDAN 1971
Via Dolorosa (Way of the Cross) in the old city of Jerusalem.

CZECHOSLOVAKIA 1967
Alchemists' Alley, Prague Castle.

CAMBODIA 1966
Angkor Wat, the largest of the Angkor Wat temples with its irrigation pool.

LEBANON 1967
The citadel of Saida (Sidon), a crossroads for trade.

MALTA 1999
Fort Sant'Anglu (16th century), belonging to the Order of Malta.

TUNISIA 1954
Tabarka Fort, part of a defense network built around the Mediterranean in the 13th century by the city of Genoa to protect merchants.

SAN MARINO 1996
Citadel of San Marino (13th century).

CAMBODIA 1966
Angkor Wat, the largest of the Angkor Wat temples with its irrigation pool.

MOROCCO 1980
Ksar (fortified town) in southern Morocco.

TUNISIA 1981
The Skifa el-Kahla Gate (16th century) in the port of Mahdia.

BHUTAN 1966
Simtokha Dzong (1629), captured by the Tibetans.

SYRIA 1925
Kasr el-Heir Fortress, dating from the time of the Crusades.

KAMPUCHEA (CAMBODIA) 1983
Temple consumed by the jungle.

GERMANY (GFR) 1969
Medieval city of Rothenburg (15th–16th centuries).

Castles

PALACES FOR POMP AND PLEASURE

A sovereign's need to display his power and magnificence through splendid palaces is universal and ageless, from the emperors of China to the tsars of Russia. Furthermore, the desire to have the largest possible number of servants and followers at the palace (and under their watchful eye) led to the creation of vast structures – for example, the Hermitage Palace in St. Petersburg has no fewer than 1,000 rooms. In those of more modest standing, the desire to be noticed was just as strong. It is interesting to follow the development of such buildings, from the feudal castle (page 68) to the stately palace, in the numerous stamps issued on this theme by many different countries. From the Renaissance onward, the area set aside for the accommodation of the lord and his family, which had been very restricted in

castles, became the predominant feature, and the defensive function became less important, allowing larger, more pleasant window openings to replace the narrow loopholes of the past. Fortifications disappeared in pursuit of aesthetics, expressed in harmonious façades looking out onto gardens. Today, in countries with old monarchies, historical palaces continue to provide accommodation for royal families, while other national leaders often choose to construct palaces of their own during their time in power. In countries where the monarchy no longer exists, palaces have now been converted into administrative buildings and museums.

But regardless of who owns these palaces, most countries have issued stamps to celebrate this prestigious part of their heritage.

CHINA 1996
The Imperial Palace at Shenyang (1625), built by the nomadic chief of the Manchu clan who founded the Qing dynasty.

JAPAN 1969
Himeji Castle or White Heron Castle (1601), in Kyoto, constructed of wood and covered in plaster to prevent fire. It is easy to get lost in the labyrinth of the tower.

ALGERIA 1975
Palace of the Dey of Algiers.

CAMBODIA 1951
The Throne Room at Phnom Penh.

VIETNAM 1990
Roadway leading to a pavilion in the imperial city of Hue.

USSR 1986
- 10 kopeck stamp: Hermitage Winter Palace in St. Petersburg (1754), former residence of the tsars.
- 15 kopeck stamp: Summer Palace at Petrodvorets (1721), St. Petersburg, built by Peter the Great.

CANADA 1982
Government House, Saskatchewan Province. This building, with its palatial appearance, was built in 1908 in Regina, a city founded by the prairie pioneers in 1882.

TURKEY 1978
Ishakpasa Palace (16th century), at the foot of Mount Ararat.

CZECHOSLOVAKIA 1976
Prague Castle (painting of 1572).

SPAIN 1989
The Royal Palace of Aranjuez.

PORTUGAL 1997
Pena Palace (19th century), Sintra.

HONG KONG 2003
The Potala Palace at Lhassa in Tibet: this white palace has been the residence of the Dalai Lama since the 7th century; the red palace is the sacred site of Tibetan Buddhism.

POLAND 1999
Ksiaz Palace, on a rocky peak in the Sudeten Mountains (rebuilt 16th–18th centuries).

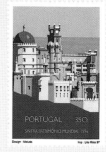

SWEDEN 1991
Drottningholm Palace (1662–1700).

DENMARK 2004
Frederiksberg Palace (1700), known as the "yellow palace," summer residence of Frederik IV.

NETHERLANDS 1981
Huis Ten Bosch Royal Palace (1645) in The Hague, official residence of Queen Beatrice.

PHILIPPINES 1973
Presidential Palace of President Marcos and his wife in Manila, built during their reign.

GREAT BRITAIN 1980
• Buckingham Palace, official residence of the British royal family.
• Kensington Palace (1760), childhood home of Queen Victoria, residence of Princess Diana, then of close members of the royal family.

FRANCE 1989
Château of Vaux-le-Vicomte, 17th-century masterpiece that Louis XIV sought to surpass by building the Palace of Versailles. The king imprisoned the château's owner, his finance minister Nicholas Fouquet, out of jealousy.

MONACO 1970
Royal Palace of Monaco, fortress built by the Genoese in 1215 and enlarged from the 15th to 17th centuries.

GERMANY 1998
The Wurtzburg Residence, one of the most beautiful Baroque palaces in Germany, built in the 18th century for a prince bishop.

NORTH KOREA 1973
The People's Culture Palace.

ROMANIA 1968
Jassy Palace of Culture.

FRANCE 1944
Château de Chenonceaux (1517), Renaissance residence bought by the French Crown and given by King Henry II to his mistress, Diane de Poitiers.

ITALY 1986
Villa Palagonia (1749) at Bagheria, Sicily, one of the most original Baroque buildings in the world, whose fantastical caricatures have intrigued visitors since the 18th century.

ITALY 1973
Main staircase and arcaded peristyle at the royal palace (18th century) of Caserta, Campania.

PARKS, GARDENS, AND FOUNTAINS

The aesthetic and symbolic desire to glorify nature by taming it in a park or garden is universal. It dates back to ancient times, from the gardens of Babylon to the landscaped spaces of today. The beauty of such gardens has been celebrated in stamps from all over the world.

For the Chinese, the garden is a place of contemplation, an intellectual pleasure, with curving pathways, successive panoramas, and tableaux that change with the seasons and are sometimes lost in the mist. For the Japanese, the garden has an imaginative appeal, contrasting the fragility of reeds with the solidity of stone, featuring water burbling gently over carefully placed pebbles, and exploring with refinement subtle differences of color.

The Persian or Arab garden divides space into rectangular areas in which water plays a dominant role, either standing tranquil in large pools or tumbling in cascades in flower-filled patios decorated with basins and mosaics. These principles can be found in the Arab gardens of Andalusia.

Italian Renaissance gardens and gardens in the 18th-century French style impose rigorous symmetry on tamed nature, with their carefully clipped trees and bushes. Yet there are surprises waiting to be discovered at the end of the straight pathways, with hidden "rooms" enclosed by foliage, and fountains and statues.

The English gardens of the 18th and 19th centuries gave the impression of untouched nature but were in fact carefully designed, taking the most picturesque elements of nature and alternating large landscaped areas with more intimate spaces, appealing to the Romantic imagination. At the end of the 19th century, the introduction of metal architecture led to the construction of vast glasshouses used to house tropical plants, creating indoor gardens. Fountains, once merely functional objects, became places where people could meet. They were later transformed into decorative features in both gardens and towns. They exist in all manner of styles, their gushing water bringing life to their surroundings.

SOUTH KOREA 1964
Secret garden in Seoul.

JAPAN 1966
Japanese lantern in the Kerokuen Garden, Kanazawa, in winter.

JAPAN 1
Screen by Hideyori K
maple trees at Ta

Chinese and Japanese gardens

CHINA 1980
Liu Yuan Chinese Garden (or Tarrying Gardens), Suzhou: the Yuancui pavilion in summer and Hanbi Shanfang pavilion in fall.

French and Italian gardens

SPAIN 2001
Patio in the Andalusian gardens of the Generalife in Granada.

MOROCCO 1955
Oudaya Arab garden, Rabat.

PAKISTAN 1961
Shalimar Gardens, Lahore, created in 1641 by a Mogul emperor.

Persian and Arabian garde

FRANCE 2001
The gardens of the Château of Versailles, designed by Le Nôtre in 1661.

USSR 1988
Fountain at Petrodvoretz (summer palace, St. Petersburg): the Oak Fountain.

ITALY 1995
The Boboli Gardens at the Pitti Palace, Florence (Renaissance 1549).

SPAIN 1988
Rural scene in the period of Charles III (18th century) in the gardens of a château.

ITALY 1997
Miramare public garden, Trieste (1860).

ITALY 1975
The baths at the Montecatini spa in Tuscany.

MEXICO 1978
Moorish fountain in the town of Chiapa de Corzo (1528).

DENMARK 1966
Tree-lined avenue at Bregentved Manor House, Holte.

AUSTRIA 1990
The Schönbrunn orangery, a tropical greenhouse erected in 1882.

AUSTRIA 1989
The Lusthauswasser, Vienna Prater, a vast green space between the two arms of the Danube.

SWEDEN 1987
Botanical Gardens, Stockholm.

UNITED STATES 1969
Beautifying America: plants for the city of Washington and park on the Potomac river.

NEW CALEDONIA 1976
Bandstand in a square in Noumea old town, planted with flame trees.

MOROCCO 1981
The Nejarine Fountain in Fez, decorated with glazed tiles on the front and roof.

FRANCE 2001
Wallace Fountain, one of a hundred installed in Paris during the 19th century, a gift from a wealthy British patron to provide fresh water to the people of Paris.

Fountains

ITALY 1973
The Baroque Trevi Fountain in Rome, much frequented, and setting for the famous bathing scene in evening dress in the film *La Dolce Vita*.

ITALY 1979
The Melagrano Fountain (wrought iron pomegranate tree) at Issogne Castle (Aosta Valley).

VATICAN 1975
The fountain in St. Peter's Square, Rome.

CZECHOSLOVAKIA 1988
Fountain at Prague Castle.

PUBLIC BUILDINGS

Throughout the world the existence of towns and cities relies on the activities carried out there, on commerce, and the services offered to the public. These can only thrive if the town becomes sufficiently large or specializes in a particular field; for example, Oxford and Cambridge depend on education. The architecture of a city's commercial, financial, administrative, and cultural buildings is a reflection of a country's identity and has been the subject of many stamps. In communist countries the architecture tends to be purely functional, whereas in wealthy countries, and those with a long history, the approach to architecture is based more on aesthetics.

In principle, the size of public buildings is proportional to that of the town or city, although these can reach excessive proportions for reasons of prestige or propaganda, as has been the case under totalitarian regimes. In addition to houses and public buildings, other structural elements in the urban environment, such as street lamps, kiosks, subway entrances, etc., contribute to a town's overall identity.

Countries all over the world have issued stamps featuring urban buildings that their postal authorities have deemed appropriate to highlight. In large cities where, over the course of the centuries, many buildings of different styles and periods have been erected, the construction of new buildings and the enlargement of old ones requires that the architect find the optimum solution, both aesthetically and technically, that will allow new and old to stand together harmoniously and in compliance with planning regulations. An example is the glass pyramid that now stands in the courtyard of the Louvre in Paris. In developing countries concerned above all for their future, and in Anglo-Saxon countries ruled by pragmatic considerations, the architect's work is facilitated by more freedom of design.

Administrative offices and town halls

JAPAN 1990
Hokkaido Hall, Sapporo, western-style architecture.

ST. PIERRE AND MIQUELON (FR) 1993
Prefect's official residence in the town of St. Pierre.

MALI 1970
Segou town hall.

NAMIBIA (FORMERLY SOUTH WEST AFRICA) 1984
Former imperial district office, now residence of the president of the republic.

ITALY 2004
6th centenary of Turin University.

GREAT BRITAIN 1971
University of Southampton.

INDIA 1995
150th anniversary of La Martinière College, Lucknow.

UNITED STATES 1982
Illinois Institute of Technology, Chicago.

Health and hospitals

Schools and universities

MAYOTTE (FR) 2000
New hospital in the territory of Mayotte.

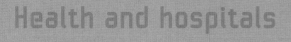

FRENCH EQUATORIAL AFRICA 1956
Office of the World Health Organization in Brazzaville (Congo).

Post offices

ALGERIA 1975
El-Kantara post office.

COLOMBIA 1949
Santo Domingo post office, built in the colonial style.

USSR 1987
Central Post Office, Moscow.

Subways and stations

CONGO 1966
Pointe-Noire railroad station, built to the same design as Deauville railroad station in France.

USSR 1965
October Square subway station, Moscow.

GERMANY (BERLIN) 1979
Five-branch candelabra-style street lamp.

PORTUGAL 1985
Kiosk in Lisbon.

Urban details

FRANCE 1994
Cast iron motif by Guimard (1900) at the entrance to the Paris Metro.

IVORY COAST 1980
1st anniversary of the West African States Central Bank, Dakar (Senegal).

UNITED STATES 1979
Philadelphia Stock Exchange.

Law courts and ministries

BRAZIL 1976
Ministry of Foreign Affairs, Brasilia.

JAPAN 1974
Supreme Court.

GERMANY (GFR) 1966
Berlin Philharmonic Hall.

CHINA 1983
Building of the National Congress of the People's Republic.

AUSTRIA 1984
Vienna Law Courts with Statue of Justice.

FRANCE 1989
Glass pyramid designed by Icoh Ming Peik in the Napoleon courtyard at the Louvre Museum in Paris.

UNITED ARAB EMIRATES 1990
10th anniversary of the Central Bank of the United Arab Emirates.

PAKISTAN 1999
Siege of the Islamic Development Bank.

ARGENTINA 1981
Centenary of the Military Circle, Buenos Aires.

Finance

Theaters, museums, and cultural venues

GREAT BRITAIN 1975
The National Theatre, London, with three auditoriums.

CZECHOSLOVAKIA 1988
Trade Union Leisure Center, Prague.

HUNGARY 1993
Budapest Opera House.

PORTUGAL 2004
Museum of the Presidency of the Republic.

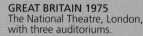

MAJOR CITIES AND THEIR MONUMENTS

Today, one out of two of the planet's population lives in a city. Cities offer an extraordinarily diverse environment because of their size, layout, style, and architecture. Their combination of various features (such as houses, palaces, gardens, and public buildings), makes them truly multifaceted. The numerous stamps issued by so many different countries offer a veritable kaleidoscope of the world's major cities.

It is said that one can grasp the history of a city by looking carefully at its architecture. It Is certainly true that the overall appearance of a city — whether unified architecturally or an anarchical juxtaposition of buildings of different periods — says a great deal about the way development has been managed, whether by strict regulation (for example, in Paris) or through an innovative approach giving free rein to the blossoming of new ideas (for example, in London).

A city's bridges and squares give it structure and are among the main features responsible for its charm. Bridges have their own particular symbolic value, connecting two shores of the same city, which are themselves often very different in character.

Cities in developing countries have been affected more recently than older, historical cities by the influx of the rural population into their urban centers, but they too are faced with the problem of creating new, modern districts close to their historic hearts. This does not present a problem where new cities have been created from scratch, such as Brasilia and Abu Dhabi. In some places, including a number of towns in China, a radical solution has been found by tearing down the old quarters to build anew.

City panoramas

ALGERIA 1998
View of hill terraces in the old town of Algiers.

NORTH KOREA 1972
Pyong-Yang, completely rebuilt in 1953 after the Korean War, adopted a Stalinist approach to city planning.

CANADA 1972
Quebec: from just a handful of inhabitants in 1609, it has developed into a dynamic city of over a million.

PORTUGAL 1993
Lisbon, its hillsides overlooking the River Tagus, is now a thriving intellectual and cultural center.

GERMANY 1992
2,000th anniversary of the city of Koblenz, founded by Teutonic knights at the confluence of the Moselle and the Rhine.

GREAT BRITAIN 1999
The City, London's financial district, boasts exciting new architecture thanks to the freedom of Britain's planning laws.

FRANCE 1995
Paris, Avenue des Champs-Élysées at night.

FRANCE 1989
Paris monuments: the Eiffel Tower and the Arche de la Défense. French town planning regulations are very strict.

CZECHOSLOVAKIA 1967
Bratislava, formerly Presburg, dominated by its castle overlooking the Danube, now the capital of Slovakia.

INTERNATIONAL STAMP EXHIBITION

SWITZERLAND 1984
Zürich, opulent Protestant city, economic and financial center of Switzerland.

GREAT BRITAIN 1980
Montage showing the monuments of London.

GERMANY 1996
The neo-classical Gendarme Square in the heart of historical Berlin, with its theaters.

PERU 1961
100-year-old cedar tree in the main square in Pomabamba, a small town almost 1,000 ft (300m) above sea level.

USSR 1972
Market Square in Lvov, one of the oldest towns in Ukraine.

INDIA 1990
Hyderabad, regional capital of southern India, with its 16th-century mosque straddling the road, and the Golconda fortified palace overlooking the city.

ITALY 1973
St. Mark's Square, Venice, threatened with being submerged: this image was designed for impact as part of the "Save Venice" campaign.

Public squares

HUNGARY 1993
The Chain Bridge, Budapest, with view of the palace.

FRANCE 1947
The bridges of Paris, and view of the Île de la Cité and Notre-Dame Cathedral.

ITALY 2001
Bridge and canal at Comacchio, a town in the Po delta.

TURKEY 1973
Bridge over the Bosphorus. This drawing shows the symbolic meeting between a child from Asia and one from Europe made possible by this bridge.

BOLIVIA 1990
Bolivia's capital city has four names: Sucre, Charcas, La Plata, and Ciudad Blanca (the appropriately named "white city"), famous for its Spanish colonial architecture.

GREAT BRITAIN 2002
Tower Bridge, London. The bridge used to be raised 50 times a day, but is now lifted only 30 times a month.

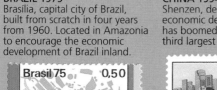

Bridges

UNITED STATES 1983
Centenary of Brooklyn Bridge, New York.

UNITED STATES 1999
United Nations Headquarters, New York: an example of the 1940s international style of architecture.

Modern cities

BRAZIL 1975
Brasília, capital city of Brazil, built from scratch in four years from 1960. Located in Amazonia to encourage the economic development of Brazil inland.

CHINA 1994
Shenzen, designated a special economic development zone, has boomed, becoming China's third largest city.

CHINA 1996
View of Hong Kong and the Bank of China. This stamp celebrates the return to China of the British territory of Hong Kong in 1997.

SINGAPORE 1995
Tomasek Boulevard, in the heart of Singapore's new business and commerce district.

MALAYSIA 1990
Kuala Lumpur, a mixture of modern buildings and ancient mosques.

SHARJAH 1964
View of Manhattan, New York, celebrating the World's Fair of 1964.

SWEDEN 1976
Modern building and sculpture ("Cave of the Winds") at Vasteras.

CENTRAL AFRICAN REPUBLIC 1970
Modern building, with witchdoctor in the bush.

BELIEFS AND CUSTOMS

BUDDHISM AND HINDUISM

In the 6th or 7th century before Christ, at a period when Hinduism was the dominant religion in India, a young nobleman was born into the Gautama family. At the age of 30, the young prince, who was accustomed to a life of refinement and luxury, suddenly discovered the poverty and suffering that existed in the world when he went outside his palace.

Immersing himself in deep reflection, he abandoned his family to take up a life of wandering and privation. However, he did not find the peace he was seeking until one day when he experienced the enlightenment of a middle way between a life of vain pleasure and one of sterile renunciation. He then became Buddha ["the Enlightened One"] or Siddhartha ["he who has accomplished his aim"], and set off to preach a new doctrine: man can escape the cycle of reincarnation of Hinduism if he attains Nirvana [the state of supreme wisdom], having eliminated all desires, which are the sources of evil. Buddha died at the age of 80, having converted many poor

people as well as kings, but left no written record of his teachings. His teachings were propagated in India, China, Tibet, and the Far East, splitting into various branches — all with the same aim of enlightenment, though differing perceptibly as to how this can be achieved. The most important are the Small Vehicle and the Large Vehicle, the latter admitting a pantheon of "bodhisattvas": beings who have attained enlightenment but have chosen to wait before reaching Nirvana in order to help other human beings. The Zen doctrine, which appeared in China in the 6th century, advocates meditation rather than the reciting of sacred texts, and devotes considerable time to manual work and martial arts.

The large number of statues of Buddha in Asia, showing all the different ritual positions of the body and hands, can be seen on numerous stamps issued by countries in the Far East. India and the countries of Indochina have also devoted stamps to various Hindu deities.

SRI LANKA 1976
The conception of Buddha: a white elephant pierces his mother's side.

LAOS 1957
Hair-cutting ceremony at Buddha's departure and renunciation of worldly things.

THAILAND 1992
Birth of Buddha.

SRI LANKA 1986
Breaking his fast with his five companions, Buddha accepts a bowl of rice.

Life of Buddha

THAILAND 1992
Seated under a fig tree, Buddha attains enlightenment.

CHINA 1997
Seated Buddha in the Maiji grotto: his left hand symbolizes listening and his right hand appeasement.

CAMBODIA 2001
Bayon Temple (12th century) at Angkor: the 400 giant faces of the Buddha with their enigmatic smiles.

THAILAND 1993
Preaching, Buddha converts more and more people.

SRI LANKA 1993
Patachara lost her husband to a snake bite, and her son was carried away by an eagle. She rediscovers serenity thanks to Buddha.

SRI LANKA 1995
Vesak Festival of the Ten Virtues: compassion – a man offers a drink to the crew of a boat.

THAILAND 1992
Death of Buddha: his ashes are placed in eight containers.

CHINA 1982
Bodhisattva (Liao dynasty sculpture).

VIETNAM 1978
Two of the 62 polychrome wooden statues (18th century) in the Tay Phuong pagoda.
• Jayata, 20th patriarch of Buddhism (4th century BCE).
• Ananda, assistant to Buddha and 2nd patriarch of Buddhism (5th century BCE).

JAPAN 1968
Gakko Bosatsu, assistant to Kannon Bosatsu, goddess of compassion.

JAPAN 1977
Seitaka Doji, assistant to Fudo (one of the guardians of the faith), ready to do combat against the enemies of Buddhism.

The ritual positions of Buddha

CHINA 1997
Bodhisattva and disciple of Buddha (Maiji grotto, Gansu province).

LAOS 1998
Golden statue of the Phabang or Prabang Buddha (14th century) after which Luang Prabang is named: both his hands are raised in a sign of appeasement and protection.

MONGOLIA 1991
Buddha seated in the Lotus position, his hands joined in the meditation position.

LAOS 1953
Buddha standing, arms pointing downward: posture of generosity, calling heaven to be his witness.

MONGOLIA 1999
The tallest golden statue of Buddha, at Ulan Bator, 92 ft (28 m) high.

LAOS 1953
Reclining Buddha: this position is rare.

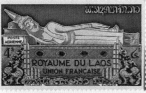

Hindu deities

CHINA 2003
The great seated Buddha of Leshan.

LAOS 1971
Ganesh, god with the head of an elephant, symbol of wisdom and domestic harmony.

LAOS 1971
Rahu, god of reconciliation and protector against poison.

CHRISTIANITY AND JUDAISM

The world's largest group of religions in terms of number of believers (1.7 thousand million), the Judeo-Christian tradition is based on the belief in a single God, revealed to us by the Old Testament, which is shared by Jews and Christians alike – though for the latter the Old Testament constitutes only the first part of the Bible.

The Jewish people are still waiting for the Messiah to appear on Earth, as announced by biblical prophets, whereas Christians believe that the Messiah was Jesus Christ, the son of God, who came to Earth 2,000 years ago in Palestine, at the time of the Roman Empire, and whose teachings are contained in the Gospels written by his disciples.

According to these gospels, Mary, the mother of God, was betrothed to Joseph, a carpenter in Nazareth. Told by an angel that she would give birth to the son of God (the Annunciation), Mary left for Bethlehem with her husband Joseph to take part in the obligatory census and gave birth there, in a stable. Shepherds and wise men, who had been told of the birth by angels and followed a star, came to adore the divine child.

At the age of 12, Jesus astounded the doctors of the Law with his knowledge. At 30, he preached the word of God, choosing as his disciples a group of 12 men (the apostles), and performed miracles. His popularity troubled the authorities, who condemned him to death. He carried his own cross on the painful road to Calvary, wearing a crown of thorns. He was subsequently crucified and his body placed in a tomb: this is known as the Passion of Christ. After three days he rose again (Easter Sunday), and ascended into heaven "at the right hand of God" 40 days later: this is known as the Ascension. The concept of the final resurrection replaced that of Hindu and Buddhist reincarnation, with all men being summoned to rise again like Christ. Christianity is, by far, the religion most abundantly represented on stamps from all over the world. These include scenes from the life of Christ, which celebrate each of the Christian festivals (Christmas, Easter, etc.) and representations of the Virgin, who, as depicted in art, has been a great source of inspiration to philately portrayed both maternally and in apparitions, which have given rise to pilgrimages in Europe and South America.

The life of Christ

God and the prophets

FRANCE 1970
The Annunciation (by a 15th-century primitive artist from Savoy).

EGYPT 2000
The Flight into Egypt: warned by an angel that King Herod had ordered all newborn male infants in Palestine to be killed to ensure the death of the son of God, the Holy Family fled into Egypt.

VATICAN 1988
The miracle of the wedding at Cana (detail from the painting by Veronese).

FRANCE 1973
The Last Supper, the final meal Christ ate with his apostles (capital in Issoire church): a circular band is cleverly used to represent the table and tablecloth.

ISRAEL 1973
Jewish biblical prophets: Isaiah.

GREAT BRITAIN 1979
Mary and Joseph's journey to Bethlehem.

SRI LANKA 1993
Jesus at the age of 12, with the Doctors of the Law.

MONTSERRAT 1985
The birth of Jesus is announced to the shepherds.

GREAT BRITAIN 1992
Stained glass window: the Three Kings offer gifts of precious perfumes (myrrh and frankincense).

The Nativity

VATICAN 1994
"And God created Man" (ceiling of the Sistine Chapel in Rome, by Michelangelo).

PERU 1978

CYPRUS 2003

AUSTRALIA 1965

SPAIN 1965
Pilgrim on his way to Santiago de Compostela: this site, where St. James the Great is believed to have come ashore, became the most important place of pilgrimage in medieval Europe.

GABON 1980
St. Matthew, apostle and author of one of the four Gospels (sculpture in Bizangobibere church).

MALTA 1967
The beheading in Rome of St. Paul, apostle and martyr.

VATICAN 1967
The three children and the appearance of the Virgin at Fatima in Portugal (1917).

BRAZIL 1979
Coronation of the Virgin of the Apparition (1904).

DAHOMEY 1966
Crucifixion scene.

SERBIA 2004
Death of Jesus on the cross.

HUNGARY 1999
The face of Christ imprinted on the holy shroud.

ANGUILLA 1970
The Ascent to Calvary (painting by Murillo).

PALESTIAN AUTHORITY 2000
Descent from the Cross (painting by Giotto).

LITHUANIA 1994, WALLIS AND FUTUNA (Painting by Jean Michon), **CHAD 1984**
The same attitude of maternal love can be seen on all three representations of the Virgin and Child.

VIETNAM 1962
Our Lady of La Vang.

SPAIN 1988
The Virgin of Hope, Malaga.

ECUADOR 1972
Our Lady of Sorrows (Caspicara, 18th century).

POLAND 1982
The Black Virgin of Czestochowska, object of pilgrimages to the monastery of Jasna Gora since 1382.

ISLAM AND MOSQUES

The world's second largest religion in terms of number of believers (around one thousand million), Islam forbids the reproduction of images of living beings to prevent idolatry. As a result, with the absence of images of Mohammed and his disciples, Islam, unlike Christianity, is rarely celebrated on stamps. But to compensate, the interlacing patterns and calligraphy of Muslim decoration are often transformed into veritable works of art. Mohammed was born in Mecca in 570, into a family descended from Abraham. At the age of 30 — like Buddha and Christ — the angel Gabriel appeared to him and revealed his mission to be the prophet of a single God. This ran counter to the polytheistic beliefs of the Arabs, and Mohammed was forced to flee to Medina in 622, the date of the "Hijra" ["expatriation"] and starting point of the Muslim calendar.

The army he assembled conquered the Arabian peninsula and destroyed all its idols. At his death, in Mecca in 632, the Muslim faith split into a number of different branches (Shiite, Sunni, etc.) and spread very rapidly throughout the Middle East, thanks to the great simplicity of its precepts, which are

easy to assimilate, and to the way it is organized, merging spiritual and temporal power, and leaving those conquered with very little choice about which religion to follow. Caliphs were installed in Damascus, Baghdad, and Cairo. The Koran, written three centuries after Mohammed's death, is the official transcription of the precepts handed down to him by God.

The principal stamps on the subject of Islam show the Kaaba, the black stone at Mecca, an object of the pilgrimage which is one of the five essential precepts of the Koran. Other images include prayer scenes and even the Dome of the Rock, the deeply symbolic mosque in Jerusalem built on the site of the Jewish temple of Solomon.

Many stamps from various countries show mosques. These invariably take the form of a main carpeted inner hall, where the faithful can pray, facing the mihrab, a richly decorated niche facing Mecca, where the imam recites prayers. Larger mosques often have madrasas attached. Madrasas are Islamic schools where clerics are trained, and whose reputation extends far and wide.

MAYOTTE (FR) 2004
A warm welcome awaits pilgrims returning from Mecca.

ALGERIA 1978
The holy Kaaba, a site of pilgrimage in Mecca, against a background of illuminations.

ALGERIA 1975
The richly decorated oratory of the Sidi Bou Mediene madrasa at Tlemcen.

MOROCCO 1978
The Dome of the Rock, the bitterly disputed mosque in Jerusalem.

MOROCCO 1992
The Kutubia minaret in Marrakesh and its twin, the Giralda of the former mosque of Seville (12th century Almohad dynasty).

SYRIA 1969
The Khaled Ibn al-Waleed mosque at Homs.

TURKEY 1957
The Soliman mosque (1557).

SENEGAL 1939
The great mosque of Djourbel at Touba, city of peace, constructed during colonial times.

EGYPT 1978
Minaret of the El-Rifaei mosque in Cairo.

IRAN 1984
Anniversary of the birth of the Prophet Mohammed.

IRAN 1985
Week of the "Hajj," the pilgrimage to Mecca.

The Kaaba and the pilgrimage to Mecca

SAUDI ARABIA 1976
The Medina mosque, commemorating Mohammed's exile in 622.

IRAN 1984
The conquest of Mecca by Mohammed, and the destruction of the idols.

MALI 1980
Celebrating the 15th century of the Hirja (Muslim calendar, starting in 622).

ALGERIA 1983
Among the Tuaregs, it is the men whose faces are completely concealed.

COMOROS ISLANDS (FR) 1974
The Grand Mufti of the Comoros Islands, Said Omar Ben Soumeth, a jurist expert in Muslim canon law, who issues "fatwas" (religious judgments).

CORMOROS ISLANDS (FR) 1970
The "Chiromani," an all-concealing Islamic religious veil worn by women in Anjouan.

FRENCH TERRITORY OF AFARS AND ISSAS 1973
Djibouti mosque and Muslim woman wearing a veil. The fact that images of people are shown is due to the colonial administration of the territory.

The veil and Islamic dress

USSR 1991
14th-century mausoleum in Pendzhikent (Tajikistan).

MALAYSIA 1990
Zahir mosque (1912) at Alor Setar (Kedah).

TUNISIA 1985
Aziza Othmana, wealthy 17th-century philanthropist who devoted her fortune to the needy.

ALGERIA (FR) 1949
Marabout, mausoleum of a holy man and place of prayer.

BOSNIA-HERZOGOVINA 1997
"Bairam," Islamic festival: 14th-century mosque at Banja Luka.

BAHRAIN 2001
• Stained glass window with Islamic interlacing.
• Beit al-Qu'ran Islamic museum, holds the largest collection of sacred manuscripts, originating in every part of the world – from China to Spain.

PAKISTAN 1985
Inauguration of a new mosque in Karachi.

UZBEKISTAN 1992
Registan Square, Samarkand.

IRAN 1988
Shahid Mottahari mosque in Teheran and its theology college.

Mosques

INDIA 1967
The Taj Mahal (17th century), magnificent mausoleum built by the Emperor in honor of his wife, Empress Mumtaz Mahal.

PLACES OF WORSHIP: PAGODAS, TEMPLES, AND CATHEDRALS

There is a certain homogeneity of design among the places of worship of most religions. They are often enclosed (to restrict access only to the initiated), and consist of a sanctuary, an inner, central space containing relics or the most sacred objects. This is true of pagodas situated at the heart of Buddhist temples, the main altar in a Christian church, and the placement of the books of the Torah in a synagogue.

Around the sanctuary is a second area, reserved for priests: the vestibules and inner courtyards of a temple or the choir of a church. Beyond this is a third area for the faithful, who carry out a purification ritual before entering: hence the basins in a temple and the holy water fonts in a church. This space often provides access to secondary places of worship: the side chapels in a church, the small "pagodons" devoted to secondary deities in a Buddhist temple, and Buddhist stupas housing sacred relics. The largest

places of worship have a fourth area for other members of the public, such as the merchants who occupied part of the temple in Jerusalem, non-believers in cathedral porches, and adjacent buildings in Hindu temples. These different religious buildings have been depicted on stamps from all over the world: from the most modest places of worship to giant pagodas and magnificent cathedrals – the finest of which were erected during the 12th to 14th centuries, in an age of great popular religious fervor. The more austere Protestant places of worship tend to appear less frequently on stamps than Catholic churches and cathedrals.

An interesting difference to notice is that Buddhist temples do not have vaults, unlike Romanesque and Gothic cathedrals, but that pagodas can be 12 or 15 stories high in order to house the various bodhisattvas, unlike Christian churches.

CHINA 1994
12-story pagoda at Kaihua temple.

NORTH VIETNAM 1968
One Pillar Pagoda, Hanoi: in the shape of a lotus flower.

CHINA 1990
Mount Huangshan temple (Henan province).

CHINA 1995
Forest of pagodas in the 3rd precinct of Shaolin temple.

MONGOLIA 1974
Buddhist temple at Bogdo Gegen palace.

LAOS 1959
That Luang stupa at Vientiane, the most important in Laos: it contains a hair of the Buddha.

CAMBODIA 1966
Preah Koh temple (12th century).

INDIA 1983
Pilgrims' ritual ablutions in the Ganges, on the ghats at Varanasi (Benares).

JAPAN (NARA) 2004
Five-roofed pagoda of the Muro-ji temple with rhododendrons in spring.

THAILAND 1982
Loha Prasat temple, Bangkok.

AUSTRIA 1977
St. Stephen's Cathedral, Vienna:
15th-century Flamboyant
Gothic.

SPAIN 1990
Pre-Romanesque church of
San Miguel de Lillo (9th century),
in Asturias.

USSR 1978
One of the first Christian
cathedrals (4th century) at
Etchmiadzin, in Armenia.

CZECH REPUBLIC 2004
Brno Gothic cathedral
(14th century).

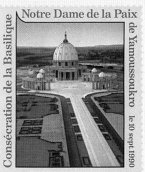

IVORY COAST 1990
Our Lady of Peace Basilica at
Yamoussokro, the second
largest after St. Peter's in Rome.

Churches and cathedrals

VATICAN 1991
St. Paul's Basilica, Rome,
the first (324) and largest
in Christendom after being
rebuilt in the 16th century.

POLAND 1977
Plock Romanesque cathedral
(12th century).

FRANCE 1964
Chapel of Notre Dame de
Ronchamp, designed by
Le Corbusier (1960).

ICELAND 2001
Chapel in the snow at
Brantarholts.

UNITED STATES 1980
Trinity Church, Boston
(architect: Richardson).

ARGENTINA 1988
St. Anne's Chapel.

NORWAY 1978
Wooden church at Heddal
(12th century).

FRANCE 1944
Chartres, one of the first
great Gothic cathedrals in
Europe (12th century),
and its stained glass
windows.

USSR 1989
St. Basil's Cathedral
(16th century) in Red Square,
Moscow.

GREAT BRITAIN 1969
Canterbury Cathedral
(13th–15th centuries, Gothic).

GREECE 1967
Small church on the island of Skopelos.

ISRAEL 2004
Centenary of the Great
Synagogue of Rome.

PORTUGAL 2004
Centenary of the
Shaaretikva Synagogue.

MONKS AND MISSIONARIES

The monastic life forms part of all the world's great religions. Monks seek the path to perfection by renouncing the world, and through penitence and prayer in a monastic community.

In Buddhism, this concept is, in fact, the very realization of Buddha's wisdom. Buddhist monasteries were in existence as early as five centuries before the beginning of the current era, and continued to develop in both China and Japan (from the 7th to the 8th centuries onwards). In Tibet, the country of the Dalai Lama, one out of five inhabitants was a monk before the Chinese communist invasion.

In Hinduism, where living as a wandering hermit or retiring into the forest were the preferred ways of life, monasteries did not appear until after the 8th century.

Christian monasteries began to appear from the 4th century in the Eastern Church, following for the first time the rules of living set down by St. Basil, and from the 6th century in the western Church, where St. Benedict of Nursia established the first Benedictine order. Monasteries soon began to proliferate throughout Europe, where the principal contemplative orders were those of Cluny, then Cîteaux in the 12th century. Mendicant orders began to emerge, such as the Franciscans and Dominicans, who, having taken a vow of poverty, preached outside the monasteries. In the 11th century, the strong Christian desire to deliver the tomb of Christ in Jerusalem from Muslim hands led to the Crusades and the creation of knight monks — the Templars, the Knights of Malta, etc.

From the 16th to the 19th century, preaching orders took part in the evangelization of the peoples of the New World discovered by the Europeans, then in countries in Asia, Africa, and Oceania, supported by religious orders such as the Jesuits. There was stiff competition between Protestant and Catholic missionaries to convert the populations of remote lands.

In Islam, where (according to Mohammed) monastic life is ruled out, "monks" (Sufis) still exist. In the 11th century, "soldier monks" began to appear (in the Almoravid and then the Almohad dynasties of southern Morocco), who streamed across North Africa and into Spain from their *ribats* (monastery fortresses) to impose the rigor of the Koran among the invaded populations by force of arms.

CHINA 1995
Shaolin Temple under snow (495).

CHINA 1995
Practice of martial arts, introduced at Shaolin in the 6th century by the Zen doctrine.

CHINA 1991
The hanging temple at Mount Huangshan monastery.

INDIA 1991
Jainist religious leader: non-violent, the monks wear a veil to avoid the risk of inhaling an insect and killing it.

ARGENTINA 1983
Father Mamerto Esquiu (1826–1883), Franciscan preacher.

ALBANIA 2003
Mother Teresa (1910–1997), founder of the Missionaries of Charity in Calcutta; awarded the Nobel Peace Prize.

LAOS 1957

INDIA 2001
2,600th anniversary of Jainism and symbols: hand with seal, swastika (the arms face right, a sign of good fortune in Hinduism and Buddhism).

INDIA 1997
Kavi Sunderlas, Hindu theologian.

LAOS 1957
Meditation.

Buddhist monks

PORTUGAL 1997
The Jesuit priest Luis Frois, the first missionary in Japan (1564), with a Kyoto dignitary.

FRANCE 1981
Anne-Marie Javouhey (1779–1851), founded the Sisters of St. Joseph of Cluny.

FRENCH POLYNESIA 1988
Great missionaries.
• Protestant: Pastor Henry Nott (1774–1844).
• Catholic: Monsignor Mazé (1885–1976).

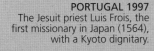

Monasteries

GREECE 1972
St. Paul's Monastery, one of 20 monasteries on Mount Athos (9th to 11th centuries), closed to women.

TUNISIA (FR) 1954
The fortified walls of Monastir, formerly a Muslim monastery.

Le Mont-Saint-Michel

FRANCE 1998
Mont St. Michel Abbey, founded in 966 by Benedictine monks.

UKRAINE 2003
Monks of the Maniavskyi and Carpathian monasteries.

ITALY 1980
St. Catherine of Siena (1347–1380), first woman Doctor of the Church.

BELGIUM 1941
Present-day Trappist monks at Orval Abbey (founded in 1070).

FRANCE 1958
St. Vincent de Paul (17th century).

SPAIN 1982
St. Teresa of Avila (1515–1582), Doctor of the Church.

GERMANY (GFR) 1980
St. Benedict of Nursia, founder of the Benedictine Order in 480.

BELGIUM 1965
Affligem Abbey (1615).

REPUBLIC OF IRELAND 1978
Catherine McAuley (1778–1841), founder of the Sisters of Mercy in Ireland.

SPAIN 1989
Monastery of San Lorenzo del Escorial (1584), laid out in the form of a grid in memory of the torture suffered by St. Lawrence on the grid iron.

SPAIN 1995
Monastery of Santa Maria de Guadalupe (1389), whose statue of the Virgin became a symbol of the conquest of the New World in 1492.

ITALY 1980
Monastery of Fonte Avellana, founded in 980.

ANIMIST RITES AND BELIEFS

Alongside the great religions of Christianity, Judaism, and Islam (which are based on the propagation of the belief in a single God), and Buddhism and Hinduism (which are directed more toward achieving inner harmony), a great variety of other beliefs and rites survive in the world. From the Inuits of Greenland to the Native Americans, from the Polynesians and Melanesians of the South Pacific and the figures of Scandinavian mythology to the initiatory rites of African witch-doctors — all these beliefs have one thing in common: the existence of a creator spirit, and of various deities that embody the elements of nature (water, trees, etc.). In closer proximity to man's everyday life, these deities must be honored to ensure health and prosperity. If not, they may become angry and unleash fearsome evils. Worship of the dead and respect for elders are also universal constants,

and the purpose of a number of rites, each very different, is to honor dead ancestors, not only to ensure the continuity of traditions but also to accustom the living to the idea of death.

Some beliefs are sufficiently powerful to survive the fragmentation of societies and cultures. Examples include the original voodoo of Togo and Dahomey, which was brought by slaves to Brazil and the Caribbean, and which became the official religion of Haiti. These rites have also been perpetuated through immigrants today in the major cities of Europe. Many stamps from Africa and the Pacific feature the masks and fetishes used in the various ceremonies to promote agriculture or the initiation rites of adolescents, for example, while the Scandinavian countries focus on figures of Norse mythology.

FRENCH POLYNESIA 1984
Old engraving: scene of human sacrifice (drum, warriors, victim).

FRENCH POLYNESIA 1985
Polynesian Tikis (ritual statues).

FAEROE ISLANDS (DENMARK) 2004
Norse mythology: Thor (god of thunder) and Ran (goddess of the sea, who catches those who venture too far in her nets).

NEW HEBRIDES 1979
Ritual puppet.

CHILE 1965
Head of a giant statue on Easter Island.

America and the Pacific

NEW CALEDONIA 1998
Kanaka mask; the wearer looks through the mouth of the mask, making him appear taller and more impressive.

BRAZIL 1976
Baikiri ceremonial mask.

UNITED STATES 1980
Native American mask.

NORWAY 2003
Troll: a hideous gnome of Norse mythology who stirs up discord.

CANADA 1980
Bird spirit of the Inuits.

IVORY COAST 1960
Senufo mask in the shape of a warthog (agricultural rituals).

BURKINA FASO 1988
Dance mask with two statuettes of young girls and a raffia veil to conceal the dancer's face.

MALI 1982
Dance mask used in agricultural ceremonies.

IVORY COAST 1979
Statuette of the mother figure (promotes fertility).

TOGO 1971
Annual ceremony of the holy stone: trance scene.

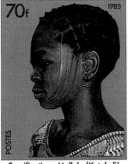

TOGO 1985
Young child whose cheeks show ritual scarification marks.

SWAZILAND 1968
Traditional customs: the reed dance.

GUINEA 1965
Ceremonial initiation mask.

BENIN 1977
"The fight against witchcraft": propaganda stamp issued by the People's Republic of Benin.

DAHOMEY 1975
Voodoo dance (fetishist dance).

GABON 1966
Copper Bakota mask: the diamond shape symbolizes femininity.

GABON 1966
Balumbu mask: heart-shaped face with trilobate hairstyle.

TRANSKEI 1990
African soothsayers: initiation of a novice.

NIGERIA 1993
Head of a Nok statuette.

CENTRAL AFRICAN REPUBLIC 1973
Africa in Europe.

African masks and rites

THE NEW YEAR AND THE ZODIAC

As early as two thousand years ago, astronomers in Mesopotamia charted the route followed by the sun, the moon, and the planets among the stars of the night sky, then divided it into 12 areas occupied by constellations that they identified and named after animals. This system enabled them to establish a precise calendar, making it possible to predict the length of the day according to the seasons, and to set the dates of festivals and crop-sowing times. Scholars in the service of those in power also developed an astrological "science" using these 12 signs to predict the outcome of future events – for example, a battle or the birth of a child – according to whether or not the stars were in a favorable position.

This knowledge spread to the eastern and western worlds and today survives in the astrological form of the signs of the zodiac. In the West there is one sign for each of the 12 months of the year; in the East one sign for each year, each sign re-appearing every 12 years. The two systems contain several of the same signs (one has the bull, the other the ox; one has capricorn, the other the goat), but they are not connected.

The signs of the zodiac have often featured on stamps issued by countries in the West, but mainly by countries in Asia and the Pacific region. In China the fact that the signs change annually lends itself to the production of regular stamp issues. Moreover, the Chinese zodiac plays a part in the Chinese New Year, which is celebrated over several days. The first day is dedicated to honoring dead ancestors, the following days to various festivities, feasting, visits, gifts, and entertainments. The New Year is also celebrated in other places, for example with the Tet celebration in Vietnam.

BOSNIA-HERZEGOVINA 2004
Virgo (August–September).

POLAND 1996
Libra (September–October).

RUSSIA 2004
Scorpio (October–November).

POLAND 1996
Leo (July–August).

BOSNIA-HERZEGOVINA 2004
Sagittarius (November–December).

Season's greetings

GREAT BRITAIN 2003

RUSSIA 2004
Cancer (June–July).

UNITED STATES 1995

FRANCE 2004

UNITED STATES 1998

MALDIVES 1974
Capricorn (December–January).

JAPAN 1998

BOSNIA-HERZEGOVINA 2004
Gemini (May–June).

RUSSIA 2004
Aquarius (January–February).

Signs of the zodiac

BOSNIA-HERZEGOVINA 2004
Taurus (April–May).

POLAND 1996
Aries (March–April).

POLAND 1996
Pisces (February–March).

The Chinese zodiac

FRENCH POLYNESIA 1993
The Year of the Rooster.

CHINA 1994
The Year of the Dog.

NORTH KOREA 1995
The Year of the Pig.

CANADA 2004
The Year of the Monkey.

VIETNAM 1996
The Year of the Rat.

SRI LANKA 1986
Singhalese and Tamil
New Year.

SOUTH VIETNAM
1975
The Tet Festival
(Vietnamese New
Year): throwing
firecrackers.

CHRISTMAS ISLAND
(AUSTRALIA) 2003
The Year of the Goat.

HONG KONG
(CHINA) 2004
Chinese New Year
Parade.

CHINA 1985
The Year of the Ox.

Chinese New Year

FRENCH POLYNESIA 2002
The Year of the Horse.

CHINA 1986
The Year of the Tiger.

NEW CALEDONIA 2001
The Year of the Snake.

UNITED STATES 2000
The Year of the Dragon.

MONGOLIA 1999
The Year of the Rabbit.

MAJOR RELIGIOUS FESTIVALS

Of the religious festivals celebrated on stamps from all over the world, Christmas, a festival of Christian origin, is by far the most popular. The stamps issued each year by a large number of countries are sufficient in themselves to form a thematic collection of interest for its novelty and variety with Santa Clauses shown in the snow or in the tropics, and manger scenes conceived by every country and every race.

It also provides an opportunity to collect reproductions of works of art as many stamps from Europe, Africa, and the Americas issued for Christmas and Easter feature paintings and sculptures on the subject produced by great artists throughout the ages – and in particular of the Virgin and Child, and scenes of Christ's Passion.

A number of stamps celebrate Jewish festivals such as Hanukkah and Lag b'Omer. By contrast, Muslim festivals are relatively rarely shown on stamps, with the exception of Id al-Fitr ("the Feast of Breaking Fast," celebrating the end of Ramadan) and Id al-Adha ("the Feast of Sacrifice," celebrating Abraham's faith by slaughtering sheep and goats as Allah substituted a sheep for Abraham's son Isaac).

A number of Asian countries also commemorate their religious festivals: as well as the New Year, there is the Water Festival marking the end of the "fasting" of the bonzes (Buddhist priests), the That Luang ceremonies of Laos, and the Day of the Wandering Souls in Vietnam.

ISRAEL 1976
The feast of Lag b'Omer: dancers from Meron.

UNITED STATES 2004
Hanukkah (or Chanukkah), Jewish festival commemorating the reconstruction of the Temple of Jerusalem, and traditional dreidl.

Jewish festivals

GHANA 1984
Easter: the cross and crown of thorns of Christ's Passion, with the inscription "INRI" (Jesus of Nazareth, King of the Jews).

GERMANY (GFR) 1984
The Oberammergau "Passion Play": 2,000 actors have enacted this scene every ten years since 1634.

Christian festivals

African festivals

Muslim festivals

UNITED STATES 2004
Kwanzaa, a non-religious, pan-African festival celebrating family, community and culture, restored in 1966 – based on an ancient tradition and celebrated from December 26 to January 1.

FIJI 1975, IRAN 1986
Id al-Fitr, Muslim festival celebrating the end of the fasting of Ramadan, and group prayer scene.

UNITED STATES 2001
EID greetings: stamp celebrating the two principal Muslim festivals: Id al-Fitr and Id al-Adha, a sacrificial feast at the end of the week of pilgrimage to Mecca.

FIJI 1975
Diwali: the Hindu festival of lights.

Asian festivals

SOUTH VIETNAM 1966
Day of the Wandering Souls: written messages are offered and burned.

LAOS 1972
The That Luang Festival: offerings of wax castles.

ITALY 2002

GREAT BRITAIN 1987

FINLAND 2002

WALLIS AND FUTUNA 1991
Santa Claus and his sleigh in a Polynesian interpretation.

GREAT BRITAIN 1990

WALLIS AND FUTUNA 1987

AUSTRALIA 1981

RUSSIA 1994
Russian Santa Claus: it was not until the 1990s and the end of communism that Russia began issuing stamps celebrating this Christian festival.

GREAT BRITAIN 1998

MEXICO 1983,
BELGIUM 1968

UNITED STATES 2002

BRAZIL 1978

SENEGAL 1985

GREAT BRITAIN 1994

SENEGAL 1972
Manger scene with figures from Goree Island.

Melchior   Balthazar   Jésus et Marie   Joseph   Gaspard

P. OPIC – M. JACQUES   DELRIEU

TRADITIONAL MUSIC

Drums, tambourines, xylophones, and other percussion instruments mark the rhythm and lead the dance. Drums may be very small (providing an accompaniment to the words of a traditional African storyteller) or enormous (as in initiation ceremonies). The tom-tom drum is used to spread news in the bush. It is an essential part of African life, beating out the rhythm in fertility and harvest ceremonies.

Wind instruments bring melody to the rhythm, producing a wide range of sounds, from the highest to the lowest, from the Andean flute, via the khene (a reed mouth organ) of Laos, to the trombones played by town bands in Europe.

String instruments are the most numerous and provide a full range of tones with their countless varieties of strings, plucked and strummed, on the myriad guitars, viols, lutes, and harps found in every region of the world. Many countries have celebrated their most typical musical instruments by showing them on stamps, making music a particularly rich and varied theme for collectors.

TAJIKISTAN 2002
Tambourine players.

DAHOMEY 1966
Griot (African storyteller) accompanying himself on a small drum.

BENIN 1980
The sato, a 10-ft-tall (3m) ceremonial bass drum, played by jumping up and striking it on top with long, curved wooden sticks.

TOGO 1983
Communicating by tom-tom in the bush and, in the background, modern means of communication in the form of satellite dishes.

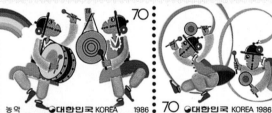

SOUTH KOREA 1986
Drummer and gong player, dancers with ribbons.

MALI 1973
Balafon (African xylophone), fitted with round calabash resonators.

KAMPUCHEA (CAMBODIA) 1984
Circle of drums.

NORTH VIETNAM 1972
Dancer with sunshade and xylophone player.

COMOROS ISLANDS 1975
Tambourine player (stamp surcharged "État Comorien" following independence).

IVORY COAST 1978
Drum used by town crier.

Percussion instruments

Wind instruments

RWANDA 1973
Horn player.

BRAZIL 1978

LIECHTENSTEIN 1980
Town band.

MOROCCO 1978
Flute player.

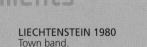

LAOS 1957
Khene player.

INDIA 2003
Sangeet Natak, National Academy of Traditional Indian Music and Dance.

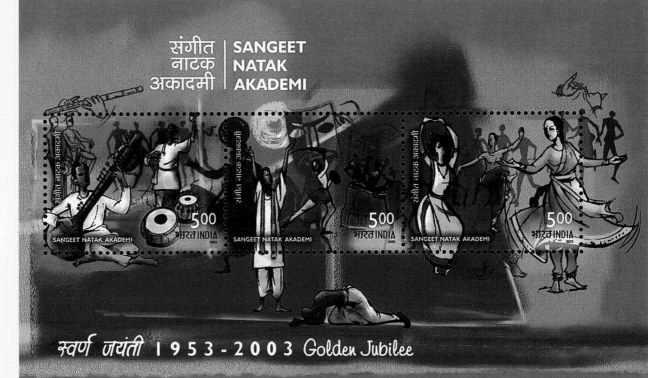

MALI 1979
Kora musicians: this traditional African instrument is made from a calabash fitted with numerous strings.

FRENCH WEST AFRICA 1958
Women playing the ardin (Mauritanian harp) in a tent.

AZERBAIJAN 1997
Harpist.

KYRGYZSTAN 1995
Old man playing a string instrument.

FRENCH POLYNESIA 1958
Wahine: Polynesian woman.

CAMEROON 1978
Man playing the mvet (zither with round resonators).

String instruments

Song

ANDORRA 1996
The "Petits Chanteurs" National Choir.

JAPAN 1981
"Cherry Tree in Blossom," a popular Japanese song.

FRENCH POLYNESIA 1989
Group of folk singers.

TRADITIONAL DANCE

African dances are associated with invocations to the spirits, seeking their goodwill – for example, for a good harvest. Typically, they involve movement of the whole body to the rhythm of an African drum, sometimes transporting the dancer into a state of trance.

In Asian dance, the rhythm is more subtle and the body movements often very slow. Movement is very graceful and expressed to the very tips of each individual finger.

For Europeans, dance provides an opportunity to show off one's finery, to have a good time, and shine before one's partner. In South America, the indigenous Pre-Colombian cultures were drastically changed by the arrival of the Europeans, and particularly of the Africans; nevertheless, they retained their own culture, of which their most spectacular expression is carnival. Countries all over the world that value their cultural legacy have produced stamps celebrating their traditional dances.

CHINA 1979
Popular celebratory dances with drum, tambourine, and banjo.

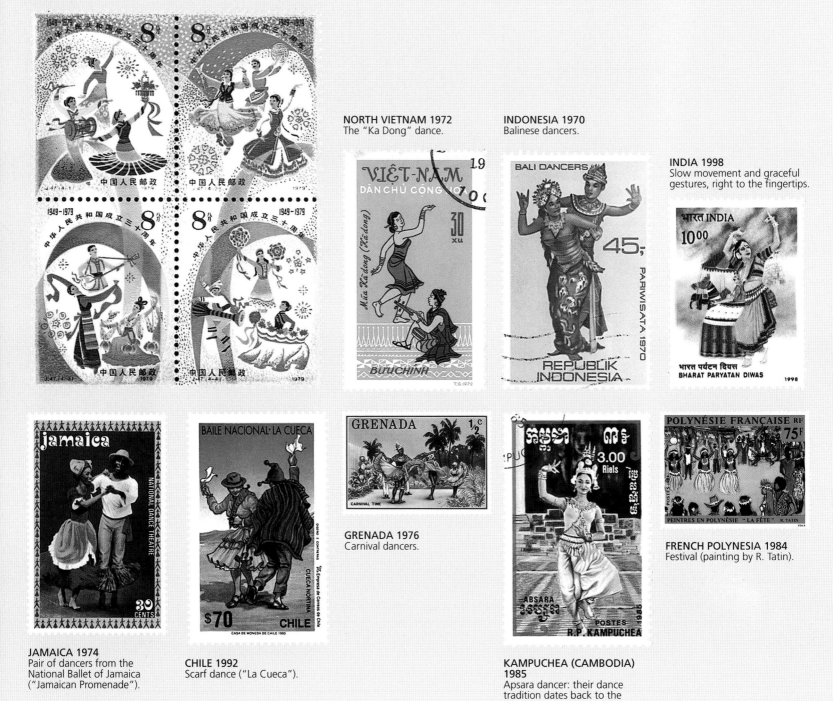

NORTH VIETNAM 1972
The "Ka Dong" dance.

INDONESIA 1970
Balinese dancers.

INDIA 1998
Slow movement and graceful gestures, right to the fingertips.

JAMAICA 1974
Pair of dancers from the National Ballet of Jamaica ("Jamaican Promenade").

CHILE 1992
Scarf dance ("La Cueca").

GRENADA 1976
Carnival dancers.

KAMPUCHEA (CAMBODIA) 1985
Apsara dancer: their dance tradition dates back to the temples of Angkor.

FRENCH POLYNESIA 1984
Festival (painting by R. Tatin).

DAHOMEY 1964
Somba dance.

CAMEROON 1976
Traditional dance.

MALI 1972
The Gomba-Malinke (dance from Bamako).

ANGOLA 1993
Popular celebration at Luanda Bay.

CHAD 1971
Dancers from M'Boum.

ROMANIA 1977
Popular Calusari dance.

POLAND 1969
Dancers in the traditional costume of Lodz.

HUNGARY 1977
Folk ballet from *Nagyrede Wedding*.

UNITED STATES 1993
Folk dance from the musical *Oklahoma*.

MOROCCO 1970
Seated dancer (the "Guedra").

USSR 1961
The Piatnitzky State Choirs (formed in 1911).

FRANCE 1981
The "bourrée croisée."

GERMANY (GFR) 1981
Dancers in the traditional costume of northern Germany.

USSR 1991
Popular celebration in Uzbekistan (dancers with flowers).

GREAT BRITAIN 1976
Bagpipe player and Scottish dancers.

GREAT BRITAIN 1976
Morris dancers.

CARNIVALS AND FESTIVALS

Tracing their origins back to the bacchanalian revels of Greek and Roman times and Christian festivals at which effigies were burned, carnivals are now an opportunity to dress up in disguise and have a good time. These disguises usually take the form of grotesque or frightening masks — a chance to exorcize our fears and demons. It is surprising to note the similarity between these grimacing masks from regions as different as Mongolia, Hungary, and Bolivia.

As well as popular traditional events held in towns and based on local themes — for example, the Il Palio horse race in Siena — there are parades of masked dancers, giant figures, and floats decorated with flowers in many countries in Europe and South America.

Festivals provide an opportunity to stage dramatic and musical performances that are extraordinary either because of the quality of the performance or because of their specialized nature, making them much-awaited events from year to year. The major festivals, the oldest of which date back to the 18th century, are organized around a famous composer — for example, Mozart in Salzburg — but the musical field has been extended with events such as the sacred music festival held in Fez, Morocco. Festivals are also held to celebrate exceptional historical events.

Of course, philately has been used to promote festivals in many countries, though unfortunately Italy has yet to honor its famous carnival masks that are the hallmark of Venice.

Carnivals

MONGOLIA 1991
Mask with fangs.

HUNGARY 1973
Buso mask at the Mohacs Carnival.

BOLIVIA 1985
Devil mask.

GABON 1967
Libreville Carnival.

GREAT BRITAIN 1998
Notting Hill Carnival, London.

GERMANY (GFR) 1973
Cologne Carnival.

SPAIN 1984
Santa Cruz de Tenerife Carnival.

SPAIN 2000
Walking on red hot coals in San Pedro Manrique (Soria).

CZECHOSLOVAKIA 1974
The "Little Queens," a popular folk event.

ITALY 1981
Il Palio, a traditional horse race held in Siena since the 17th century.

FRANCE 2003
Witch and pumpkin, celebrating Halloween — an ancient Celtic feast remembering the dead.

SLOVENIA 2001
Folk mask and wedding scene.

FRANCE, INDIA 2003 (JOINT ISSUE)
15th-century French miniature (with cockerel motif) and
19th-century Indian jewelry (peacock motif).

JAPAN 1985
Okinawa silks.

GERMANY (GDR)
1983
Sundial with cannon
gnomon (1800).

CZECHOSLOVAKIA
1979
French Rococo clock
(18th century).

AUSTRIA 1975
Painted fan: scene from Salzburg
provincial theater (18th century).

GREAT BRITAIN 1993
Precision marine
chronometer by John
Harrison (1759).

CENTRAL AFRICAN
REPUBLIC 1972
Man pursued by a
rhinoceros (African clock).

CHINA 1982
Fan decorated with a bird.

Lamps

CHINA 1985
"Good fortune" lantern
with dragon and phoenix.

Timepieces

GERMANY (GDR) 1989
Decorative ceiling light from
the Erzebirge region.

Weaponry

ALGERIA 1970
Damascene guns (18th century).

PORTRAITS OF WOMEN

A number of countries specialize in the commercial issue of stamps intended solely for collectors, and many of them produce stamps showing works by the world's most famous artists (such as Rubens and Picasso), but most countries also dedicate series of stamps to their own famous and lesser-known artists, and to works held in their national museums.

Several countries, such as Russia, France, Hungary, Poland, and Japan, have produced a higher-than-average number of stamps on this theme.

Generally speaking, the works presented are traditional, representational art, with the exception of two countries — France and Austria — which for some years have taken the risk of issuing stamps featuring abstract works of art. Rather than presenting these by period, country, or school — an approach more fully explored in books on art history — the selection here is based on themes. The first of these is the eternal and universal theme for artists of woman. She is shown idealized in her many different guises, regardless of her status or the style of the work: there are mystical women, portraits of great ladies and humble peasants and working women, nudes (in praise of the beauty of the female body), and women seen through the distorting prism of modern art.

YUGOSLAVIA 1971
Young girl in Serbian bourgeois costume, by Katarina Ivanovic (1817–1882), the first Serbian woman painter.

POLAND 1987
Portrait of a woman, by Léon Wyczolkowski (1852–1936).

SAN MARINO 1963
Lady with a Unicorn by Raphael (1506).

CZECHOSLOVAKIA 1969
Seated woman, by Alphonse Mucha (1860–1939).

Ladies

SPAIN 1958
Portrait of Doña Isabel Cobos de Porcel, by Goya.

Peasant women and workers

BULGARIA 1972
Peasant woman, by Vladimir Dimitrov (19th-century painter).

Women and religion

FRANCE 1999
Stained glass window at Auch Cathedral, by Arnaud de Moles (1513).

BOLIVIA 1972
The Idol's Kiss, by Cecilio Guzmán de Rojas (1929).

USSR 1971
Miner's wife, by Kasatkine (1894).

JAPAN 1985
Peasant woman in snowy woods, by Yumeji Takehisa (1884–1939).

GERMANY 1996
Seated Nude, by Max Pechstein (1881–1955).

FRANCE 1961
Blue Nudes, by Matisse (1952).

FRENCH POLYNESIA 1981
And the Gold of their Bodies, by Gauguin (1848–1903).

SINGAPORE 1995
Women on the beach in Bali, by Cheong Soo Pieng.

INDIA 1973
18th-century miniature: rajah's wife.

FRANCE 1967
Half-figure of a Bather, by Ingres (1820).

JAPAN 1982
Woman's back with fabric decorated with irises, by Saburosuke Okada (1869–1939).

COLOMBIA 1977
La Cayetana, by Enrique Grau (1962).

BRAZIL 1990
The Bathers, sculpture by Alfredo Ceschiatti in Brasilia.

Female nudes
Women in modern art

FRANCE 1980
Woman with Blue Eyes, by Amedeo Modigliani (1884–1920).

JAPAN 1982
Srimhadevi, by Shiko Munakata (1903–1975), the "Japanese Picasso."

BELGIUM 1970
Women, by Paul Delvaux (1897–1994).

FRANCE 2003
Marilyn Monroe, by Andy Warhol (1967).

FRANCE 2004
Galatea of the Spheres, by Salvador Dalí (1952).

AUSTRIA 1982
Muse of the Republic, by Ernst Fuchs (1930).

POLAND 2003
Vanitas, by Wieslaw Walkusi.

ITALY 1976
Woman at a Table, by Umberto Boccioni (1882–1916).

FRANCE 1989
Dancer, by Jean Arp (1925).

JAPAN 1979
Reclining Woman, by Yorozu Tetsugoro (1885–1927).

PORTRAITS OF MEN AND COUPLES

The second theme chosen in the field of painting and sculpture is that of portraits of men and self-portraits of artists, many of which display similarities that transcend periods.

To complete this brief overview there are some images of couples, intertwined in dance or simply sitting together, or embracing and captured in the purest and most passionate of kisses. A few portraits of children bring a certain freshness to the selection.

FRANCE 1980
Peasant Meal, by Louis Le Nain (1603–1648).

HUNGARY 1967
Godfather at Breakfast, by Istvan Csok (1865–1961).

TAIWAN 1975
Old man, ancient Chinese painting.

USSR 1973
Portrait of the sculptor S. Komenkow, by Korin (1947).

Old men

ITALY 2002
Christ on the Cross, by Cimabue (1240–1302).

GREECE 1950
Ephebe from Marathon.

ITALY 2000
Perseus brandishing the head of Medusa, sculpture by Cellini (1500–1571).

YUGOSLAVIA 1971
Portrait of a young man, by Konstantin Danil (1830).

Young men

UNITED STATES 2004
Native American effigy from the Mississippi region.

NIGER 1977
Carved negro head with a crest of small figures.

SPAIN 1959
Self-portrait by Velázquez (1599–1660).

MEXICO 1975
Self-portrait by David Alfaro Siqueiros (1896–1974).

Men and religion

Self-portraits

Couples

ARGENTINA 1988
Love, detail from a mural by Antonio Berni (1905–1981).

SPAIN 1978
Portrait of Jaime Sabartes by Pablo Picasso (1881–1973).

AUSTRIA 1978
Adam, by Rudolf Hausner (1886–1971).

GERMANY (GFR) 1974
Man Resting, by Erich Heckel (1883–1970).

Men in modern art

FRANCE 2000
Waltz, sculpture by Camille Claudel (1864–1943).

FRANCE 2002
Dancers, by Fernando Botero (born 1932).

GREAT BRITAIN 1995
Dancers at the Moulin de la Galette (detail), by Renoir (1841–1919).

BELGIUM 1970
Sculpture by Henry Moore (1898–1986) in Middleheim Park in Antwerp.

UNITED STATES 2004
Love, sculpture by Isamu Noguchi (1904–1988).

ITALY 2003
A chaste kiss: *The Meeting at the Golden Gate*, by Giotto (1266–1337).

AUSTRIA 1964
An enigmatic kiss: detail from *The Kiss*, by Gustav Klimt (1862–1918).

GREAT BRITAIN 1995
The Kiss, sculpture by Rodin (1840–1917).

Kisses

Children

BELGIUM 1963
Nicolas, the artist's son, at the age of two, by Peter Paul Rubens (1577–1640).

FRANCE 1962
Rosalie, the artist's daughter, by Fragonard (1732–1806).

BRAZIL 1980
Little Girl with a Glass of Water, by A. de Figueiredo (1843–1905).

ROMANIA 1984
Child, by Nicolae Grigorescu (1838–1907).

PAINTINGS OF DAILY LIFE

The third theme chosen for painting is that of everyday life, a subject that has inspired numerous painters to capture on canvas a fleeting moment in people's daily lives: the joy of motherhood, dances, village fairs, hunting scenes, religious services, or people simply taking a rest from their work.

Stamp producers have demonstrated a preference for happy scenes, as can be seen in the numerous stamps based on paintings by the French Impressionists, with their joyful scenes of Sunday outings in the country, and in the 17th-century Japanese engravings of people at leisure. A few stamps featuring 20th-century art photography complete the theme.

NORTH KOREA 1976
Evening in the village street, modern social painting.

JAPAN 1983
Women at work in the kitchen, by Utamaro Kitagawa (1753–1806).

UNITED STATES 1994
Family meal (*Freedom from Want*), by Norman Rockwell (1894–1978).

POLAND 1969
Nursing Time, by Stanislav Wyspianski (1869–1907).

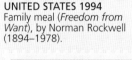

FRENCH POLYNESIA 1984
Leaving church, by Jacques Boullaire (20th century).

SOUTH AFRICA 1988
After service at the church of the Oath, by J. H. Pierneef (commemorating the Great Trek of 1838).

FRANCE 1970
Dancer on Stage with Bouquet, by Degas (1834–1917).

GREAT BRITAIN 1995
Indian dancers, painting from the Aurengzeb period (17th century).

FRANCE 2001
The Peasant Dance, by Peter Brueghel the Elder (1525–1569).

Leisure

INDIA 1996
The seasons: spring, Indian miniature.

FRANCE 1972
Women in the Garden, by Claude Monet (1867).

FRANCE 1993
The Muses, by Maurice Denis (1870–1943).

USSR 1978
Country fair, by Boris Kustodiev (1878–1927).

Daily life

TURKEY 1968
Musicians, 16th-century miniature.

Cultured pursuits

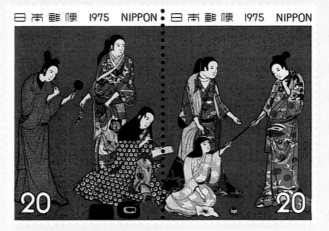

JAPAN 1975
Courtesans engaged in various pursuits, screen painting by Matsuura (early 17th century).

ALGERIA 1969
Hunting in the Djebel, by Nasreddine Dinet (1861–1929).

Work

GERMANY (GDR) 1972
Young girls selling grapes, by Max Lingner (1949).

GREAT BRITAIN 1979
The Liverpool Great National Steeplechase, watercolor by F. C. Turner (1839).

LEBANON 1971
Peasants at work, 12th-century Arab painting.

CYPRUS (KIRVIS, TURKISH SECTOR) 1987
Shepherd, by Feridun Isiman.

HUNGARY 1966
Yawning Apprentice, by Mihaly Munkacsy (1844–1900).

GERMANY (GDR) 1972
Bird hunting in Egypt, painting dating from 2400 BCE.

Art photography

FRANCE 1999
Schoolchildren, by Robert Doisneau (1912–1994).

GREAT BRITAIN 2000
Cyclist near Fife (Scotland).

AUSTRALIA 1991
On the beach, by Max Dupain.

UNITED STATES 2001
Driver, by Dorothea Lange (1895–1965).

LANDSCAPE AND ANIMALS IN ART

Animals in art, the fourth and final theme of painting and sculpture, shows us nature as seen through the artist's personal vision.

Chinese art is particularly successful at conveying the beauty and serenity of the landscape, and has celebrated this in large-format stamps, while western artists are adept at painting the sea in its many different moods in their seascapes.

The more restricted nature of the subject in still-life paintings allows comparison between different periods and regions.

Landscapes

TAIWAN 1980
Landscape by Ch'iu Ying (1494–1552).

JAPAN 1969
Pine trees, painting in ink on a scroll by Hasegawa Tohaku (1539–1610).

USSR 1986
Sunlit pines, by Yvan Chichkine (1896).

AUSTRIA 1975
Spiral tree, by Friedensreich Hundertwasser (1975).

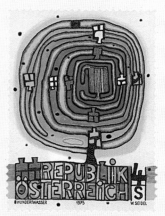

GREAT BRITAIN 1968
Landscape, by John Constable (1821).

USSR 1978
Shrove Tuesday, by Boris Kustodiev (1916).

CZECHOSLOVAKIA 1990
Landscape, by Jan Zrzavy (1923).

TUNISIA 1984
Mediterranean landscape, by Jilani Abdul Waheb (1890–1961).

FRANCE 1977
The Bridge at Mantes, by Jean-Baptiste Camille Corot (1868).

FRANCE 1982
Embarkation at Ostia, by Claude Lorrain (1600–1682).

GREAT BRITAIN 1975
Peace, Burial at Sea, by J. M. W. Turner (1775–1851).

Seascapes

CANADA 1997
York Boat on Lake Winnipeg, by Walter J. Phillips (1930).

Animals

JAPAN 1982
Walking in a snowy landscape, by Torii Kiyonaga (c. 1800).

VIETNAM 1989
Horse, by Ngua-tu Bi Hong.

LIECHTENSTEIN 1978
The Piebald Stallion at the Eisgruber Stud, by J Hamilton.

CHINA 1979
Manchurian tiger roaring, by Liu Jiyou.

UNITED STATES 1998
Black Cascade, mobile sculpture by Alexander Calder (1959).

FRENCH POLYNESIA 1988
Landscape with waterfall, painting on tapa (fabric made from bark).

UNITED STATES 1963
Birds, by John James Audubon (1785–1851).

SINGAPORE 1995
Gibbons, by Chen Wen Hai.

USSR 1981
Stag, by J. Pirosmanishivili (1863–1918).

FRANCE 1976
Still-life, by Maurice de Vlaminck (1876–1958).

ARGENTINA 1978
Still-life, by Ernesto de la Carcova.

Still-life

POLAND 1969
May sunshine, by Joseph Mehoffer (1869–1946).

LITERARY CLASSICS

Many countries celebrate their national writers by producing stamps of philosophers, poets, and novelists.

While the ideas of philosophy are universal, the dissemination of novels, and of poetry in particular, is inhibited by barriers of language and culture. In the West, for example, traditional Chinese and Japanese novels and the Indian poets are relatively unknown. However, thanks to the medium of cinema and the large audiences it attracts, the heroes of many 19th-century adventure novels — such as *Moby Dick* and *The Three Musketeers* — have reached a new public, and achieved international popularity.

Access to the cultural heritage of African countries is hindered by their oral tradition; furthermore the great multiplicity of African dialects has forced African writers to express themselves in the languages of the West.

TAIWAN 1975
Lao-Tseu, philosopher of the 6th century BCE, riding an ox.

GERMANY 1974
Emmanuel Kant (1724–1804), wrote *The Critique of Pure Reason*.

FRANCE 1978
Voltaire and Rousseau: new ideas of the 18th century, the Age of the Enlightenment.

GERMANY 2000
Friedrich Nietzsche (1844–1900), nihilism.

GERMANY (GFR) 1983
Franz Kafka (1883–1924), the inextricable universe.

Philosophers

Poets

TAIWAN 1985
Poetry from *The Book of Odes*, compiled by Confucius: leaves dropping in the fall.

RUSSIA 1998
Pushkin (1799–1837), self-portrait.

GREAT BRITAIN 1992
Alfred Lord Tennyson and "I am half sick of shadows" (1864).

GERMANY (GFR) 1982
Johann Wolfgang von Goethe (1749–1832).

SENEGAL 1996
Léopold Senghor, statesman in Senegal, poet and academic in France.

DJIBOUTI 1992
Arthur Rimbaud and "The Drunken Boat" (1871).

ROMANIA 1975
Mihail Eminescu (1850–1889) and the folly of his dreams.

INDIA 1976
Subhadra Kumari Chanban, poet (1904–1948).

JAPAN 1999
Bochan, short story by Natsume Soseki.

GREAT BRITAIN 1980
Emily Brontë and *Wuthering Heights* (1847).

HUNGARY 1980
Margit Kaffka (1880–1918).

GREAT BRITAIN 1996
Daphne du Maurier (1907–1989) and her typewriter.

UNITED STATES 1999
Ayn Rand and skyscraper illustrating *The Fountainhead*.

URUGUAY 2001
Moby Dick, by Herman Melville.

REPUBLIC OF IRELAND 1967
Gulliver's Travels, by Jonathan Swift (1667–1745).

GREAT BRITAIN 1970
Oliver Twist, by Charles Dickens (1812–1870).

UNITED STATES 1972
The Adventures of Tom Sawyer, by Mark Twain.

FRANCE 1982
Twenty Thousand Leagues under the Sea, by Jules Verne.

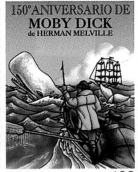

SPANISH SAHARA 1958
Don Quixote rescuing the lion.

HAITI 1935
The son and grandson of a black general, Dumas father and son wrote cloak-and-dagger fiction such as *The Three Musketeers* and *The Count of Monte Cristo*.

FRANCE 2003
Esmeralda and *The Hunchback of Notre-Dame*, by Victor Hugo.

USSR 1952
Nikolai Gogol and *Tarass Bulba*.

ISRAEL 1994
The Dreyfus Affair and *J'Accuse*, by Émile Zola.

CRIME FICTION, FANTASY, AND COMIC STRIPS

Originating in the 19th century and popularized in the early 20th century by characters such as Sherlock Holmes (Conan Doyle's detective hero) and Hercule Poirot (created by Agatha Christie, one of the world's best-selling authors), crime fiction has now developed — as has science fiction — into a literary genre in its own right, with its own audience and literary prizes. Many crime and science fiction novels have also been successfully transferred to the screen, achieving great popularity, which explains the presence of these fictional characters on stamps.

Comic strips came later, appearing in the 1920s, initially as a simple extension of literature in which text and drawing shared the page equally in serials published in newspapers and magazines. Their great popularity has transformed them into a genre in their own right, with the best-known heroes originating from the United States, Belgium, and Japan.
The transition from comic strip to animation was rapid, first in the United States with Walt Disney's productions, then later in Russia, Czechoslovakia, and France. With the advent of computer technology, other countries such as Japan have also become important players in the world of animation.

GREAT BRITAIN 1995
The War of the Worlds, science fiction novel by H. G. Wells.

BELGIUM 1994
Georges Simenon and Inspector Maigret.

UNITED STATES 1984
"Take a bite out of crime": Mac Gruff, The Crime Dog.

FRANCE 1996
Fantomas, by Souvestre and Allain (1911).

GREAT BRITAIN 1993
Sherlock Holmes and Doctor Watson, *The Reigate Squire* (1901).

Crime fiction

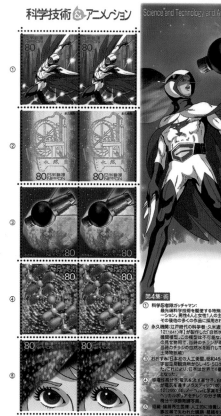

JAPAN 2003
Scenes from animated films.

Animation

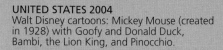

UNITED STATES 2004
Walt Disney cartoons: Mickey Mouse (created in 1928) with Goofy and Donald Duck, Bambi, the Lion King, and Pinocchio.

USSR 1988
The White Horse, animated film (1947–1975).

UNITED STATES 1995
Little Orphan Annie (1925).

UNITED STATES 1995
Popeye (1929).

UNITED STATES 1995
Dick Tracy (1931).

UNITED STATES 1995
Flash Gordon (1934).

BELGIUM 2001
Tintin in the Congo, by Hergé (1931).
© Hergé/Moulinssart 2005.

BELGIUM 2004
Blake and Mortimer by E. Jacobs (1946).
© Dargaud Lombard. 2005.

BELGIUM 1993
Natacha the airhostess,
by F. Walthéry (1987).
© Marsu 2005 by Walthéry
www.natacha.comics.com

SWITZERLAND 2004
Titeuf, by Zep (1992).

PORTUGAL 2004
Guarda Abilia, by Julio Pinto
and Nuno Saraiva.

BRAZIL 2003
Pluft the little ghost and Maribel,
by Maria Clara Machado.

NETHERLANDS 1997
Bob and Bobette, by
Willy Vandersteen (1945).

ITALY 1996
Corto Maltese, by Hugo Pratt
(1975).
© Cong S. A. Lausanne.
www.cortomaltese.com

SPAIN 2002
Captain Alatriste, by Arturo
Perez-Reverte.

NORTH VIETNAM 1972
"Professor Toad," traditional
engraving from the village of
Dong Ho, ancestor of the comic
strip.

FRANCE 2001
Gaston Lagaffe, by Franquin.
© Marsu 2005 by Franquin
www.gastonlagaffe.fr

FRANCE 1999
Asterix, by Goscinny and Uderzo
(1959).

Comic strips

THE CIRCUS, AND CHILDREN'S LITERATURE

Children's books have featured on many stamps.
Puppets, which form part of a long theatrical tradition in various regions of the world, appeared thousands of years ago in China and India, then in Japan in the 7th century, blossoming and giving rise to the Banraku theater in the 17th century. In Europe, the most notable puppet figures, often of a mischievous and even cynical nature, are Karagoz, who appeared in Turkey in the 14th century in the form of a shadow theater puppet (to avoid the Islamic ban on human representation), Polichinello in 17th-century Italy (later becoming Mr Punch in Great Britain), Guignol in 18th-century France, Kasparek in Czechoslovakia, and Kasper in Germany at the end of the 19th century.

The circus dates back to the wild beasts of Egypt and ancient Rome, and to the minstrels, jugglers, and bear and monkey trainers who performed at fairs in the Middle Ages. It was not until the 18th century in Great Britain and France that the circus took its modern form, first with acrobats on horseback, but gradually introducing the best acts and performers from all over the world, notably Chinese acrobats and jugglers, and trainers of performing Russian bears. In the 19th century, the world's largest circuses were in the United States, a country keen on size, with acts by trapeze artists, acrobats, and stunning illusionists.
Today, many circus acts, particularly clowns, are celebrated in the form of stamps.

GREAT BRITAIN 1997
Enid Blyton's "Famous Five."

UNITED STATES 1993
Little Women, by Louisa May Alcott.

FRANCE 1999
Les Petites Filles Modèles (Model Little Girls), by the Comtesse de Ségur.

GERMANY (GFR) 1970
The Adventures of Baron Munchausen, by Rudolf Erich Raspe (1785).

Children's literature

MALI 1976
Children's literature: "And the elephant's child pulled and pulled …"

GREAT BRITAIN 1985
Fairy tales.

GREAT BRITAIN 1998
Alice through the Looking Glass, by Lewis Carroll.

FRANCE 1994
Guignol, hand puppet by Laurent Mourguet (1769–1844), used as a means of criticizing his contemporaries.

VIETNAM 2000
Water theater puppets.

Puppets

CHINA 1995
Ancient puppet.

TAIWAN 2001
Puppet theater.

JAPAN 1972
The Banraku puppet theater. The puppeteers are concealed beneath black sheets.

TURKEY 1986
Karagoz, a deceitful, greedy, mocking character whose influence pervaded the Mediterranean.

The circus

MONGOLIA 1973
Ballerina on horseback.

GERMANY (GDR) 1978
The bear's kiss.

UNITED STATES 1993
Clown, ringmaster, trapeze artist, and elephant.

USSR 1979

GREAT BRITAIN 1999
Clown performing a slack wire act.

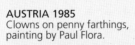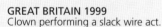

AUSTRIA 1985
Clowns on penny farthings, painting by Paul Flora.

NETHERLANDS 1977

MALTA 2002

SLOVAKIA 1990

USSR 1989
Illusionist act.

LITHUANIA 2002
The weightlifter
J. Ramanauskas
(1912–1996).

UNITED STATES 2003
The illusionist Harry
Houdini (1874–1926).

JAPAN 1982
Entertainers, by Seiji Togo.

THEATER

Theater existed in China as early as 2,000 years ago and expanded across Asia with the spread of Buddhism. This was a very symbolic and highly codified form of drama: the audience was already familiar with the plot, the set was non-existent – everything depended on the actor, concealed behind a mask or heavy make-up, on his mastery of voice and gesture, through the execution of which he conveyed a wide range of coded meanings.
Stamps from Asian countries have featured many examples of Chinese and Vietnamese theater, including traditional scenes, the Japanese Noh theater of the ancient Samurai, and popular traditional Kabuki theater. The theater of India and Laos relates episodes from the heroic epics of Rama and Sita, recounted in a 48,000-verse Sanskrit poem; unlike Chinese and Japanese theater, women are allowed to perform the female roles.

Western theater is derived from Greek theater and developed over the centuries, abandoning the symbolic use of masks and ascribing greater importance to plot and the psychology of the characters.
In Europe, troops of actors performed in the streets throughout the Middle Ages, and began performing indoors in Spain in the 15th century; the 16th century saw the construction of the Elizabethan theaters and the work of England's most celebrated playwright, William Shakespeare, who also developed a growing reputation in Italy and France.
The art of theater has been celebrated in numerous stamps featuring much admired playwrights and performers.

Asian theater

INDIA 2002
Japanese (Kabuki) theater and popular Indian (Kathakali) theater.

TAIWAN 1992
Mime of a boat in a Chinese drama.

SOUTH VIETNAM 1975
Vietnamese theater scene.

LAOS 1997
Laotian theatrical mask, variant of those used in Indian theater.

VIETNAM 1994
Vietnamese theatrical mask.

SINGAPORE 1990
Chinese theatrical mask.

JAPAN 1984
Male characters of Kabuki theater.

LAOS 1955
Laotian theater: Sita and Rama.

Stage actresses

FRANCE 1945
Sarah Bernhardt (1844–1923).

ITALY 1977
Dina Galli (1877–1951).

GERMANY (GFR) 1976
Hermine Körner (1878–1960).

POLAND 1996
Pola Negri (Apolonia Chalupiec).

LAOS 1971
Laotian theatrical costume (Rama).

GREECE 1999
Masks of ancient Greek theater and Japanese Noh theater, unchanged since the 14th century.

GREECE 1987
Scene from an ancient Greek tragedy.

TUNISIA 1989
Carthage drama festival.

ISRAEL 1971
The Inn of Ghosts, at the Cameri theater.

GREAT BRITAIN 1995
Elizabethan theaters: The Swan (1595), The Rose (1592), and The Globe (1599).

GREAT BRITAIN 1982
Scene from *Hamlet*, by William Shakespeare (1564–1616).

FRANCE 1973
Molière, playwright and actor (died 1673), dressed as Sganarelle.

ITALY 1974
Commedia dell'Arte: Pulcinella.

ARGENTINA 1983
Auditorium of the Teatro Colón (1908).

ITALY 2002
Auditorium of the Teatro della Concordia, Perugia.

USSR 1954
Anton Chekov (1860–1904).

REPUBLIC OF IRELAND 1980
George Bernard Shaw (1856–1950).

UNITED STATES 1995
Tennessee Williams (1911–1983).

GERMANY 1998
Bertolt Brecht (1898–1956).

Western theater

CLASSICAL MUSIC

In ancient civilizations, music was not considered an art but fulfilled a religious and social purpose. It was in the Middle Ages that it gradually developed into a form of entertainment.

Originally handed down by oral tradition, music began to be written down in ancient Greece, becoming gradually codified from the Middle Ages onward and eventually transformed into the new genres developed in 17th-century classical music such as the suite, sonata, toccata, and concerto.

In Europe, in the 18th and 19th centuries in particular, music was considered an art in its own right. Following the success of Baroque and then Romantic music, the 20th century saw the emergence of music that relied heavily on deliberate dissonance. European stamp producers have celebrated composers from Germany, Austria, France, Russia, and other countries, as well as the principal musical instruments used to perform classical music – including pianos, violins, and organs.

AUSTRIA 1991
Bicentenary of Mozart's death (1756–1791).

1756 ✱ WOLFGANG AMADEUS MOZART ✱ 1791

ISRAEL 1996
Felix Mendelssohn (1809–1847) and the Elijah oratorio.

FRANCE 1983
Hector Berlioz (1803–1869) and French horn.

GERMANY (GFR) 1970
Ludwig van Beethoven (1770–1827).

GERMANY (GFR) 1976
Conductor interpreting a symphony by Carl Maria von Weber (1786–1826).

CROATIA 1999
Jelacic March, by Johann Strauss the elder (1804–1849).

AUSTRIA 1959
Joseph Haydn (1732–1809).

GREAT BRITAIN 1985
Water Music, by George Frideric Handel (1685–1759).

Ancient music

GREECE 1985
Duet by Marsyas and Apollo.

FRANCE 1979
Music, 15th-century miniature.

AUSTRIA 1947
Franz Schubert (1797–1828).

POLAND 1980
The Frederick Chopin Piano Competition (1810–1849).

HUNGARY 1986
Franz Liszt (1811–1886) and piano.

GREAT BRITAIN 2000
Harp.

GREAT BRITAIN 1984
The promotion of the arts by the British Council.

SWEDEN 1983
Violinist.

Musical instruments

GERMANY (GDR) 1956
Maurice Schumann (1810–1856) and score by Schubert (in error).

NORWAY 1993
Edward Grieg (1843–1907) and river symbolizing Peer Gynt.

FINLAND 2004
Jean Sibelius (1865–1957).

GERMANY (GFR) 1981
Philipp Telemann (1681–1767).

UNITED STATES 1973
George Gershwin (1898–1937) and *Porgy and Bess*.

RUSSIA 1991
Sergei Prokofiev (1891–1953).

FRANCE 1974
Francis Poulenc (1899–1963).

AUSTRIA 1996
Organ Symphony by Anton Bruckner (1824–1896).

JAPAN 1989
Conductor.

ITALY 1967
Arturo Toscanini (1867–1957).

BRAZIL 1987
Heitor Villa-Lobos (1887–1959).

Conductors

OPERA, BALLET, AND SONG

The classical form of opera really dates back to 1607 and Monteverdi's *Orfeo*. Librettos and venues proliferated from the 17th to the 19th centuries with the success of Italian *bel canto*, German Romanticism, French *opéra comique*, and operas glorifying Russian nationalism.

Classical ballet underwent a renaissance and developed considerably from the 19th century with the work of composers such as Tchaikovsky. This period saw the beginning of the romantic ballet. At balls dancing changed, with the introduction of the waltz to replace the minuet.

Music for dance became more diversified with the polonaise, the Czech polka, Spanish flamenco, the Argentinian tango, and the Cuban habanera. In the early 20th century, while in Paris Swedish ballets continued a modernized classical tradition, in Great Britain and the United States in particular a new kind of musical theater began to blossom, and popular song underwent an extraordinary expansion conquering a vast audience from every corner of the globe.

Opera and classical ballet, as well as more popular genres such as jazz, blues, rock, and reggae, have all been celebrated in stamps, as well as traditional national songs.

DENMARK 1959
Ballerina performing *La Sylphide*.

CUBA 1978
Cuba National Ballet in a "pas de quatre."

JAPAN 1997
Ballerina and Samurai at the National Theater.

USSR 1961
Romeo and Juliet, by Prokofiev (1936).

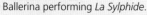

ARGENTINA 2000
Tango dancers.

FRANCE 1981
Jacques Offenbach (1819–1880) and *La Vie Parisienne* (Life in Paris).

JAPAN 1998
The Argentinean tango as seen by the Japanese.

SPAIN 1996
Carmen Amaya, flamenco dancer.

RUSSIA 1992
The Nutcracker, by Tchaikovsky (1840–1893).

Ballet and dance

Opera

VATICAN 2000
Giuseppe Verdi (1813–1901) and *Othello*.

GERMANY 1998
Auditorium of Bayreuth Opera House (1748).

AUSTRIA 1970
Die Fledermaus, opera by Johann Strauss.

USSR 1989
Mussorgsky (1839–1881) and *Boris Godunov*.

ITALY 1973
Enrico Caruso (1873–1921).

URUGUAY 1972
The "Coros del Este" sing Beethoven.

UNITED STATES 2000
Cats, musical showing on Broadway (1982).

GREAT BRITAIN 1992
The Yeomen of the Guard, operetta by Gilbert and Sullivan (late 19th century).

Musical theater

AUSTRALIA 2004
Dame Joan Sutherland (born 1926).

GREECE 1980
Maria Callas (1923–1977).

BELGIUM 1997
Ernest Van Dijck (1861–1923).

UNITED STATES 1997
Lily Pons (1904–1976).

Opera singers

JAMAICA 1981
The reggae singer Bob Marley (1945–1981).

FRANCE 1990
The singer Maurice Chevalier (1888–1972) in his trademark boater hat.

BRAZIL 1997
Jazzband musician Pixinguinha (1897–1973) with boater hat.

Jazz and popular singers

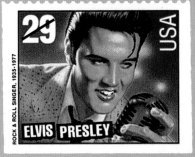

UNITED STATES 1993
Rock and roll singer Elvis Presley (1935–1977).

UNITED STATES 1993
Blues singer Dinah Washington (1924–1963).

UNITED STATES 1995
Jazz trumpeter Louis Armstrong (1901–1971).

CINEMA

Since its invention by the Lumière brothers in Lyons in 1895 and the first projection of *L'Arroseur arrosé* (The Sprinkler Sprinkled), cinema has undergone amazing development during the course of the 20th century, underpinned by decisive advances such as the advent of the "talkie" and of color. The big screen has overtaken other forms of entertainment in popularity, experimented with every genre, and has proved to be a medium of expression that has tempted producers from many countries.

Its global audience has brought fame and glory to film-makers, actors, and actresses – some of whom have been idolized by the public, with others going on to make a career in politics. The powerful domination exercised over cinema by the United States is balanced to some extent in the stamp world by the number of other film-producing nations (such as Japan, India, Brazil, and many countries within Europe) that have devoted stamps to their own home-grown films.

ITALY 1997
Ugo Tognazzi in *Amicei Miei* (My Friends) (1975).

FRANCE 1998
The actress Romy Schneider (1938–1982).

SENEGAL 1995
L'Arroseur arrosé (The Sprinkler Sprinkled), first short film, by Louis Lumière (1895).

GERMANY 1997
The actress Marlene Dietrich (1901–1992).

FRANCE 1955
The Lumière brothers, the inventors of cinema (1895).

GERMANY 1995
The robot in the film *Metropolis*, by Fritz Lang (1925).

FRANCE 1986
Les Belles de Nuit, by René Clair (1952), with Gérard Philippe.

SPAIN 1994
Luis Buñuel (1900–1983) and Spanish cinema.

GREECE 1995
Melina Mercouri, actress *Never on a Sunday*, and politician.

FRANCE 1982
Amarcord by Fellini wins the Palme d'Or at the 35th Cannes Film Festival.

World cinema

USSR 1965
• *Ballad of a Soldier*, by Gregory Chukrai (1959).
• *Battleship Potemkin*, by Sergei Eisenstein (1925).

ISRAEL 1995
One hundred years of cinema: The Marx Brothers, Simone Signoret, Peter Sellers, Danny Kaye, etc.

SWEDEN 1981
Cries and Whispers, by Ingmar Bergman (1972).

GREAT BRITAIN 1999
Actor and film-maker Charlie Chaplin (1889–1977).

GREAT BRITAIN 1996
Actress Vivien Leigh (1913–1967).

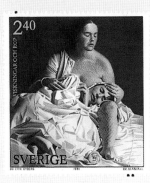

BRAZIL 1986
Film-maker Glauber Rocha (1938–1981).

JAPAN 2000
The Seven Samurai, by Akira Kurosawa
(1954).

INDIA 2001
Film-maker V. Shantaram.

SRI LANKA 1990
Actress and singer Rukmani
Davi (*The Goddess,* 1960).

American cinema

UNITED STATES 2003
Actress Audrey Hepburn
(1929–1993).

UNITED STATES 1995

UNITED STATES 1995
Actress Marilyn Monroe
(1926–1962).

UNITED STATES 2002
Actor Cary Grant
(1904–1986).

UNITED STATES 1998
Film-maker Alfred Hitchcock
(1899–1980) and signature
silhouette evoking the brief
appearances he made in his
own films.

AUSTRIA 2004
Arnold Schwarzenegger, actor and
governor of California.

UNITED STATES 1990
*The Wizard of Oz, Gone with
the Wind, Beau Geste,* and
Stagecoach.

UNITED STATES 2003
Special effects: creation of
Steven Spielberg's character
E.T. (1982).

UNITED STATES 1997
Actor Boris Karloff in make-up
for *Frankenstein* (1931).

NEW ZEALAND 2003
The character Gollum in *Lord of the
Rings* (2003).

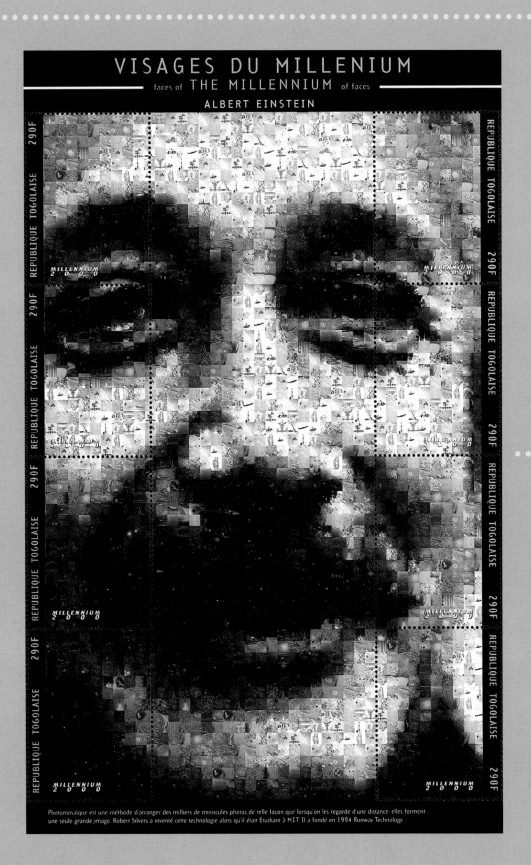

DISCOVERIES, INVENTIONS, AND MANUFACTURING

FROM SEDAN CHAIR TO COACH

The evolution of transport across ages and civilizations is a popular theme among philatelists, and many countries have issued a large number of stamps on the subject.

Boats powered by man with the aid of oars or paddles plied the waterways long before roads came into existence, while important figures and the sick were carried on litters by bearers.

Among all the animals used for transport, the horse is by far the most widely used. Its domestication appears to date back to the Neolithic period. Other animals, such as camels and elephants, have also played their part, valued for their skill or simply because of their availability in certain areas of the world. After these first means of locomotion came the invention of the wheel during the Bronze Age; this was a decisive factor in the

extraordinary development of transport, although certain civilizations, such as the Incas, never discovered it.

The coach is also a popular subject, and has been featured by many postal authorities – principally with illustrations of the mail coaches used in the 17th century and particularly in the 19th century to transport mail as well as passengers.

The bicycle, too, has been the subject of many retrospective looks at transport: from the penny farthing to the bicycles of today. However, it is mainly in Asia that the pedal rickshaws known as trishaws or "pousse pousse" are found.

The first of our pages devoted to transport looks at the different means of locomotion used in ancient times, all of which rely on human or animal strength as their source of energy.

DAHOMEY (FWA) 1939
Dugout propelled by pole.

COMOROS ISLANDS (FR) 1964
Dugout with outriggers.

SOUTH VIETNAM 1974
Passenger boat with oarswoman rowing with crossed oars.

CANADA 1953
Inuit in a kayak.

MADAGASCAR 1965
Filanzane, a chair carried by bearers to transport dignitaries.

CONGO 1975
Tipoy, an ancestral carrying chair.

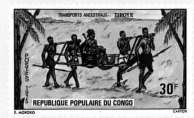

LAOS 1974
Cycle trishaw, a passenger vehicle.

LAOS 1958
Elephant carrying a palanquin.

KAMPUCHEA (LAOS) 1985
Buffalo cart.

INDIA 1973
A pair of lovers on a camel (Indian miniature).

VIETNAM 1993
Chinese sedan chair (the wheels are further back than on the western version).

VIETNAM 1993
Hand-pushed cart.

NICARAGUA 1982
19th-century mail coach.

FRANCE 1967
Old Man Juniet's Trap, by Douanier Rousseau (1908).

INDONESIA 1997
Ceremonial coach (16th century).

LIECHTENSTEIN 1978
Prince Joseph's golden coach (18th century).

GREAT BRITAIN 1984
Attack on the Exeter Mail, 1816.

POLAND 1964
18th-century stage coach.

REPUBLIC OF IRELAND 1987
Horse-drawn tram, Galway.

GERMANY (GFR) 1981
Stage coach at a coaching inn in 1855.

SWEDEN 1971
Timber sled.

USSR 1981
Muscovite sled (19th century).

GREAT BRITAIN 1978
Penny farthing, 1878, and late 19th-century bicycle.

CZECHOSLOVAKIA 1978
Cyclists in 1910.

POLAND 1986
Cyclist in 1886 (the pedal drives the rear wheel via the chain).

DENMARK 1985
Young woman riding a bicycle (celebrating the women's decade).

FRANCE 1983
Velocipedes, designed by the Michaux brothers (the pedal is on the front wheel).

GREAT BRITAIN 1978
Cyclists of the 1930s.

SWITZERLAND 1983
Bicycle and racing bike.

RAIL TRANSPORT

The second of this series of stamps on transport is devoted to the train. This was a 19th-century invention, if one excludes the first small trucks that ran on rails in the mines in the 18th century. Stephenson's development of the locomotive (which reached a speed of 8 mph/13 km/h) led to the first genuine railroad line in the world being opened to passengers in England in 1825; it ran between Stockton and Darlington. Other countries soon followed suit, including France in 1827, to facilitate the movement of coal from the Loire to Paris, and the United States in 1829.

Engineers from the great industrial countries of the world vied with one another to perfect the locomotive and to build railroads in areas considered to be inaccessible, while the drivers of steam trains plied their hard and dangerous trade battling against the heat of the boiler and the dangers of railroads. The legend of the railroad was enriched by the colorful and epic conquest of the American West in the 19th century, a period that still lives on in the minds of people today.

In towns and cities electric tramways gradually replaced horse-drawn trams: the world's first tramway was opened in Berlin in 1881. The world's first underground railroad opened in London in 1863, but experienced ventilation problems due to the amount of steam. The subways that followed, Budapest in 1896 and Paris in 1900, were electric.

During the 20th century, the railroad system developed with the rail network expanding, the increasing automation of motor units and signaling, and speed increases made possible by section rails and increasingly powerful traction equipment. Two countries drove the development of high-speed trains (over 185 mph/300 km/h at top speed): Japan, with the Shinkansen (bullet trains, running between Tokyo and Osaka, 1964); and France, with the TGV (trains à grande vitesse/high-speed trains), running between Paris and Lyons, 1981).

Most countries have chosen to celebrate not only their own trains but also the world's most famous trains in blocks or series aimed at collectors.

GREAT BRITAIN 1980
1830 train on the Manchester–Liverpool line.

MALI 1972
The first locomotive, which reached Bamako in 1906.

GREAT BRITAIN 1985
The *Golden Arrow*, a luxury Pullman train between London and Paris (1926).

LIBERIA 1996
Pacific class steam locomotive and Canadian Pacific Railway opened in 1866 (stamp block produced for the Canada philately exhibition).

UNITED STATES 1999
The *Super Chief*, train of the Hollywood stars in 1937 and other legendary trains.

KAZAKHSTAN 1992
Train on the steppes of central Asia (1922).

FRANCE 1937
Pacific class streamlined steam train.

CZECHOSLOVAKIA 1968
Centenary of the Ceske Budejovice–Pilsen railroad.

ARGENTINA 1949
Allegory illustrating the nationalization of the Argentinian railroads.

FRENCH WEST AFRICA 1947
Arrival of the passenger autorail at Dakar station.

MAURITANIA 1962
Mine train.

NORWAY 1954
Railroad man and centenary of the Norwegian railroads.

FRANCE 1943
Railroad man and centenary of the Paris–Orléans and Paris–Rouen railroads.

UNITED STATES 1950
Homage to the American railroad engineers.

LOS TRANVÍAS EN CUBA

CUBA Correos 2004

CUBA 2004
Tramway in Havana.

Subways and tramways

EIRE 24
Cork Electric Tram

REPUBLIC OF IRELAND 1987
Electric tramway, Cork.

NIPPON 80

JAPAN 1999
Tokyo tramway in 1903.

UNITED STATES 1971
Cable car in San Francisco.

SAN FRANCISCO CABLE CAR
U.S. 8¢
HISTORIC PRESERVATION

CHINA 1973
Diesel and steam trains passing.

JAPAN 1990
Streamlined electric locomotive.

NIPPON 62
EF 55形

NORTH KOREA 1987
Subway station and transport worker.

10 DPR KOREA

FRANCE 1987
Construction of the Paris metro by the engineer Bienvenüe in 1900.

250 RÉPUBLIQUE FRANÇAISE
F. BIENVENÜE

First high-speed trains

S 100 JAHRE SCHAFBERGBAHN 6
REPUBLIK ÖSTERREICH

AUSTRIA 1993
The Schafbergbahn mountain railroad (1893).

DEUTSCHE BUNDESPOST 50
75 JAHRE WUPPERTALER SCHWEBEBAHN

GERMANY (GFR) 1976
75th anniversary of the Wuppertal suspended railroad.

85 HELVETIA

SWITZERLAND 2003
Reflecting the passion for punctuality displayed by Swiss railroads.

RÉPUBLIQUE FRANÇAISE 0,60
TURBOTRAIN T.G.V. 001

FRANCE 1974
The TGV 001 high-speed turbo train.

0,23€ 1,50F RF LA POSTE 2001
EUROSTAR

FRANCE 2001
The high-speed Eurostar between London and Paris.

日本郵便 50
NIPPON 九州新幹線「つばめ」と桜島・鹿児島県

JAPAN 2002
The new Shinkansen bullet train.

Modern high-speed trains

1964 日本郵便
東海道新幹線開通記念 10

JAPAN 1964
The first high-speed Shinkansen bullet train, running between Tokyo and Osaka.

CARS, MOTORBIKES, AND TRUCKS

The car is a great classic among stamp collectors, from the earliest vehicles at the end of the 19th century to the cars of today. Every period, every category, and every country that produces cars has been featured on stamps (note that racing cars appear in the chapter on sport). As a means of transport, but also and primarily as an outward display of social status, the car is of universal interest. This is reflected in the abundance of stamps featuring the handsome cars produced between the war years, bathed in the aura of nostalgia and splendor that accompanies that period.

The British postal service has been artistically bold in celebrating its post-war sports cars with nothing more than the radiator grilles of prestigious marques such as Triumph, MG, Morgan, and Austin Healey.
Luxury limousines, utility vehicles, and even trucks have appeared on stamps — as have associations and events linked to the motor car, such as automobile clubs and motor shows.
Even motorized two-wheelers, from Vespas to Harley-Davidsons, have found a place in the world of philately.

UNITED STATES 1988
1932 Packard and 1935 Duesenberg.

GABON 1977
French car by Louis Renault in the Paris–Vienna race (1902).

REPUBLIC OF IRELAND 2003
Homage to Henry Ford and the American Model T Ford (1908), sold cheaply thanks to the industrial revolution and mass production.

SPAIN 1977
The 1916 Hispano Suiza.

NEW ZEALAND 1992
"The 1920s: The motor car brings freedom."

POLAND 1987
The 1936 Lux-Sport.

FRANCE 2000
The German Volkswagen "Beetle" (1936), the world's best-selling car.

GABON 1978
Front-wheel-drive saloon designed by André Citroën (1934).

ITALY 1985
Fiat Uno (1983).

FRANCE 2002
2 CV (1948), purposely simplified, popular with young people.

GREAT BRITAIN 1996
Sports car radiator grilles: Triumph TR3 (1957), Austin Healey, and MG (1955).

UNITED STATES 1995
Tail fin on an American car of the 1950s.

GERMANY 1999
Centenary of the German automobile club (1899) and Maybach DSH (1934).

UNITED STATES 1952
50th anniversary of the American Automobile Association (1902).

ITALY 1954
60th anniversary of the Touring Club Italia (1894).

GREAT BRITAIN 2001
The evolution of the London double-decker bus.

CHINA 1996
The "Red Flag" car used by Chinese officials.

USSR 1976
ZIS 154 bus (1947).

FRANCE 2003
Vintage Paris bus.

USSR 1976
ZIS 110 saloon car (1945).

ITALY 1996
50th anniversary of the Vespa (1946).

HUNGARY 1985
The legendary Harley-Davidson: the 200 cc Duo Glide 1 (1960).

FRANCE 2000
The Citroën DS 19 (1955), known for its revolutionary hydraulic suspension.

JORDAN 2003
Rolls-Royce (1960s) from the royal fleet of cars, now in a museum.

EGYPT 1926
Motorcyclist delivering express post.

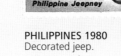

MAYOTTE (FR) 2001
Loading a shared bush taxi ready for departure.

PHILIPPINES 1980
Decorated jeep.

GERMANY (GFR) 1983
50th anniversary of the Frankfurt Motor Show (1933).

FRANCE 1998
Centenary of the Paris Motor Show (1898).

SAILING SHIPS AND LINERS

Navigation is a particularly vast theme, stretching from Antiquity to the present day. These pages are devoted to 19th-century sailing vessels, warships, liners, and submarines. Canoes, fishing boats, leisure, and racing yachts appear in the chapters on ancient modes of transport, occupations, leisure, and sport.

The turning point for marine technology came in the 19th century, first with the arrival of steam power, which, for a time, was used cautiously together with sail power on cargo-passenger boats, and second with the invention of the propeller, which replaced the picturesque but rather inefficient paddle wheels. During this period of transition, sailing ships like the *Cutty Sark* were still the fastest: the Tea Races between sailing ships traveling from China to Europe, each competing to arrive first with their cargo of tea, remain legendary.

All the last great four- and five-mast sailing ships, launched at the end of the 19th century and used exclusively for the transport of heavy goods, disappeared during the 1920s and 1930s. The expertise of the sailors who crewed these sailing ships, of the topmen in the rigging, and of the crews adept at maneuvers, lives on today in the naval sail training ships of various countries.

The glory years of the liner were between the two world wars, before commercial aviation reached the stage of development it has today. The battles between the great liners to win the prestigious Blue Riband – awarded to the fastest crossing of the Atlantic – still remain in the national memory.

Many countries have issued stamps, and in some cases entire series, on this theme.

FRENCH POLYNESIA 1985
Sailing ship in the 19th century in Papeete Bay.

AUSTRALIA 1984
The *Cutty Sark* (1869), the fastest three-master in the Tea Race, and later in the transport of wool from Australia.

ARGENTINA 1969
The frigate *Hercules*.

USSR 1981
Great school ships of the USSR: the *Sedov*.

NEW CALEDONIA 2001
The *France II*, a five-master used for transporting nickel ore.

JAPAN 1975
The *Tenchi-Maru*, a 17th-century galley.

VIETNAM 1999
Junk, with characteristic batten sail rigging.

DENMARK 1976
Cargo-passenger boat running on both sail and steam on the transatlantic crossing between Denmark and the United States.

GREAT BRITAIN 2004
The steamship *PS Great Western* in a storm (1838).

NORWAY 1981
Topmen climbing the rigging of a tall ship.

FRENCH SOUTHERN AND ANTARCTIC LANDS 1978
The *Aviso Doudart de Lagrée*.

UKRAINE 2004
Modern aircraft carrier with plane taking off.

USSR 1970
The cruiser *Aurora* during the Russian Revolution of 1917.

CUBA 1973
10th anniversary of the Revolutionary Navy.

UNITED STATES 1995
US Naval Academy racing yacht.

ALAND (FINLAND) 1998
Ferry boat unloading.

GREAT BRITAIN 1966
Hovercraft, ferry mounted on a cushion of air, used to cross the English Channel.

CENTRAL AFRICAN REPUBLIC 1968
The *Governor Ballay* river steamboat (Bangui, 1891).

NEW CALEDONIA 1973
The liner *El Kantara* on the Marseilles–Nouméa route via Panama (1923).

SOUTH AFRICA 1996
The liner *Oranje* in Cape Town port.

FRANCE 1962
The liner *France* (1960), renamed the *Norway* in 1979.

UNITED STATES 1996
River paddle steamers (19th century).

GREAT BRITAIN 2004
MS *Queen Mary 2*.

GERMANY (GFR) 1989
Liner arriving in the port of Hamburg.

GERMANY 2004
The *Dampfer Bremen*, holder in 1929 of the Blue Riband (for the fastest liner crossing of the North Atlantic).

UNITED STATES 1999
Second World War Gato class submarine after Pearl Harbor.

GREAT BRITAIN 2001
Swiftsure class 1 submarine (1973).

USSR 1973
Red Guard class D3 submarine, decorated with the red flag.

AIRCRAFT AND AEROSTATS

These pages represent a selection of the great moments of aviation and aircraft celebrated in stamps from all over the world. Although balloons had been in existence since the 18th century (developed by the Montgolfier brothers in 1783), and a few experimental flying machines had been produced, the true development of aviation extended across just one century, starting in 1903 with the Wright brothers, and punctuated by numerous adventures and great moments of glory.

The technology of dirigibles, which derived from balloons, came to an end in 1937 with the Hindenburg disaster when the hydrogen on board caught fire. The first aircraft inventors were also fearless pilots, for example Blériot, who, after several accidents, took off to cross the English Channel in 1909 on an incredibly fragile old crate of an aircraft. Many are those who lost their lives in the conquest of the air.

In the 1920s, competition was furious between the great western nations to open new airlines and conquer this emerging market. The French and Germans, for example, battled it out over the South Atlantic for the airmail service between Europe and South America. The exploits of pilots and engineers — such as those of Lindbergh over the North Atlantic and Mermoz over the Andes — captured the public imagination. A number of women also carried out great feats of aviation.

The jet plane, invented by the British in 1931, became more common in the 1950s, and was used in both military aviation (for speed of attack) and civil aviation (giving shorter flight times). However, the technological triumph of the supersonic craft *Concorde* was not matched by commercial success. Nowadays, flying is no longer an elite form of transport. With ever larger and increasingly reliable aircraft it has become a mass mode of transport.

FRANCE 1983
The first balloon ascent by Pilâtre de Rozier and the Marquis d'Arlandes (1783).

GERMANY 1992
Ferdinand von Zeppelin (1838–1917) and his hydrogen-filled dirigible.

FRANCE 1934
First crossing of the English Channel by aircraft, by Louis Blériot in his monoplane (Calais–Dover, 1909).

FRANCE 1973
The Brazilian Santos-Dumont, who built dirigibles and "demoiselle" or "grasshopper" planes in Paris (1907).

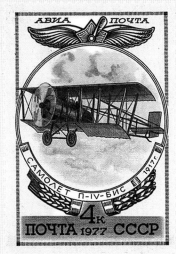

UNITED STATES 1999
Charles Lindbergh's *Spirit of St. Louis*; Lindbergh was the first person to cross the North Atlantic by plane (1927).

FRANCE 2000
Antoine de Saint-Exupéry (1900–1944), pioneer of the airmail service (Africa and the Andes), and writer.

UNITED STATES 1978
The Wright Brothers and the first manned flight (1903).

USSR 1977
Antonov R3 biplane (1925).

SENEGAL 1966
Disappearance at sea (1936) of Mermoz's French Latecoère 300 seaplane *Croix du Sud*; Mermoz made the first air crossing of the South Atlantic in 1930.

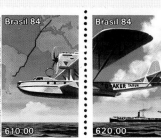

BRAZIL 1984
German seaplane on the first regular air route between Germany and Brazil (1934).

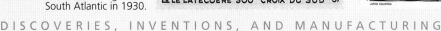

UNITED STATES 1991
Harriet Quimby, first American female pilot (1911).

UNITED STATES 1995
Bessie Coleman, first black female pilot to obtain her license (in France, 1921).

INDIA 1998
Homage to Indian women in aviation.

FRANCE 1955
Maryse Bastié, holder of the women's South Atlantic record (1936).

USSR 1984
C. B. Illyouichin (1894–1977), civil and military aircraft builder.

FRANCE 1988
Marcel Dassault (1892–1986), designer of the Mystère IV, Mirage III, and Falcon.

UNITED STATES 1997
The elegant Lockheed Constellation (1955).

UNITED STATES 1997
Second World War Flying Fortress.

SOUTH AFRICA 1995
Vintage and modern fighter planes (De Havilland 9 and Cheetah D).

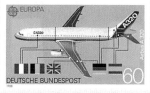

BRAZIL 1985
AMX fighter aircraft construction program.

UNITED STATES 1995
US Air Force Thunderbirds flying in formation.

GERMANY (GFR) 1988
The European Airbus A320 program, and the flags of the various countries involved in its construction.

FRANCE 2002
Final models of the Franco-British supersonic aircraft *Concorde*, built from 1969 to 1979.

USSR 1969
The Tupolev TU 144, direct competitor of *Concorde* from 1968 to 1978.

UMM AL QIWAIN 1972
BOAC Boeing 747.

USSR 1980
The M1 10K helicopter.

FRENCH SOUTHERN AND ANTARCTIC LANDS 1981
Alouette II helicopter in flight over the Atlantic.

NATURE'S WRATH

While stamps sometimes celebrate the beauty of meteorological phenomena (such as storms, the polar lights, and cloud formation), certain unusual natural phenomena (flooding, earthquakes, tidal waves, cyclones, and volcanic eruptions) can often be tragic and have dramatic consequences. Stamps that depict these often carry a face value plus an additional tax for payment into a charitable fund. Some countries have chosen to feature famous shipwrecks, but the principal theme of most maritime countries

remains that of their rescue services, which need funding in order to replace or purchase new equipment.

Many countries have also issued stamps on the theme of lighthouses. These allow us to trace their development from the early days of lanterns hanging from the ends of poles at the top of a cliff, to the modern, completely automatic lighthouse, which has meant the disappearance of the demanding and solitary job of lighthouse keeper, who lived on an isolated rock in the ocean.

CHILE 1995
Passing the legendary Cape Horn, much feared for its storms.

MAURITIUS 1994
Shipwreck of the *Saint-Géran* (1744) off Cape Malheureux.

TRANSKEI 1994
Shipwreck of the *Clan Lindsay* (1898).

FRENCH SOUTHERN AND ANTARCTIC LANDS 1995
The *Tamaris* in distress in the Southern Isles (1887). The giant petrel in the foreground, carrying a message of distress, was found seven months later in Australia, 4,000 miles (6,500km) away. When rescue arrived the crew had disappeared.

LAOS 1966
The 1966 flooding with the airport site under water.

MADAGASCAR 1998
Shipwreck of the *Titanic* in 1912, after it hit an iceberg.

USSR 1984
The arctic expedition ship *Cheliuskin* run aground (1934).

USSR 1965
Volcano erupting in the Kamchatka Peninsula.

NORWAY 1944
Shipwreck of the coaster *Baruy*, torpedoed by a submarine.

JAPAN 1963
Tsunami or giant wave with Mt. Fujiyama on the horizon.

INDONESIA 1967
People fleeing an erupting volcano.

GREAT BRITAIN 2000

NORWAY 2001
The aurora borealis above the polar circle with its iridescent, electro-magnetic shroud of light.

GREECE 1953
Reconstruction fund for the Ionian Islands ravaged by an earthquake.

ICELAND 1964
Formation of the volcanic island of Surtsey: erupted in November 1963; lava cooled in April 1964.

MAURITIUS 1995
Aerial view of a cyclone.

UNITED STATES 2003
Cumulonimbus and tornado forming.

GREAT BRITAIN 1972
19th-century coastguard.

REPUBLIC OF IRELAND 1974
Rescue of the *Daunt Rock*
lightship (1824).

ICELAND 1978
Rescue by winch (50th
anniversary of the Icelandic Sea
Rescue Society).

FRANCE 1974
French National Sea Rescue
Society boat manned by
volunteers.

NORWAY 1991
The *Skomvaer III* (centenary of
the Sea Rescue Society).

FINLAND 2003
Maritime lighthouses.

FRENCH POLYNESIA 1988
Point Venus lighthouse (1868).

DENMARK 1960
16th-century coastal lighthouse:
lantern suspended from a pole.

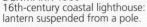

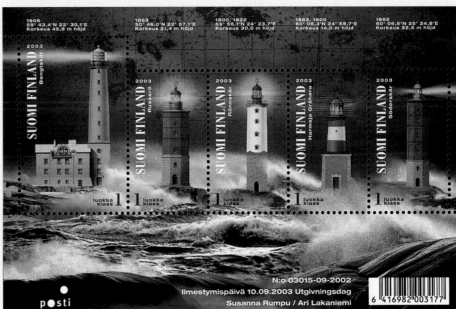

GREAT BRITAIN 1998
St. John's Point lighthouse
(County Down).

JAPAN 2000

USSR 1983
Coastal lighthouse, Tallin.

UNITED STATES 1995
Lighthouses on the American Great Lakes.

INVENTORS AND SCIENTISTS

In response to the interest man has always shown in astronomy – the most ancient of the sciences and for many years associated with religious beliefs – the world of philately has paid homage to Copernicus, to Galileo (whose heliocentric model was judged to be heretical by the Church), and to other great astronomers and mathematicians. It is also interesting to compare the different ways in which postal authorities have interpreted a subject as abstract as mathematics.

With the exception of China, some of whose inventions date back over a thousand years, most inventions with modern applications postdate the 16th century. Many were discovered in the 19th and 20th centuries, largely in the most industrialized countries of the period: in Europe and the United States. Some inventions appeared simultaneously in a number of places, but individual countries like to commemorate their own inventors, whether universally known or simply local celebrities. This is also true of inventors who left their country of birth and are now celebrated both in their country of origin and in their adopted country. (An example here is the physicist Enrico Fermi, who is celebrated both in Italy and in the United States.)

As the disciplines of science are too numerous for all to be represented here, a few of the more accessible fields have been chosen, such as electricity, electronics, and atomic physics.

POLAND 1969
Nicolas Copernicus and his heliocentric model.

VATICAN 1994
The solar system, considered heretical by the Church at the time of Galileo and Copernicus.

GREAT BRITAIN 1986
Caricature of Edmund Halley and his famous comet.

FRANCE 1989
Augustin Cauchy (1789–1857), author of theorems on integrated series.

USSR 1969
Mendeleiev, creator of the periodic table of chemical elements (1868).

GERMANY 1996
Wilhem Leibnitz (1646–1716), developed infinitesimal calculus.

UNITED STATES 1958
International Year of Geophysics: allegory of the creation of the world by Michelangelo.

AUSTRIA 1980
Alfred Wegener, produced the theory of continental drift (1915).

CHILE 1976
The European Southern Observatory of La Silla (1969) in the Andes.

GREAT BRITAIN 1987
Illustration of Newton's gravity principle (1687) and the apple that led to his discovery.

RUSSIA 1996
Ekaterina Dachkova (1744–1810), director of the Academy of Sciences in St. Petersburg.

GREAT BRITAIN 1991
First flight of a jet-powered plane by Sir Frank Whittle (1931) over East Anglia.

GERMANY (GFR) 1958
Invention of the compression engine by Rudolf Diesel (1893).

SPAIN 1983
Discovery of wolfram (tungsten) by the De Elhuyar brothers (1783).

INDONESIA 1999
Allegory illustrating fear of the "millennium bug" on computers.

ITALY 1999
Invention of the electric battery by Alessandro Volta (1799).

GREAT BRITAIN 1991
Charles Babbage, pioneer of the calculating machines (1821) that eventually led to computers.

FRANCE 1938
Discovery of radium by Pierre and Marie Curie (1898).

GERMANY 1994, FRANCE 1994
Quantum theory equations (Max Planck) and wave theory equations (Louis de Broglie): "h" represents Planck's constant.

UNITED STATES 1955
"Atoms for Peace."

UNITED STATES 1996
Computer technology (tube computer, 1949).

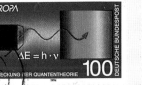

UNITED STATES 1979
Albert Einstein, author of the Theory of Relativity ($E = mc^2$, 1905).

UNITED STATES 2001, ITALY 2001
Enrico Fermi (1901–1954), Italian atomic scientist who emigrated to the United States in 1938; he developed the first atomic battery using fission.

DENMARK 1985
The physicist Niels Bohr (Nobel Prize, 1922) with his wife.

HUNGARY 1988
Human head drawn by computer.

GERMANY (GDR) 1972
15th Young Inventors' Exhibition.

UNITED STATES 2004
Buckminster Fuller (1895–1983), inventor of the geodesic dome, mathematician, and visionary.

FRANCE 2001
Invention of the smart card (Roland Moreno, 1974).

POST, COMMUNICATIONS, RADIO, AND TELEVISION

A number of postal services existed before the advent of the stamp with the cost of delivery being paid by the recipient. The world's first stamp was produced by Rowland Hill in England in 1840; this enabled the sender to pay the delivery charge. It is believed that the system occurred to him one day when the recipient of a letter refused to pay the delivery charge for a letter from her fiancé because she was able to read a message written on the envelope in an agreed code.

Tribute is also paid to the instigator of the UPU (Universal Postal Union), created in 1874. The UPU, is one of the few international organizations whose usefulness is recognized by all: without the UPU, sending a letter from one country to another would have been paralyzingly complex.

It is interesting to note that the advent of the Internet and electronic mail — which provides an alternative to the postal service, and may even threaten the very existence of the stamp — is nevertheless celebrated in philately (for example, see the Australian stamp).

Telephone, radio, and telecommunications have also been celebrated on stamps from many countries, often highlighting the striking contrast between ancient and modern means of communication. However, television, despite its importance in the home, is relatively rarely featured. Closer to home, the evolution of the postal and telecommunications services across the ages is a theme that postal authorities the world over have chosen to celebrate in abundance.

GREAT BRITAIN 1979
Sir Rowland Hill (1795–1879), inventor of the postage stamp (1840).

DENMARK 1976
19th-century postilion.

SPAIN 1963
Centenary of the first International Postal Conference in Paris (1863): mail coach at the Paris postal headquarters.

POLAND 1962
The decisive moment of posting a letter.

FRANCE 1955
Post by piloted balloon during the siege of Paris (1871).

CHILE 1994
First transport of Chilean post by car.

GERMANY 1994
Postman on ice skates in the Spreewald (c. 1900).

GERMANY 1995

IVORY COAST 1964
Postal delivery with soldier escort (1914).

MOROCCO 1953
Having a letter written by the public scribe.

GERMANY 1997
Heinrich von Stefan, creator of the Universal Postal Union (1874).

NEW CALEDONIA 2004

UNITED STATES 1973
Sorting the post.

USSR 1977, CANADA 1979
Campaigns to promote the use of postcodes on mail.

BHUTAN 1973
Collecting the post from a rural postbox.

AUSTRALIA 1985
Allegory illustrating email — in direct competition with the postal service.

ITALY 1995
Guglielmo Marconi, inventor of wireless telegraphy and TSF radio (1897).

UNITED STATES 1976
The first telephone: Alexander Graham Bell (1876).

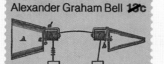

JAPAN 1990
Centenary of the introduction of the telephone in Japan.

UNITED STATES 2000
Mobile cellphones, popular all over the world.

AUSTRALIA 1991
Group of singers from the golden age of radio.

GREAT BRITAIN 1972
50th anniversary of the BBC (1922).

GERMANY (GFR) 1973
50th anniversary of German radio (1923).

NIGER 1965
Helping people through the use of radio: interview with a farmer.

JAPAN 1985
Night scene with cherry trees in blossom: commemorating the 50th anniversary of Japanese radio (1925).

DJIBOUTI 1991
Marseilles–Djibouti–Singapore underwater telephone cable.

CZECHOSLOVAKIA 1974
Intersputnik, International Organization of Space Communications.

FIJI 1983
Ancient and modern means of communication.

BRAZIL 1990
Television tower illuminated at night, Brasília.

UNITED STATES 1999
The birth of commercial entertainment on television (1941).

FRANCE 1962
The Nançay radiotelescope, listening for transmissions from outer space.

USSR 1984
25th anniversary of space television (1959).

ROADS AND CANALS, BRIDGES, AND DAMS

In the process of building roads and other communication routes, man has had to overcome natural obstacles, and this in turn has led to the creation of remarkable constructions. Bridges, which were originally nothing more than simple tree trunks laid down as a crossing point, then built in stone or from woven liana, have today become incredible structures thrown across the void between earth and sky.

The wooden and stone bridges of the Middle Ages required great expertise to construct, having to withstand the power of rivers in flood, as the dams that today regulate flow did not exist in those times.

With the exception of the vast medieval water reservoirs of Angkor, it was not until the 19th and 20th centuries that the great dams were built, first for irrigation and later to supply hydraulic electricity.

Road development underwent a renaissance with the advent of motorized transport. The remarkable network of Roman roads, which ran in long, straight lines providing the fastest possible link between the great cities of the Empire, had been abandoned in the Middle Ages as it no longer met the needs of merchants, who traveled slowly from place to place selling their wares. The building of canals, the waterway equivalent of the road, required massive investment regardless of the period because of the scale of the work required. Important examples include Suez, Panama, and the recent canal-building program in China.

Many countries have chosen to commemorate their feats of civil engineering on stamps. These can form a collection on a specific theme or part of a wider-ranging collection on "architecture."

Ancient bridges

The ancient Chupu bridge, Kuanhsien.

CHINA 1997
Covered bridge over the River Nanjiang (Dong architecture).

IVORY COAST 1965
Liana bridge at Lieupleu.

Other bridges

GREAT BRITAIN 1989
The Iron Bridge in Shropshire, cradle of the industrial revolution.

Ironbridge, Shropshire

BRAZIL 1974
The President Costa E. Silva Bridge.

FRANCE 1952
The Garabit Viaduct (Cantal), constructed by Eiffel (1880).

Roads

GREAT BRITAIN 1968
The prehistoric Tarr Steps causeway on Exmoor (1000 BCE).

FRENCH WEST AFRICA 1956
Road from Abidjan to Abengourou, Ivory Coast.

THAILAND 1981
Opening of the first highway.

MEXICO 1961
Railroad tunnel on the Chihuahua–Pacific line.

GREAT BRITAIN 1994, FRANCE 1994
Opening of the Channel Tunnel (joint issue of two pairs of stamps).

Tunnels

SWITZERLAND 1964
The Great St. Bernard Tunnel: first transalpine road tunnel.

GERMANY 2000
The Blue Miracle Bridge over the river Elbe at Dresden (1893).

MEXICO 1974
The Tepotzotlan Viaduct (commemorating Engineers' Day).

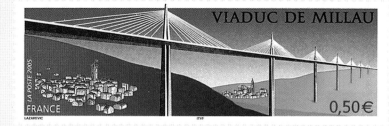

FRANCE 2005
The Millau viaduct, the highest bridge in the world: the central stay pillar is 1,125 ft (343m) high.

INDIA 1998
Train and viaduct on the Konkan line.

JAPAN 1988
The great Seto road and rail bridge.

SWEDEN 1979
Lock for leisure craft on the Göta Canal.

EGYPT 2001
Cable-stayed bridge over the Suez Canal.

CAMEROON 1953
Inauguration of the Edea Dam.

URUGUAY 1959
The Baygorria Dam (1958).

SOUTH AFRICA 1991
Tetrahedral stone dyke.

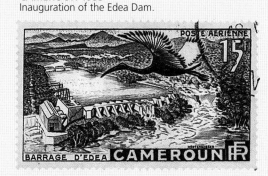

GREAT BRITAIN 1993
Barge port on a canal.

GERMANY (GDR) 1968
The Rappbode arch dam.

BRAZIL 1989
Dam of the first hydroelectric power station in South America (1889).

CHINA 1972
Red Flag irrigation channel, built along the mountainside.

CHINA 1998
Bridge over the Lingqu Canal.

MINES, INDUSTRY, AND ENERGY

Beginning in England in the 18th century, the industrial revolution was at the root of Europe's power during the 19th century, and spread to the rest of the world in the 20th century.

Today, our mindset has changed and our admiration for technical prowess has been tempered by concern for preserving the environment. This changing attitude has been reflected in stamps on this theme: a careful comparison will show that the subjects chosen between 1930 and 1950 – for example, pride in our great iron and steel works – has now been replaced by images of former factories converted into green spaces, and museums. The gap is even greater when it comes to nuclear energy. Nuclear power stations were originally promoted on stamps, whereas now the dangers of nuclear power are stressed, and the adoption of renewable energy sources and non-polluting industries is advocated.

Industry is one of the less common themes featured in philately, but is one that is educationally rich. A few examples of stamps on mining have been included to round off the theme.

GREAT BRITAIN 1989
Historic 18th-century industrial sites: cotton production powered by watermill (Strathclyde).

GREAT BRITAIN 1999
The power of steam in the 19th century.

GREAT BRITAIN 1976
A 19th-century coal miner and Thomas Hepburn's social reforms.

GERMANY (GDR) 1978
Inspector of mines in ceremonial dress (19th century).

FRANCE 1949
Miner using a pneumatic drill.

CHILE 1971
Nationalization of the copper mines.

BRAZIL 1980
Coal wagons.

USSR 1981
Giant excavator and ore train at Ekibastouz.

MAURITANIA 1975
Iron ore mine belonging to the Mauritania Mining Company.

GERMANY 2003
Coal mines in the Ruhr, surrounded by trees.

SPAIN 1938
Tribute to the foundry workers of Sagunto.

PERU 1986
Alpacas and the textile industry.

GREAT BRITAIN 1999
The ship-building industry.

GERMANY 1996
The old iron and steel mill at Völklingen, now a world heritage site.

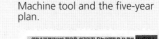

NORTH KOREA 1972
Machine tool and the five-year plan.

CHINA 1957
First Chinese trucks on the assembly line.

USSR 1946
New five-year plan for the steel industry.

AUSTRIA 1961
15th anniversary of the nationalization of industry (1946): generator.

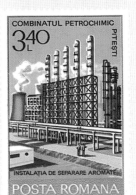

CHINA 1959
The chemical industry.

UNITED STATES 1957
"American and Steel Growing Together."

MAYOTTE (FR) 2002
Remnants of the sugar industry.

DUTCH ANTILLES 1959
Opening of the water distillation plant in Aruba.

ROMANIA 1978
Petrochemical complex: aromatic distillation unit.

DUBAI 1969
Commemorating the first oil exports.

FRANCE 1965
20th anniversary of the Atomic Energy Commission (1945).

USSR 1981
Atommach nuclear power plant.

GREAT BRITAIN 1966
Windscale nuclear reactor.

GREAT BRITAIN 1986
North Sea oil platform and electricity produced (illuminated light bulb).

AUSTRALIA 2004
Renewable energy: sun, wind, water, biomass.

NEW ZEALAND 1995
Symbols of nuclear disarmament.

BELARUS 1996
Boarded-up windows on houses contaminated by the Chernobyl nuclear disaster (1986).

MEXICO 1977
Ten years of the Tlalelolco nuclear non-proliferation treaty (1967).

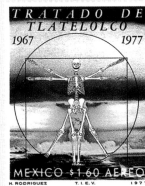

MEDICINE AND BIOLOGY

As with inventors and scientists, many countries have paid tribute through their stamps to their great doctors, sometimes going back as far as Antiquity and the Middle Ages.

The selection chosen here focuses on some of the great names in the field of vaccination and the fight against infectious diseases, although many other fields are equally valuable. Advances in modern medicine are increasingly the result of teamwork, and this is sometimes acknowledged on stamps through

a less personalized representation. A number of British stamps have recently paid tribute to genetic research, although the applications of this research can pose serious ethical problems. Medical scanning and medical conferences have also provided subjects for stamps, which can be appreciated for both their aesthetic appeal and their originality.

To round off the theme of science, some naturalists and zoologists featured on stamps have also been included.

GREECE 1996
Hippocrates (460–377 BCE), doctor and surgeon, devised the oath sworn by all future doctors.

MEXICO 1980
Illustration from the *Codex borbonicus* promoting a surgeons' congress.

GREAT BRITAIN 1999
First vaccination against smallpox by Jenner (1796), using a serum extracted from an infected cow.

IRAN 1992
Doctor in ancient times examining a patient.

REPUBLIC OF IRELAND 1978
Worldwide eradication of smallpox, illustrated by a vaccination scene, by Hamman (19th century).

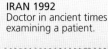

FRANCE 1948
Dr Albert Calmette, inventor of the BCG vaccine (Bacillus Calmette–Guérin, 1899–1921) against tuberculosis.

JAPAN 1958
Picture of a stethoscope promoting a bronchopathology congress.

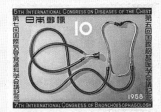

FRANCE 1952
Dr René Laennec, inventor of the stethoscope (1816).

AUSTRIA 1981
Dr Sigmund Freud (1856–1939), founder of modern psychiatry.

FRANCE 1973
Louis Pasteur (1822–1895), discovered the vaccine against rabies and invented food pasteurization.

GREAT BRITAIN 1999
Discovery of penicillin by Alexander Fleming (1928), thanks to a chance discovery on a patch of mold.

NIGER 1975
Dr Albert Schweitzer, doctor, musician, theologian, humanist, founder of the Lambaréné hospital in Gabon (1913).

VIETNAM 1994
Dr Alexander Yersin, produced a serum against plague (1896).

FRANCE 1994
Discovery of the AIDS virus in the United States and France (1983).

CAMEROON 1954
Dr Eugene Jamot, found a cure for sleeping sickness (1916).

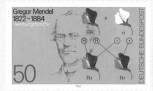

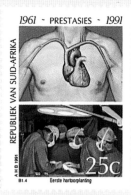

GERMANY (GFR) 1984
Gregor Mendel, discovered the laws of modern genetics (1866).

JAPAN 1977
Surgeon preparing to operate.

CHINA 1975
Tribute to the success of Chinese surgery.

SOUTH AFRICA 1991
The world's first heart transplant, by Dr Christiaan Barnard (1967).

GREAT BRITAIN 1999
Birth of the first test tube baby (1978). Work by Antony Gormley.

GREAT BRITAIN 2003
The completion of DNA genome decoding.

ARGENTINA 2003
The application of nuclear medicine: cobalt therapy equipment.

GREAT BRITAIN 1994
Ultrasound medical images.

GREAT BRITAIN 1989
150th anniversary of the Royal Microscopical Society.

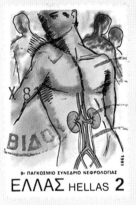

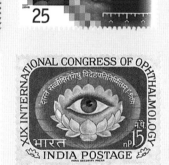

GREECE 1981
World Nephrology Congress in Athens.

SPAIN 1966
World Psychiatry Congress in Madrid.

AUSTRIA 1980
Celebrating 175 years of health studies in universities.

INDIA 1962
International Congress of Ophthalmology, New Delhi.

BRAZIL 1977
World Rheumatism Year. This stamp shows the aspirin molecule, used to treat rheumatism.

USSR 1949
Ivan Petrovich Pavlov, physiologist, known for his animal experiments into conditioned reflexes (1928).

MAURITIUS 1997
Reconstruction of a Dodo skeleton by George Clark and Sir Richard Owen (1865). The bird became extinct in the 18th century.

THE CONQUEST OF SPACE

After years of looking up into the heavens and at the stars, of imagining voyages into space in science fiction novels, man finally embarked on the conquest of space in 1957 with the launch of *Sputnik*, the first artificial Russian satellite. During the decades that followed, the two superpowers – the United States and the USSR – confronted one another with their vast space programs, each hoping to seize the honors in this prestigious showcase for technology: the first man was sent into orbit in 1961 (the Russian Yuri Gagarin); the first man landed on the moon in 1969 (the American Neil Armstrong); and automatic probes were launched into deepest space.

However, the space race ran out of steam, first with the collapse of Soviet communism in 1991, then with the failure of the American space shuttle *Columbia* in 2003, resulting in the death of seven astronauts. However, in 2003 a newcomer, China, launched Shenzhou 5, its first manned space mission, and then Shenzhou 6 in 2005, thus joining the very select club of "space" nations.

Naturally, the space race has been featured on stamps produced by various nations, including those who have sent their own nationals to work on third-party projects with one of the two superpowers.

EXPLORING THE SOLAR SYSTEM, 2000.

SCIENCE FICTION, 1998: FUTURISTIC VISION OF SPACE TRAVEL.

SKYLAB IN ORBIT, 1974.

FIRST MAN ON THE MOON, 1969.

THE FUTURISTIC SPACE SHUTTLE PROJECT, 1993.

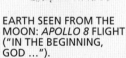

EARTH SEEN FROM THE MOON: *APOLLO 8* FLIGHT ("IN THE BEGINNING, GOD …").

APOLLO–SOYUZ JOINT FLIGHT WITH THE USSR, 1975.

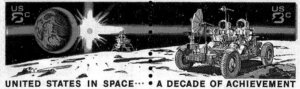

LUNAR EXPLORATION, 1971: A DECADE OF ACHIEVEMENT.

United States

MAN IN SPACE, 1967: *GEMINI 4*.

USSR

SPACE WALK, 1980.

FRENCH–SOVIET FLIGHT, 1989:
SPACE WALK BY JEAN-LOUP
CHRÉTIEN.

VOSTOK V (V. BIKOVSKI) AND VOSTOK VI (V. TERESHKOVA) GROUP FLIGHT, 1963.

China

COMMEMORATING THE
FLIGHT OF THE FIRST
SPUTNIK SATELLITE, YURI
GAGARIN'S FLIGHT AND THE
FIRST SOYUZ STATIONS.

THE FIRST MAN IN SPACE:
YURI GAGARIN, ON BOARD
VOSTOK, APRIL 12, 1961.

THE BLACK DOG
"CHERNUSHKA," LAUNCHED
INTO SPACE, MARCH 9, 1961.

FIRST CHINESE MANNED
FLIGHT, OCTOBER 2003:
ON BOARD THE CRAFT
SHENZOU.

SPACE WALK, 1967.

THE FIRST WOMAN IN
SPACE: VALENTINA
TERESHKOVA, JUNE 1963.

BEIJING PALACE AND THE FIRST CHINESE MAN IN SPACE, 2003.

ASTRONAUTS IN THE SALYUT SPACE STATION, 1976.

LUNAR EXPLORATION, 1971
BY LUNA 17 AND
LUNOKHOD.

LAUNCH OF THE LUNA 10 ROCKET, 1967.

ALLEGORY OF THE CONQUEST OF SPACE, 1984:
COSMONAUT SUPPORTING SPUTNIK.

CONQUEST OF THE POLES AND OCEANS

The conquering of the poles is one of the finest chapters in the history of human endurance, and has been recorded in the stamps of the countries concerned with some superb examples.

While the surface of the North Pole is composed of a frozen sea of great thickness, the continent of Antarctica at the South Pole is a land covered by a gigantic ice cap (over 13,000 ft (4,000m) thick), reachable only during the brief summer period when the break-up of the outlying ice makes it accessible. The crews led by Jules Dumont d'Urville (1840), then James Clark Ross (1841) had to face the storms of the southern seas (the "roaring forties" and "screaming fifties") and the dangerous grip of the ice in simple sailing vessels.

The true conquest of the poles did not take place until the 20th century, using dog sleds, with Robert Peary and Matthew Henson in the north (1909) and Roald Amundsen in the south (1911). Other expeditions were unable to withstand the extreme conditions at the poles, and men died from cold and exhaustion. Flying over the poles was also a feat: Amundsen achieved this in a balloon at the North Pole (1926) and Richard Byrd by plane at the South Pole (1929).

Today, the Antarctic is a continent protected by international treaty, restricted to scientific research, with around ten countries participating and manning permanent bases. The Russian Vostok base has been set up at the coldest place on the planet (-128°F/-89°C), while the Dumont d'Urville French base has recorded the world's fiercest winds (almost 200 mph/319 km/h). Survival trials have also been conducted in extreme Antarctic winter weather conditions near the pole, using rudimentary survival capsules.

The pursuit of knowledge has prevailed, too, in oceanographic campaigns and has been acknowledged in a number of stamps, while the conquest of mountain summits, particularly Everest, has also inspired commemorative stamps celebrating these exploits of courage and endurance.

FRENCH SOUTHERN AND ANTARCTIC LANDS 1990
Discovery of Adélie Land by Dumont d'Urville (January 1840) and his ship, the *Astrolabe*, stuck in the ice.

FRENCH SOUTHERN AND ANTARCTIC LANDS 1984
The *Erebus*, James Clark Ross's ship, caught between icebergs in a storm (March 1842).

FRENCH SOUTHERN AND ANTARCTIC LANDS 1969
Homage to the English navigator James Clark Ross, who discovered the Ross Sea inside the ice (1841).

REPUBLIC OF IRELAND 2004
Sir Ernest Shackleton's Antarctic expedition vessel set off in 1914 but was broken on an ice floe. Shackleton successfully managed to get all his crew home after over-wintering in the harshest conditions.

Discovery

BELGIUM 1997
The *Belgica* on Adrien de Gerlache's expedition, reached the continent of Antarctica (1897).

CHILE 1966
The Chilean pilot who came to the aid of the Shackleton expedition (1916).

UNITED STATES 1986
Robert Peary and Matthew Henson reach the North Pole, accompanied by Inuits (1909).

JAPAN 1960
First Japanese Antarctic expedition, 1910.

GREAT BRITAIN 1972
Captain Robert Scott and his men arrive at the South Pole one month after Amundsen. Demoralized by their late arrival, one after another they all eventually perished of cold and hunger on the way back (1912).

NORWAY 1961
Roald Amundsen, the first man to reach the South Pole (December 1911), with four men and 52 dogs, planted the Norwegian flag.

UNITED STATES 1988
Richard Byrd flew over the South Pole in a Ford trimotor plane (1929). His flight over the North Pole in 1926 has not been officially recognized.

CHILE 1981
The Antarctic Treaty, signed in 1961 by 12 countries, making the continent a protected international territory, and prohibiting the commercial exploitation of its resources.

FRENCH SOUTHERN AND ANTARCTIC LANDS 1995
Researchers going to spend six months of Antarctic winter inside the Charcot station bid farewell.

CHILE 1984
Women's Antarctic exploration team.

SWITZERLAND 1994
Bathyscaphe diving record, held by Jacques Piccard: 35,813 ft (10,916 m).

FRANCE 2000
Commander Jacques-Yves Cousteau, inventor of the aqualung (1946) and deep-sea explorer.

BRITISH ANTARCTIC TERRITORY 2000
Caterpillar track snowcat astride a crevasse.

PERU 1989
Second Peruvian scientific expedition to the Antarctic.

FRENCH SOUTHERN AND ANTARCTIC LANDS 2002
Dog sled.

FRENCH SOUTHERN AND ANTARCTIC LANDS 1989
Scuba diving under the ice floe at Adélie Land.

USSR 1978
The icebreaker *Vassilii Pronetchichiev*.

BRITISH ANTARCTIC TERRITORY 1998
Clothing worn by Antarctic explorers in 1843 and 1998.

GREAT BRITAIN 2003
The conquest of Everest by Edmund Hillary and the Sherpa Tenzing Norgay (1953).

USSR 1982
Conquest of Everest by a Soviet expedition (1982).

FRENCH SOUTHERN AND ANTARCTIC LANDS 1995
The geologist Edgar Aubert de la Rüe and his wife Andrée, both great explorers.

MONACO 2003
Albert I promoted oceanographic studies (creation of the International Peace Institute, 1903).

NEPAL 1994
Late Pansang, first female Sherpa to conquer Everest (1993).

SOCIETY

FARMING AND ANIMAL HUSBANDRY

Farming and animal rearing were the first planned and organized activities in which man was involved. Today, all kinds of agriculture, from the most primitive to the highly industrialized, exist side by side all over the world. Stamps from many countries have celebrated a variety of farming activities such as coconut picking, traditional harvesting methods, women selling produce, and workers on collectivized farms.

Forestry and timber production are also featured, for example tree felling and the transport of timber to sawmills, including making use of the current to float trunks downriver.

The activities associated with animal rearing are similar in every part of the world: the shepherd guarding his flock and milking his ewes, and the dairy farmer milking his cows. With the appearance of large herds of cattle – often thousands in a single herd – the skills needed to move them also evolved. The cowboys familiar to us from Westerns are known as *gauchos* and *vaqueros* in South America, and *stockmen* in Australia and New Caledonia. Their skills have been featured on stamps, particularly in the form of rodeo events which keep alive the skills the early cowboys needed on long cattle drives.

FRENCH WEST AFRICA 1947
Harvesting coconuts.

ZAMBIA 1988
Tea picking.

TOGO 1972
Grating manioc.

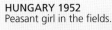

HUNGARY 1952
Peasant girl in the fields.

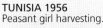

TUNISIA 1956
Peasant girl harvesting.

MADAGASCAR 1978
Socialist farming cooperative.

PERU 1969
Agrarian reform (stamp surcharged 3 soles on 90 centavos).

UPPER VOLTA 1972
Agriculture under the second five-year development plan.

LAOS 1963
Rice harvesting.

Farming

LAOS 1987
Rice fields in the mountains.

CHILE 1968
Agrarian reform in Chile.

NORTH VIETNAM 1962
State farm under the first five-year plan.

Elephant used to drag timber.

Forestry

INDONESIA 1995
Floating market.

CAMEROON (FR) 1955
Harvesting exotic timber.

FRENCH EQUATORIAL AFRICA 1955, AUSTRIA 2000
Floating timber downstream.

Animal rearing

FRENCH TERRITORY OF THE
AFARS AND ISSAS 1973

TOGO 1974
Milking cows.

ITALY 1950
Sardinian shepherd.

BELGIUM 1983
Dairymaid at the Tineke van
Heule festival, Heule.

FRENCH POLYNESIA 2002
Papeete market.

BRAZIL 1992
Gaucho hunting with a
boleadeira (lasso with pebbles).

NEW CALEDONIA 1979
Pouembout rodeo.

NEW CALEDONIA 1969
Cattle branding.

MONGOLIA 1987
Horse breaking.

Cowboys

URUGUAY 1953
Gaucho breaking a horse.

AUSTRALIA 1986
Stockman mustering a stray cow.

BRAZIL 1978
Vaquero and herd.

FISHING, INDUSTRY, AND THE SERVICE SECTOR

Along with farming and animal rearing, fishing is the third activity by which man has survived over many centuries. Again, this has been illustrated in all its different forms on the stamps of many countries. (Those relating to big game and recreational fishing can be found on pages 183 and 184.) A number of the stamps shown here feature traditional fishing methods, using the harpoon and the net. The harsh life of fishermen out at sea is also represented. Today, the sail-powered commercial fishing vessels of the 19th century have all disappeared and been replaced by trawlers and factory ships. The number of fish farms is increasing and gradually transforming the occupation of fisherman into that of fish farmer. Jobs in industry are mainly commemorated on stamps issued by socialist countries, while those in administration and finance, which are visually less interesting, rarely appear at all. Both the International Labor Organization and May 1 (Labor Day) are widely celebrated.

Fishing industry

FRENCH EQUATORIAL AFRICA 1955
Net fishing on Lake Chad.

CONGO 1975
Fishing with hoop nets.

NEW CALEDONIA 1955
Fisherman with a casting net.

LAOS 1963
Fisherman casting a net.

POLAND 1956
Fisherman and trawlers.

GREAT BRITAIN 1981
Fishermen landing a net on a trawler.

MALTA 1979
Fishermen in an open boat and warship (end of the agreements with Great Britain).

ICELAND 1963
Trawler (campaign against hunger).

REPUBLIC OF IRELAND 1991
Traditional coastal trawler.

ST. PIERRE AND MIQUELON (FR) 1974
The "Doris" boat used by fishermen, with the Church of Our Lady of the Sailors in the background.

FAEROE ISLANDS (DENMARK) 1993
Centenary of the Faeroe Islands' merchant navy school: taking measurements using the traditional sextant.

USSR 1983
Factory boat used for processing fish.

NAMIBIA 2004
Worker in the fishing industry.

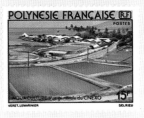

FRENCH POLYNESIA 1980
Experimental fish farming.

CHINA 1964
Worker in the chemical insecticide industry.

ROMANIA 1978
Supervisors in a factory control room.

AUSTRIA 1987
Exhibition on mass production.

USSR 1986
Factory construction technician and computer operators.

SWITZERLAND 1969
50th anniversary of the International Labor Organization: metal worker.

SWEDEN 1989
Centenary of the Swedish Workers' Movement: May Day Parade 1889.

NORTH VIETNAM 1966
80th anniversary of Labor Day.

MEXICO 1974
Campaign to promote exports: "You can export."

Industry and service sectors

AUSTRIA 1987
Working on computer.

VANUATU 1983
Telex operator.

GREECE 1965, TURKEY 1968
Images promoting the National Savings Bank.

AUSTRIA 1998
Reporter and photographer.

CHINA 1974
Oil refinery workers.

MILITARY AND PUBLIC FORCES

A symbol of state authority, of prestige and national independence, the armed forces appear on stamps issued by every country in the world, but in varying proportions. They are the subject of numerous stamp issues in communist countries and dictatorships, and in countries exposed to a latent conflict (such as India and Pakistan, for example), but are featured much less often on stamps issued in democratic countries. These stamps commemorate great military events as well as the different occupations within the armed forces.

Some countries have also produced series of stamps tracing the evolution of uniforms through the ages, which have proved extremely popular with collectors.

Other representatives of authority and public forces have also been featured, principally police and fire officers and, to a lesser extent, customs officials. Unlike military stamps, those showing the other public forces are more frequently seen in democratic countries. However, the justice service has rarely been chosen as a subject for stamps.

CHINA 1952
The People's Army: air, sea, land.

USSR 1978
60th anniversary of the Soviet army.

Armed forces

CHILE 1987
Centenary of the Infantry School.

INDIA 1989
Third cavalry regiment: 19th-century lancer and modern tank.

FRANCE 1984
The Foreign Legion: the Camerone oath (Mexico, 1863).

UNITED STATES 1955
Armed Forces Reserve (marine, coastguard, soldier, sailor, airman).

ITALY 1972
Centenary of the Alpine Chasseur corps.

NORWAY 1988
Centenary of the Broadcasting Corps.

CANADA 1985
Canada's naval forces.

GERMANY (GDR) 1971
15th anniversary of the People's National Army.

SPAIN 1971
50th anniversary of the Spanish Legion.

THAILAND 1987
72nd anniversary of the Royal Air Forces.

URUGUAY 1966
50th anniversary of the Engineer Corps.

Women in the armed forces

VIETNAM 1982
Woman serving in the maritime militia.

SOUTH KOREA 1980
30th anniversary of the Women's Army Corps.

CUBA 1985
25th anniversary of the Cuban Women's Federation: soldier.

Firefighters

CHILE 1963
Centenary of the Santiago fire service.

CANADA 2003
The important rescue work undertaken by firefighters.

Police

TURKEY 2004
165th anniversary of the Gendarmerie.

FRANCE 1970
Different activities of the National Gendarmerie.

ITALY 1964
150th anniversary of the Carabinieri.

USSR 1979

UNITED STATES 1968
"Law and Order."

CANADA 1998
125th anniversary of the RCMP (Royal Canadian Mounted Police).

GREAT BRITAIN 1980
The Metropolitan Police Force.

JAPAN 2004
Car and motorbike police patrols.

JAPAN 1979
50th anniversary of the quarantine system: police border guards.

POLAND 1983
30th anniversary of the Customs Cooperation Council.

Customs

CANADA 2000
125th anniversary of the Supreme Court.

Justice

EGYPT 2004
Centenary of administrative justice.

ROYAL AND PRINCELY FAMILIES

The lives of kings, queens, princes, and princesses attract great popular attention. Along with the popular press, philately plays its part in this fascination with royalty, issuing stamps to commemorate the main events in the lives of royal families, such as marriage, accession to the throne, golden and silver wedding anniversaries, and death.

Most of these stamps originate in the countries of western Europe, but examples can also be found in Jordan, Thailand, Morocco, and, to a lesser extent, Saudi Arabia. Of all the world's royal families, it is the British that lead the way with stamps issued both in Great Britain itself and also in its former colonies. Great Britain is followed by Spain, the Scandinavian and Benelux countries, as well as Monaco (with the much publicized marriage between Prince Rainier and Grace Kelly), and the more discreet Liechtenstein. Special mention must be made of Princess Diana, who, with her photogenic charm and humanitarian deeds, captivated the entire world, so much so that she became one of the figures most frequently portrayed on stamps, particularly those issued in developing countries. Pope John Paul II was another popular personality with the media, and his image has graced numerous stamps.

Great Britain

TOGO 1997
Princess Diana as a Red Cross helper, with the Pope, and at a reception.

GREAT BRITAIN 1997
Golden Wedding anniversary of Queen Elizabeth II and Prince Philip, showing the couple in 1947.

PITCAIRN ISLANDS 1973
Marriage of Princess Anne and Captain Mark Phillips.

GREAT BRITAIN 1997
Golden Wedding anniversary of Queen Elizabeth II and Prince Philip, showing the couple in 1997.

GREAT BRITAIN 1986
Marriage of Prince Andrew and Sarah Ferguson.

GREAT BRITAIN 1981
Marriage of Prince Charles and Lady Diana Spencer.

GREAT BRITAIN 2003
Golden Jubilee of the coronation of Queen Elizabeth II (1953).

GREAT BRITAIN 2005
Marriage of Prince Charles and Camilla Parker Bowles.

GREAT BRITAIN 2003
Prince William, in the year he turned 21.

UNITED STATES 1993
Grace Kelly (1929–1982).

MONACO 1956
Marriage of Prince Rainier III and Grace Kelly.

Monaco

MONACO 1989
Princess Caroline, president of the Princess Grace Foundation (1964).

Greece and Spain

GREECE 1956
Queen Sofia of Greece (Potsdam 1870–Frankfurt 1932).

SPAIN 1975
Juan Carlos I (proclaimed King of Spain) with his wife Sofia of Greece.

NETHERLANDS 1991
25th anniversary of the marriage of Queen Beatrix and Prince Claus.

NETHERLANDS 1990
Four queens in one century: Emma, Wilhelmina, Juliana, and Beatrix.

LUXEMBOURG 1978
Silver Wedding anniversary of Grand Duke Jean and Princess Joséphine-Charlotte of Belgium (1953).

Benelux countries

LIECHTENSTEIN 1982
Princess Marie Aglaé and Prince Jean Adam, heir to the throne.

BELGIUM 1935
Death of Queen Astrid.

BELGIUM 1960
Marriage of King Badouin I and Queen Fabiola of Spain.

BELGIUM 1999
Marriage of the heir to the throne, Prince Philippe, and Mathilde d'Udekem d'Acoz.

Scandinavia

NORWAY 1982
25th anniversary of the coronation of King Olav V at Trondheim Cathedral.

NORWAY 1997
King Harald V.

DENMARK 2004
Marriage of the heir to the throne, Prince Frederik, and Mary Donaldson.

SWEDEN 1976
Marriage of King Carl XVI Gustav and Sylvia Sommerlath.

Middle East and Asia

JORDAN 1997
62nd birthday of King Hussein, with his wife Queen Noor.

MOROCCO 1968
Heir to the throne, future King Mohammed VI.

THAILAND 1975
Silver Wedding anniversary of King Bhumibol and Queen Sirikit.

THAILAND 1972
20th birthday of Prince Vajiralongkorn.

MOTHER AND CHILD

The relationship between mother and child is a universal theme in philately: the beauty of maternal love is portrayed with an interesting diversity, reflecting the way motherhood is perceived in different cultures. Many stamps have been issued with an educational purpose such as promoting infant health by encouraging breast feeding and appropriate medical care. International programs are used to coordinate promotional stamp campaigns, notably the International Year of the Child, and Children's Week.

Occasionally, stamps are also used to reflect strongly held convictions, an example being the Spanish anti-abortion stamp.
Other stamp issues have raised awareness of the violent abuse of children and drawn attention to famine, of which children are the first victims. In the field of child protection, UNICEF, the United Nations Children's Fund, plays a key role: stamps from all over the world make reference to UNICEF and feature its mother and child logo.

COMOROS ISLANDS (FR) 1974
Comorian Red Cross.

SOUTH VIETNAM 1968
International Day of the Child (UNICEF): mother and child.

INDONESIA 1998
50th anniversary of the World Health Organization: one of the few stamps issued showing a pregnant woman.

AUSTRIA 1968
Mother's Day.

FRANCE 1939
Stamp promoting a higher birth rate.

HUNGARY 1974
Motherhood, drawing by Janes Kass.

Breast feeding

LAOS 1985
Campaign to promote infant health.

SPAIN 1987
Infant survival campaign: breast feeding.

CONGO 1970
Mother's Day.

CUBA 1984
Technical revolution for infant survival: breast feeding for the well-being of the child.

SPAIN 1975
Pro-life campaign: "Let them be born!"

THAILAND 1982
Day of the Child.

SYRIA 1990
Mother's Day.

ALGERIA 1969
Protection of mother and child.

LAOS 1965
Foreign aid for development: Japanese health aid.

CENTRAL AFRICAN REPUBLIC 1972
Tribute to mothers: mother teaching her child to read.

№ 355311

USSR 1983
Environment and peace: mother and child with flowers.

DENMARK 1950
Stamp with surtax in support of child welfare: portrait of Princess Anne-Marie.

USSR 1961
International Day of the Child: mother teaching her child to walk.

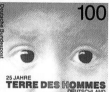

GERMANY 1992
25th anniversary of the international Terre des Hommes federation.

INDIA 1957
Day of the Child.

International Year of the Child

TURKEY 1955
Charity stamp.

UNITED STATES 2003
"Stop Family Violence."

(Note the common logo on these issues.)

NORWAY 1985
Boy and Girl, sculpture in the Vigeland museum in Oslo.

NEW CALEDONIA 1985
No more starving or imprisoned children.

BOLIVIA 1994
SOS-Bolivia children's villages: a child playing the pan pipes.

International Youth Y

EDUCATION AND TEACHING

Once the right of a select few, education has now become more widely accessible and obligatory in a growing number of countries. Stamps have reflected this evolution, promoting the image of the school and the different forms it can take in various areas of the world – for example, children are taught in tents among the nomadic tribes of Mauritania. Stamps are sometimes used with pupils as an educational tool. However, they are principally used to promote national campaigns aimed at, for example, reducing illiteracy, highlighting organizations that are working to achieve cooperation between developed and developing countries. Africa,

where the literacy rate is lowest, is one of the main sources of stamps of this type. Many people see education as the only long-term solution to Africa's problems of poverty.

Initiatives aimed at promoting books and reading as a means of development, such as International Book Week, are also accompanied by promotional stamp issues. In fact, in many countries stamps are a way of disseminating information about universities and higher education establishments to the public in general, and to future students from the country of issue and abroad.

School and reading

CZECH REPUBLIC 2004
330 years of compulsory schooling.

LEBANON 1962
Day of the Schoolchild: schoolboy.

BRAZIL 1977
150th anniversary of primary education.

ITALY 1955
Centenary of professional teaching.

ITALY 1988
9th centenary of the founding of Bologna University: low-relief of a female student.

FRANCE 2002
At the school desk, Paris 1965.

MAURITANIA 1960
Nomad schoolchildren being taught in a tent.

SOUTH VIETNAM 1972
Elderly scholar and pupils.

UPPER VOLTA (BURKINA) 1979
International Year of the Child: African storyteller and children.

UNITED STATES 1957
Centenary of the National Education Association: tribute to the teachers of the United States.

MOROCCO (FR) 1954
French–Muslim education.

RIO MUNI (SPANISH EQUATORIAL GUINEA) 1960
Boy reading and missionary.

HAITI 1966
Audio-visual teaching methods.

THAILAND 1988
Day of the Teacher.

PHILIPPINES 1989
Philately as a classroom tool.

CHILE 1972
International Book Year: "Reading is Living."

INDIA 1996
Tenth anniversary of south-east Asian cooperation for the benefit of the people.

Literacy

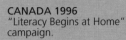

CANADA 1996
"Literacy Begins at Home" campaign.

JAPAN 1995
Japanese cooperation volunteer teaching a Bangladeshi woman to read.

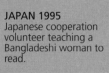

NICARAGUA 1981
First anniversary of the literacy crusade.

UPPER VOLTA (BURKINA) 1979
World Literacy Day.

SRI LANKA 1992
11th anniversary of the Mahapola educational foundation.

MADAGASCAR 1981
World Literacy Day.

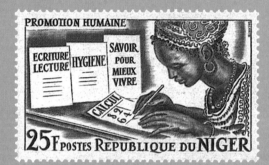

NIGER 1965
Social development: "Knowledge for a better life."

EGYPT 1998
90th anniversary of Cairo University.

VIETNAM 1996
Centenary of Hue state school.

REPUBLIC OF IRELAND 1992
400th anniversary of the impressive library at Trinity College, Dublin.

MEXICO 1979
50th anniversary of the autonomy of the national university: students reaching out toward culture.

University

INDIA 1994
St. Xavier College, Mumbai (125th anniversary).

IVORY COAST 1966
Graduate of the National Administration School.

CHILDREN'S TOYS AND GAMES

Children's games have been the subject of stamps from all over the world, highlighting certain cultural differences.

A favorite among young children the world over, the teddy bear deserves a special mention for its interesting origins. The soft toy was created after President Theodore Roosevelt could not bring himself to kill a tethered bear during a hunt.

Dolls are favorites among little girls everywhere, but the diversity of their costumes makes them collectable items with adults too. Traditional toys reflect the cultural region from which they originate, for example the

wooden crocodile on wheels on a stamp from Togo. Conversely, the children's computer games and television programs that appear on stamps tend to be more standardized.

There are many outdoor play activities that are identical or very similar throughout the world, and the imagination of children who manage to amuse themselves in original ways and at very little cost is to be admired, whether racing with old tires, as in Mayotte, holding clog races in Thailand, playing hopscotch in France, or making colored paper planes in Brazil.

TAIWAN 1979
Children Playing on a Winter's Day, Song dynasty painting.

NORTH KOREA 1979
International Year of the Child: "song of joy" in praise of the head of state.

MONGOLIA 1977
Day of the Child: boy playing the flute and little girl dancing.

USSR 1963
Traditional Russian dolls.

GREAT BRITAIN 2003
Hornby trains: locomotive and tender (1948).

TOGO 1971
25th anniversary of UNICEF: toy on wheels.

UNITED STATES 1997
American dolls: Betsy McCall and Skippy, by Percy Crosby.

UNITED STATES 2002
Centenary of the teddy bear (1902).

THAILAND 1991
Day of the Child: racing on wooden clogs.

HUNGARY 1988
Objects from Kecskemet toy museum: little train.

JAPAN 1991
30th anniversary of the administrative conciliation system: child building a toy town.

GREAT BRITAIN 2001
Child's face painted to look like
a tiger.

BRAZIL 1978
Nation Week: children playing.

FRANCE 1989
Children playing: hopscotch.

MAYOTTE (FR) 2000
Tire racing.

TAIWAN 2001
Kite.

UNITED STATES 1995
Carousel horses.

BELARUS 2003
Roller blading.

CONGO 1986
Children's hoop race.

AFGHANISTAN 1963
Child Protection Day: swing and
skipping rope.

SYRIA 1990
Day of the Child: playing
leapfrog.

FRENCH POLYNESIA 1992
Toy canoes with sails.

KUWAIT 1968
Sailing model boats.

AUSTRALIA 1987
Children fishing for crayfish.

MEXICO 1976
First Latin American forum on
children's television.

INDIA 1985
Day of the Child: young girl with
a computer.

ROMANIA 1960
Children's sports: running race.

UNITED STATES 1999
Big Bird, puppet from the children's TV show *Sesame Street*.

PARLOR GAMES AND BOARD GAMES

The first parlor games originated with the earliest ancient civilizations (Indus, Egypt, Greece), in the form of dice and knucklebones. Games have always been a source of entertainment, particularly during the long evenings of the past, but they can also serve an educational purpose, exercising our mental agility and intellectual competitiveness. Indeed, the Greeks propounded the idea that learning could take place through play, through games requiring careful thought and strategy.

Chess appeared in India in the 8th century, and in a few centuries had conquered China, Korea, Japan, as well as Persia, the Arab caliphates, Spain, and finally Europe, where the definitive rules were established around the 13th century. Card games, which had existed in China for many years,

appeared in Europe in the 14th century, and became widespread after the invention of printing in the 15th century. The Renaissance saw the invention of the lottery, the game of jeu de l'oie, and the emergence of the ground rules of many of today's parlor games. Such games became very popular in the courts of Europe, China, and Japan during the 17th and 18th centuries. Throughout history, and even when they were forbidden, betting games (such as cock-fighting and horse or greyhound racing) have always been unquestionably popular, as was reflected in the immediate enthusiasm shown for forecast betting when it was introduced in Africa in the 1970s. In philately, it is largely the richness and variety of old-fashioned games that have been celebrated.

Card games

BELGIUM 1973
Contemporary playing cards.

JAPAN 1995
Card game (screen painting by Matsuura).

CZECHOSLOVAKIA 1972
16th-century playing cards.

WALLIS AND FUTUNA 1994
The card game bridge on Wallis and Futuna.

NORTH KOREA 1995
Chess players.

VIETNAM 1983
Carved chess pieces: elephant (India).

HUNGARY 1974
21st Olympic Chess Championship: engraving from Caxton's book of chess (15th century).

USSR 1984
World Chess Championships in Moscow (men) and Volgograd (women).

ARMENIA 1996
Tigran Petrossian, ninth world chess champion.

ISRAEL 1976
Chess piece.

Chess and checkers

NETHERLANDS 1986
Game of checkers and cup of coffee with sugar cubes as pieces.

Other games of strategy and mental challenge

CHINA 1993
The game of Go.

HUNGARY 1982
Rubik's cube.

NORTH KOREA 1995
Women playing yut.

BELGIUM 1995
Crosswords and Scrabble.

DJIBOUTI 1992
Traditional game.

FRENCH POLYNESIA 1993
15th anniversary of the
Australian Mathematics
Competition.

GABON 1989
Traditional game using seeds.

IVORY COAST 1984
Game of eklan.

Betting games

MEXICO 1971
200th anniversary of the
National Lottery.

LAOS 1966
Ox fighting.

BENIN 1977
Tenth anniversary of the National
Lottery.

PERU 1970, VIETNAM 2000
Cock fighting.

MALI 1976
First forecast betting in the
newspaper *L'Essor*: the winning
horse, Roi de l'Air.

AUSTRIA 1968
Centenary of the Freudeneau
horse races.

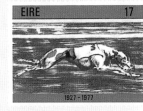

REPUBLIC OF IRELAND 1977
Greyhound racing.

COUNTRY AND MOUNTAIN PURSUITS, AND SCOUTING

The vast theme of outdoor pursuits has been illustrated on stamps in a variety of ways by many countries. This first section relates to country and mountain pursuits – in particular, hiking, hunting, and fishing. Scouting merits a special mention. The scout movement, created in 1907, grew out of Baden Powell's army experience in South Africa (originally scouts were young unarmed men sent on reconnaissance missions during the Boer War of 1898). The popularity of scouting is reflected in the number of stamps from all over the world that have taken it as their theme, so much so that there are collectors who treat it as a subject in its own right. Also interesting to

note is the South African stamp commemorating the creation in 1931 of the Voortrekker movement, the Boer equivalent of Baden Powell's scouts, their erstwhile enemies.

The selection of stamps on mountain pursuits and hiking covers a range of activities: downhill and cross-country skiing, trekking, mountaineering and rambling, cycling, and boating along rivers and canals.

In the modern world, hunting and fishing have become leisure activities, but a number of traditional techniques continue to be featured on stamps today, such as hawking, rod and reel fishing, and net fishing.

CHAD 1982
75th anniversary of the scout movement: playing host to scouts from Kuwait.

LAOS 1973
Around the campfire.

SURINAM 1961
Caribbean Girl Scouts' Jamboree: semaphore signals.

NIGER 1973
Scouts delivering first aid.

JAPAN 1972
50th anniversary of scouting in Japan.

GREAT BRITAIN 1982
Girl Guides and Brownies.

SOUTH AFRICA 1981
50th anniversary of the Voortrekker movement, the Afrikaans equivalent of Baden Powell's scout movement.

MOROCCO 1962
Fifth Arab Scout Jamboree, Rabat.

Scouting

AUSTRIA 1970
Mountaineering and tourism.

NORWAY 1983
Hiking in the mountains.

ROMANIA 1961
Cross-country skiing (stamp without perforations).

INDONESIA 1980
Mountaineering.

NEW ZEALAND 2003
Heli skiing.

LEBANON 1966
Woman skier at the International Cedars Festival.

ARGENTINA 1977
Novice skiers at San Martín de los Andes ski resort.

Mountain pursuits

Outdoor excursions

SWEDEN 1979
Traveling by barge on the Göta Canal.

TURKEY 1994

LUXEMBOURG 2004

PORTUGAL 2004
Hiking on Madeira.

NORWAY 2004

SLOVAKIA 2004
White water rafting.

SWEDEN 1983

Hunting

RUSSIA 1999
Hunting wild duck.

GREENLAND 1987
Inuit hunters on the ice floe.

PORTUGAL 1994
Hunter with falcon.

MONGOLIA 1975

AUSTRIA 1971, JAPAN 1972, HUNGARY 1971

River fishing

THE SEASIDE AND TOURISM

The second section on leisure focuses on the seaside and the various tourist attractions used by different countries to promote their image. There is also a certain humor in some of the images chosen (for example, reprinting an old poster of Monte Carlo) as well as some surprises, such as the unexpected beaches of China, and the Albanian Riviera.
Attention is also drawn to the charm of local tourist hostesses, and the delights of the coastal landscape and seaside resorts. A warm welcome is an important factor in the development of tourism, as is the landscape, with the traditional palm-trees of distant shores with exotic names.
Each country likes to highlight its tourist resources in the stamps it issues, hoping to attract tourists in search of new horizons: the resulting kaleidoscope of images makes this a highly collectable theme.

Holidays by the sea

MONACO 2004
1950s advertising poster: "What a joy to spend the summer in Monte Carlo."

ITALY 2004
Suitcase, symbolizing holidays.

CHINA 2001
Chinese seaside resort.

DENMARK 1991
Sunbathing on Fano beach.

ICELAND 1993
Bathing in the waters of the Blue Lagoon.

ALBANIA 1967
The Albanian Riviera.

ITALY 1992
The spa resort of Rimini, in existence since ancient times.

LEBANON 1961
Tourism month.

ANTIGUA 1976

ÅLAND (FINLAND) 2004

SENEGAL 1969
Beach on Goree Island.

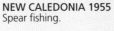

NEW CALEDONIA 1955
Spear fishing.

MEXICO 1973
Tourism: big game fishing in Baja California.

MAURITIUS 1971

Tourism

HUNGARY 1963
Centenary of marine facilities on Lake Balaton.

AUSTRALIA 2004
Old publicity poster for liners.

SOUTH KOREA 1983
Tourist Agency Congress in Seoul: tourist hostess.

BELGIUM 1978
Tourist hostess in Brussels.

SYRIA 1987
International Tourism Day: the citadel of Aleppo.

PHILIPPINES 1960
Sunset on Manilla Bay.

COCOS ISLANDS (AUSTRALIA) 1979
Christmas on the atoll.

NIGER 1987
National Tourist Office: Tuareg from the Sahara and Southern Cross pendant.

SENEGAL 1967
International Tourism Year: Niokolo Koba national park.

CHILE 1972
Tourism Year of the Americas.

COCOS (KEELING) ISLANDS
GOODWILL TOWARD MEN   CHRISTMAS 1979

SOUTH AFRICA 1995
Tourism in the north-west province: the Lost City complex.

NAURU 1973
Coastal landscape.

EGYPT 2003
Restaurant with swimming pool and view of the pyramids.

SPAIN 2001
Paradors: luxury state-run hotels in refurbished castles and convents.

TURKEY 2004
Europa theme: holidays (seaside and visits to historical sites).

FOOD AND DRINK

A country's food is an important aspect of its culture, and, along with its tourist attractions, is a key factor in bringing in tourists. However, food is very unevenly represented in philately, appearing only in those countries where the cuisine is considered culturally important – notably the countries of the Mediterranean such as Turkey and Italy. Above all, it features the cuisine of France and its overseas territories, together with certain Asian countries (such as Korea) and South America.

Stamps featuring drinks such as tea, coffee, and wine are quite common but usually restricted to producing countries. On the other hand, beer is more widely represented. It can be found all over the world, and may be brewed from imported materials – providing the country has brewing facilities and alcohol is not prohibited.

MALTA 2002
Maltese cuisine: stew with green peas.

ITALY 1994
Bread varieties.

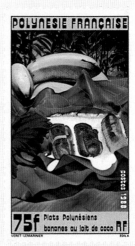

FRENCH POLYNESIA 1988
Bananas in coconut milk.

CHILE 1972
Tourism and gastronomy.

TURKEY 1994
Traditional local dish: kansik dolma.

GREAT BRITAIN 1989
Food and Farming Year: fruit and vegetables.

SWITZERLAND 2004
Cheeses: tomme cheeses and gruyère, with walnuts and grapes.

ST. PIERRE AND MIQUELON (FR) 2002
Spicy cod stew.

FRENCH SOUTHERN AND ANTARCTIC LANDS 2003
Antarctic "floating island" dessert.

FRENCH SOUTHERN AND ANTARCTIC LANDS 2003
Lobster Saint-Paul style.

FRANCE 2003
Cheeses: camembert, made with the milk of Normandy cows.

FRANCE 2003
Foie gras.

Gastronomy

Tea, coffee, chocolate

WALLIS AND FUTUNA 1957
Making the traditional drink kaua.

MAURITANIA 1980
Teatime in Mauritania.

SWITZERLAND 2001
Centenary of Choco Suisse.

NEW CALEDONIA 2002
Coffee: roasting beans; cup of coffee.

TOGO 1975
Growing palm-trees to produce palm wine.

BELGIUM 1986
The Year of Beer: glass of beer.

PHILIPPINES 1990
Centenary of beer production: ten glasses of beer.

CAMEROON 1970
Cameroon brewery: brewing equipment.

REPUBLIC OF IRELAND 1959
Bicentenary of the Guinness Brewery.

GERMANY (GFR) 1983
450th anniversary of the beer purity law: brewing, from a 1677 engraving.

Beer

Wine

FRANCE 1940
In aid of national assistance: grape harvesting.

PORTUGAL 1970
Harvesting grapes for port wine.

HUNGARY 1972
International Wine Competition: Egri Bikaver.

AUSTRIA 2004
12,320 gallon (56,000 liter) wine barrel (1704) and visitors.

LIECHTENSTEIN 2003
Grape harvesting is still carried out with a basket on the back.

SPAIN 2002
Designation of origin wines: bunch of grapes and glass of Rioja wine.

LUXEMBOURG 2001
Vineyard, chapel, and old wine press.

PRESERVING THE ENVIRONMENT

The world's population is growing at an increasing rate: one and a half billion people in 1900, two and a half billion in 1950, and over six billion in 2003. The environmental consequences are becoming visible in all areas, with air and water pollution, reduced fossil fuel reserves, and even an indirect impact on the climate.

The great complexity of the mechanisms that govern the chain of life, from plant to animal, to predator, make it very difficult to predict the future. If a significant change takes place in one aspect of the environment, the knock-on effects are unpredictable.

Most countries have used stamps as a means of raising public awareness of these issues and to support national environmental campaigns. In industrialized countries there are growing movements to preserve natural sites, save energy, and call a halt to industrial pollution, while countries with hotter climates, particularly those in the southern hemisphere, are all too aware of the dangers of drought and forest fires, and the struggle to hold back the encroaching desert.

One common concern is the preservation of water, which is a natural treasure and the source of all life.

INDIA 1990
Campaign for the consumption of clean water.

UNITED NATIONS (NEW YORK) 2003
International Year of Fresh Water.

TURKEY 1988
European campaign for the Protection of the Environment.

GERMANY (GFR) 1980
Protection of natural sites.

SPAIN 1978
Campaign for the protection of water and wetlands.

IVORY COAST 1972
Water campaign.

UNITED STATES 1984
50th anniversary of the Wetland Preservation and Migratory Bird Hunting Act.

UNITED STATES 1984
Smokey the Bear, symbol of the forest fire prevention campaign.

IRAN 1983
Ecology week.

HUNGARY 2001
Water, a natural treasure.

SWEDEN 1979
International Year of the Child: raising awareness of pollution.

GREECE 1977
Protecting the environment: the Acropolis and a factory.

USSR 1990
Atmospheric pollution: acid rain falling on a rose.

FRANCE 1978, AUSTRIA 1979
Saving energy.

HUNGARY 2003
Car-Free Day.

BRAZIL 1976
Preserving the forest.

CONGO 1988
Combating desertification: end
tree felling.

MEXICO 1976
Forest fire prevention campaign.

NIGER 1975
Combating drought: stricken
farmers.

CHINA 1994
"Make the desert green": a single
tree among the sand dunes.

RUSSIA 1991
The ecology of disaster-stricken
regions: the Aral Sea.

IVORY COAST 1983
Combating drought: forest after fire.

MALI 1978
The Hammamet Symposium:
desertification, environment, and
agriculture.

MEXICO 1977
United Nations Conference on
Desertification.

**UPPER VOLTA (BURKINA)
1980**
Combating desertification:
Operation Green Sahel.

MAURITANIA 1984
Combating drought: animal
carcasses.

NEW CALEDONIA 1975
"Stop Bush Fires."

FIRST AID AND MEDICAL CARE

Modern-day first aid began in 1864 with the creation of the Red Cross, the brainchild of Henri Dunant of Switzerland, who was moved by the suffering of those wounded and abandoned at the Battle of Solferino (1859) during the struggle for Italian unification. The mission of the Red Cross grew during peace time to include aiding those wounded in accidents and the victims of natural disasters.

The International Federations of the Red Cross and the Red Crescent now have national organizations in 181 countries, manned by volunteers, and known all over the world by the symbol of a red cross on a white background (the Swiss flag with the colors reversed). The symbol of the red crescent was created in 1876 for Muslim countries at the request of the Ottoman Empire, which felt that the symbol of the red cross was too

evocative of the Crusades of the Middle Ages. The red lion and sun symbol created in Persia was withdrawn in 1980. Most countries issue Red Cross and Red Crescent stamps regularly, levying a surtax aimed at providing financial support for the organizations.

Nurses have also been much celebrated as the subject of stamps, including several famous nurses such as Florence Nightingale, who was struck by the deplorable hygiene in hospitals at the time of the Crimean War (1854) and undertook to reform it. Another is Clara Maass, an army nurse during the war between Spain and the United States (1898), who volunteered to be tested to discover the causes of yellow fever and died as a result.

Among the various medical NGOs, Médecins sans Frontières was honored with the Nobel Peace Prize in 1999.

NETHERLANDS 1993
First Aid Centenary.
This evocative stamp
inspired many.

First aid

GREAT BRITAIN 1987
Centenary of St. John
Ambulance Brigade (1887).

AUSTRALIA 1966
75th anniversary of the Royal Life Saving Society.

SWITZERLAND 1928
Henri Dunant (1828–1910),
founder of the
International Red Cross
(1864).

NICARAGUA 1983
First-aid helpers at the
service of humanity.

THAILAND 1980
The Red Cross: extracting
venom to manufacture
serum.

BELGIUM 2001
Red Cross volunteer.

SLOVENIA 1999
Rescue dogs hunting for
survivors.

EL SALVADOR 1985
Centenary of the
El Salvador Red Cross:
rescue at sea.

HUNGARY 1965
Evacuating victims of the
Danube floods.

JAPAN 1965
Blood donor campaign.

AUSTRIA 1993
25th anniversary of medical
care via radio
communication.

SPAIN 1984
Campaign on the dangers of fire.

MONGOLIA 1977
Fighting fire the traditional way.

GERMANY 1970
Firefighter in action.

MEXICO 1978
35th anniversary of Mexican social security.

Industrial accidents and the disabled

SWITZERLAND 1978
Protecting workers:
chemical industry.

SPAIN 1984
Preventing accidents at
work: falls at construction
sites.

GREAT BRITAIN 1981, MEXICO 1981
International Year of the Disabled.

Health workers

AUSTRALIA 1955
Young nurse, and Florence
Nightingale (1820–1910) in
the background.

THAILAND 1991
Princess Maha Chaki
Sirindhorn in Red Cross
uniform.

UNITED STATES 1976
Clara Maass (1876–1901),
nurse who gave her life to
yellow fever testing.

LUXEMBOURG 1974
Princess Marie-Astrid,
president of the Red Cross
youth movement.

JAPAN 1977
16th International Nurses' Congress.

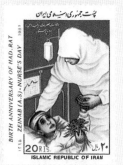

ALGERIA 1967
Surtax in aid of the Red
Cross.

**UPPER VOLTA (BURKINA)
1969**
50th anniversary of the
league of the Red Cross
and Red Crescent
(including the Lion and
Red Sun).

IRAN 1987
Day of the Nurse.

COLOMBIA 1964
Red Cross fund.

FRANCE 1998
Médecins sans Frontières, humanitarian organization
awarded the Nobel Peace Prize.

THE BATTLE AGAINST DISEASE

Under the aegis of international organizations such as the World Health Organization and UNICEF, major information campaigns have used stamps as a way of raising public awareness of health issues, including regular medical check-ups, vaccination, organ donation, and caring for the disabled. In addition to these international campaigns, various countries have issued stamps to draw attention to particular illnesses or diseases affecting the population, and to raise funds. The stamps most frequently issued relate to malaria, polio, blindness, and cancer. Providing help for the blind is also a concern shared by many countries.

AIDS, which has replaced malaria in the unenviable position of being the world's greatest killer disease, has received special treatment in philately: the message is one of information about the precautions to take to reduce the risk of contracting the disease. The crude realism of certain stamps may shock (particularly those from Africa), but it reflects the desperate struggle against this scourge that is decimating entire populations.

UNITED STATES 1957
A tribute to those who help in the fight against polio.

FRANCE 1959
The campaign against polio.

ARGENTINA 1956
Raising funds to combat polio.

MEXICO 1984
World campaign against polio.

CONGO 1977
World Health Day: "Sight is life."

FRANCE 1962
"The world united against malaria."

SWAZILAND 1976
Child blind from malnutrition.

NEW CALEDONIA 1988
40th anniversary of the World Health Organization: "Health for All."

GREAT BRITAIN 1981
Guide dogs for the blind.

CHILE 1977
Protecting handicapped children.

UNITED STATES 1974
Help for children with special needs.

SOUTH AFRICA 1978
Year of Health.

AUSTRIA 1976, NIGER 1965
The fight against cancer.

UNITED STATES 1996, ITALY 2000
Preventing breast cancer: the European stamp is more explicit.

GUINEA 1973
Preparing smallpox vaccine.

PHILIPPINES 1978
Campaign for the global eradication of smallpox.

GHANA 1988
UNICEF campaign for immunization by vaccination.

TURKEY 1988
"Vaccination against measles."

Vaccination and organ donation

SPAIN 1982, TURKEY 1988
Organ donation.

AIDS prevention

ANGOLA 1994
"AIDS is the responsibility of us all."

MALI 1994
The fight against AIDS: promoting use of condoms.

SWAZILAND 2003
"Unsterilized instruments can transmit AIDS."

RUSSIA 1993
AIDS.

VATICAN 2004
"Children, victims of AIDS."

FRENCH POLYNESIA 2001
"AIDS solidarity" and red ribbon.

VANUATU 1991
"AIDS kills."

ETHIOPIA 1991
World AIDS Day.

NATIONAL HEALTH AND SAFETY CAMPAIGNS

Information campaigns to prevent road accidents have featured on the stamps of many countries. The theme of safety is often tackled in a light-hearted way to get the message across to children. Campaigns against the consumption of alcohol have also used stamps to raise public awareness of the dangers of drinking and driving, and also the harmful effect that parents who drink can have on family life.

Originating in South America, tobacco spread to the courts of Europe during the 16th century through Jean Nicot, the French ambassador to Portugal,

and for many years was considered a harmless pleasure. It is only in recent decades that the damaging effects of tobacco on health have become the subject of information campaigns using stamps as their medium.

As with alcohol and tobacco, the same message on drugs can be found on stamps issued all over the world, but while the message may be the same there are considerable cultural differences in the way it is conveyed.

TURKEY 1987
Campaign for the wearing of safety belts.

ITALY 1987
Drive with care.

USSR 1979
Watch out for children playing on the road.

FRANCE 1981
"Drink or drive …; the choice is yours."

HUNGARY 1973
Anti-road-rage campaign.

HUNGARY 1973
Don't drink and drive.

CUBA 1970
Promoting the use of zebra crossings.

NEW CALEDONIA 1980
Road safety campaign at nursery schools.

SWITZERLAND 1969
Use pedestrian crossings.

Road safety

LUXEMBOURG 1979
International Year of the Child: road safety.

USSR 1985
Temperance campaign: in families and institutions.

ITALY 1987
The fight against alcoholism (after a painting by Degas).

The battle against alcohol abuse

TURKEY 1987
Don't drink and drive.

WALLIS AND FUTUNA 1996
Campaign against alcoholism.

BRAZIL 1991
Fighting drugs and alcohol.

FRANCE 1961
In 1561, Jean Nicot introduced the tobacco used by South American natives into Europe.

JAPAN 1987
Sixth World Conference on tobacco versus health.

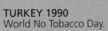

TURKEY 1990
World No Tobacco Day.

YUGOSLAVIA 1990
The fight against addiction to smoking.

BULGARIA 1980
World Health Day: anti-smoking campaign.

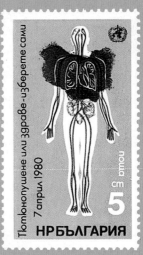

The battle against smoking

MEXICO 1980
"Tobacco or health; the choice is yours."

The battle against drugs

UNITED STATES 1971
Prevent drug abuse.

PAKISTAN 1987
"Eradicate narcotics."

TURKEY 1990
International Day against Drug Abuse.

ITALY 1977
"Drugs kill."

MONACO 1973
"Fight against drugs."

BOLIVIA 1989
"Help prevent drug dependency."

GERMANY (GFR) 1975
Fight against drug abuse.

AUSTRIA 1973
"Stop! Drugs are suicide."

BOSNIA-HERZOGOVINA 2002
"No to drugs."

HUMAN RIGHTS

In 1945, 50 founder states signed the act creating the UNO (United Nations Organization), with the aim of maintaining peace in the world and promoting cooperation between states. In 1948, the states belonging to the United Nations signed the Universal Declaration of Human Rights, deriving from the principles of the 1789 French Revolution, governing the foundations of liberty, justice, and peace in the world: "All human beings are born free and equal in dignity and rights . . ." Endowed with a simple, non-legal, moral authority, this document has gained considerable international influence over the course of time. Many organizations, funds, and programs have been created under the aegis of the UN. These are diverse and include UNICEF (the Children's Fund), UNHCR (United Nations High Commissioner for Refugees), UNESCO (United Nations Educational, Scientific and Cultural Organization), WHO (World Health Organization), FAO (Food and Agriculture Organization), and the IMF (International Monetary Fund). Naturally, many stamps have been issued celebrating the actions of these organizations and other independent non-governmental organizations such as Amnesty International and the Salvation Army.

Various countries, including India and the United States, have also used stamps to advocate family planning with a view to curbing population growth.

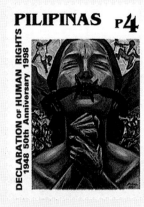

FRANCE 1998
Universal Declaration of Human Rights (Paris, 1948): René Cassin (who drafted the document) and Eleanor Roosevelt (who was the driving force behind it).

PHILIPPINES 1998
50th anniversary of the Universal Declaration of Human Rights.

UNITED NATIONS (NEW YORK) 2004
"Books not arms," designed by Michel Granger.

INDIA 1991
World Peace.

SWEDEN 1995
"Non-violence," illustration by Carl Fredrik Reuterswärd.

Peace and human rights

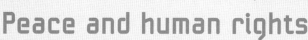

DENMARK 1986
25th anniversary of Amnesty International.

GREECE 1982
Amnesty International: campaign against "disappearings."

UNITED NATIONS (GENEVA) 2000, AUSTRIA 2001
50th anniversary of the High Commissioner for Refugees.

SENEGAL 1971
High Commissioner for Refugees 1951–1971.

Rights of refugees

AUSTRIA 1960, MOROCCO 1960
World Refugee Year.

DENMARK 1971
Aid for refugees.

EGYPT 1972
United Nations Day: refugees.

SPAIN 1986
Emigration.

GERMANY 1994
"Living together."

MAURITANIA 1971
International Year for Action to
Combat Racism and Racial
Discrimination.

RWANDA 1971
Music.

MEXICO 1978
The fight against racial
segregation.

CZECHOSLOVAKIA 1959
Racial equality.

The battle against racism

BENIN 1984
World Food Day.

BOLIVIA 1966
Aid for poor children.

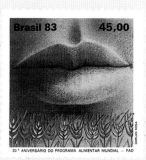

BRAZIL 1983
20th anniversary of the world
food program.

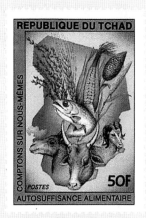

CHAD 1984
Food self-sufficiency: "Let's
count on ourselves."

NIGER 1986
The "Trucks of Hope"
humanitarian program.

Family planning

UNITED STATES 1972
Family shown with two children.

MAYOTTE (FR) 1998
Three children: "1, 2, 3 …
enough."

INDIA 1994
One child: "Small family, happy
family."

GREAT BRITAIN 1965
Centenary of the Salvation Army.

The battle against
famine and poverty

THE STATUS AND IMAGE OF WOMEN

The position of women has changed considerably over the course of the 20th century. Most women were initially confined to a domestic role, and often remained under the guardianship of their father and then their husband. However, through the actions of a few they gradually came to acquire rights and freedoms such as the right to vote, marital equality, freedom to choose whether to have children, and access to jobs traditionally held by men. These rights are far from being uniformly acquired throughout the world and the disparities between countries are still considerable.

The evolution of women's status has often been traced on stamps: from the housewife pounding millet to women prime ministers in Muslim countries. Coordinated issues (for the International Year of the Woman, for example) have been produced to raise awareness of the status of women. The subjects chosen by postal authorities are sometimes rather out of touch with everyday reality but they do reflect the objective to be achieved. Despite these advances, a number of stamps continue to remind us that violence toward women is unfortunately still a reality.

NEW ZEALAND 1993
Centenary of women's right to vote (1893).

GREAT BRITAIN 1968
50th anniversary of votes for women.

BRAZIL 1983
50th anniversary of the political emancipation of women.

CONGO 1975
Tenth anniversary of the Revolutionary Union of Congolese Women.

COLOMBIA 1962
The political rights of women.

CUBA 1970
Tenth anniversary of the Federation of Cuban Women.

EGYPT 1995
National Women's Day.

CHINA 1983
Fifth National Women's Congress.

GERMANY 2000, EQUADOR 1991
"End violence toward women."

MADAGASCAR 1982
20th anniversary of the Pan African Women's Organization.

TUNISIA 1981
25th anniversary of the Law of Personal Status, giving rights and freedoms to women.

Political rights

SENEGAL 1975, SPAIN 1975, FRANCE 1975, MAURITANIA 1975, ALGERIA 1975
International Year of the Woman.

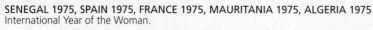

Traditional images

COLOMBIA 1959
Miss Universe.

JAMAICA 1963
Miss World.

BOTSWANA 1999
Miss Universe.

MACAO (PORTUGAL) 1999
Providing water.

TOGO (FR) 1941
Pounding millet.

ZIMBABWE 2003
Women's jobs: old and new.

MAURITANIA 1967
New jobs for women, part of the "Promoting Women" campaign.

AUSTRALIA 1990
Centenary of women doctors.

SOUTH VIETNAM 1969
Vietnamese women intellectuals.

Women at work in the modern world

UNITED STATES 1997
Women in military service.

CAMEROON 1983
Woman barrister swearing an oath.

PAKISTAN 1995
Women prime ministers of Muslim countries: Professor Tansu Ciller (Turkey) and Mothama Benazir Bhutto (Pakistan).

REPUBLIC OF IRELAND 1986
Woman civil engineer.

COMPETITIVE SPORTS

THE SUMMER OLYMPICS

The first modern Olympic Games were held in Athens in 1896. They were the result of the persevering efforts of Pierre de Coubertin, who wished to see a revival of the spirit of the games of Ancient Greece, during which all war came to a halt to allow this sporting competition to take place. Originally a sporting event for amateurs, over the course of a century the Games have grown in importance, with the public "idolizing" its sporting heroes, as in ancient times. The Games have also become an expression of national prestige with political ramifications and have therefore been at the mercy of international relations: the Games were not held during the two world wars; in 1972 Israeli athletes were shot by Palestinian militants; in 1980 the United States boycotted the Moscow Games; and in 1984 eastern bloc countries boycotted the Los Angeles Olympics.

The evolution of the Olympic Games has been followed in the world of philately: the commemoration of the Games through stamps did not in fact begin until the Paris Games of 1924, with mainly allegorical representations issued by the organizing countries. The number of issuing countries gradually increased after the Rome Games of 1960, and the Olympic Games are now a global event commemorated by blocks or series of stamps from all over the world.

The selection below presents an overview of 26 disciplines in 23 Olympic Games that have taken place over the last century, chosen randomly from various countries. An additional stamp acknowledges the Paralympics, elite sports events for athletes from six disability groups, which have also been taking place alongside the Olympics since 1960.

FRANCE 1956
Pierre de Coubertin (1863–1937), creator of the first world Olympic Games in Athens in 1896.

UNITED STATES 1932
The Los Angeles Games, 1932: athletics (running).

GERMANY (REICH) 1936
The Berlin Games, 1936: swimming (diver).

FRANCE 1924
The Paris Games, 1924: athlete (allegory).

GREAT BRITAIN 1948
The London Games, 1948: (allegory).

UNITED STATES 2004
Wilma Rudolph, the "black gazelle," sprint triple gold medal winner (Rome, 1960).

AUSTRALIA 1956
The Melbourne Games, 1956: the Olympic torch.

ITALY 1960
The Rome Games, 1960: athlete (allegory).

GREECE 1972
The Munich Games, 1972: wrestling (allegory).

LEBANON 1964
The Tokyo Games, 1964: shooting (rifle).

SPAIN 1968
The Mexico Games, 1968: sailing.

HUNGARY 1972
The Munich Games, 1972: horse-riding (show-jumping).

MEXICO 1967
The Mexico Games, 1968: hockey.

HUNGARY 1976, SOUTH KOREA 1976, CANADA 1976
The Montreal Games, 1976: canoeing, volleyball, and judo.

GERMANY (GDR) 1980
The Moscow Games, 1980: athletics (running).

**SOUTH KOREA 1984,
UNITED STATES 1984,
POLAND 1984**
The Los Angeles Games,
1984: badminton, soccer,
and fencing.

**ROMANIA 1988,
YUGOSLAVIA 1988**
The Seoul Games, 1988:
gymnastics and rowing.

UNITED STATES 1996
The Atlanta Games, 1996:
baseball.

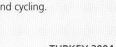

LAOS 1992, CHINA 1992, AUSTRALIA 1992
The Barcelona Games, 1992: tennis, basketball, and cycling.

TURKEY 2004
The Athens Games, 2004:
weightlifting.

PORTUGAL 2004
The Athens Paralympics, 2004: disabled swimmer.

GREAT BRITAIN 1996
The Atlanta Games, 1996: athletics (javelin).

RUSSIA 2000, NEW CALEDONIA 2000
The Sydney Games, 2000: boxing and synchronized
swimming.

GYMNASTICS AND ATHLETICS

Athletics events, which were highly regarded in the Games of Antiquity, continue in the modern games and have been enriched with new disciplines that highlight expression through movement in the form of gymnastics with freestyle and set figures.

Stamps from all over the world feature top-class athletes who compete in the Olympics. They also show many other international sporting events that attract global audiences, such as the European Championships, the Pacific Games, the Mediterranean Games, and city marathons.

Sports competitions also provide an opportunity to strengthen a common cultural identity (as in the Pan-American Games, the Commonwealth Games, and the Games of French-Speaking Countries) or a sense of belonging (university games and military competitions), all of which have been celebrated on stamps.

Despite the diversity of style — which varies according to period and country — these stamps display great uniformity in the attitudes and movements of the sporting figures represented.

BELGIUM 2001
Gymnastics: the rings.

FINLAND 1945
Gymnastics: the fixed bar.

HUNGARY 1985
International Youth Year: modern gymnastics.

SPAIN 1985
World Rhythmic Gymnastics Championship.

SOUTH KOREA 1983
National Gymnastics Meeting: the beam exercise.

BRAZIL 1991
World Physical Education Congress.

18p

GREAT BRITAIN 1988
British Amateur Gymnastics Association.

CZECHOSLOVAKIA 1960
National Spartakiade: women's combined hoops.

JAPAN 1995
World Gymnastics Championship.

POLAND 1987
World Women's Gymnastics Championship, France 1986.

INDIA 1991
Yoga exercise: ustrasana (the camel posture).

SWITZERLAND 1971
Youth and sport.

FRANCE 2003
World Athletics Championship.

REPUBLIC OF IRELAND 1979
World Cross-Country Championships.

ITALY 1981
World Athletics Cup.

GREAT BRITAIN 1991
World University Games.

CHINA 1985
National Workers' Games.

USSR 1980
The Moscow Olympics: walking and women's discus.

KENYA–UGANDA–TANZANIA 1970
Commonwealth Games.

CANADA 2001
Games of French-Speaking Countries.

CANADA 1999
Pan-American Games.

NEW CALEDONIA 1995
Sun triathlon.

ITALY 1997
Mediterranean Games.

MEXICO 1989
The Mexico City Marathon.

CZECHOSLOVAKIA 1978
European Athletics Championship: pole vaulting.

BRAZIL 1960
Spring Games.

CZECHOSLOVAKIA 1962
Military Games Spartakiade.

WALLIS AND FUTUNA 1975
South Pacific Games: javelin.

SKIING AND SKATING

The Winter Olympics were first held in 1924 in Chamonix (France) to complement the Summer Olympics and to provide a platform in the same Olympic spirit for winter sports events. They are held in the same year as the Summer Olympics; the World Championships take place every two years and the World Cups every year, making it possible to follow interim results.

Ski competitions have been featured on the stamps of most European countries (Alpine skiing, Nordic skiing, and ski jumping), with biathlons celebrated mainly by east-European countries. The United States and Canada also compete in ice hockey and speed skating, while ice dance and artistic skating are universal.

FINLAND 1945
Cross-country skiing.

NORWAY 1979
Cross-country ski race at Holmenkollen.

NORWAY 1979
Centenary of the Huseby ski jump, 1879.

ARGENTINA 1959
Winter sports at Bariloche: ski jumping.

FRANCE 1937
International Ski Championship, Chamonix.

AUSTRIA 1975
The Innsbruck Winter Olympics, 1976: cross-country skiing.

AUSTRIA 1975
Innsbruck 1976: ski jumping.

SWITZERLAND 2002
World Alpine Ski Championship at Saint Moritz (2003).

ITALY 1970
World Alpine Ski Championship at Val Gardena.

AUSTRIA 1982
World Alpine Ski Championship at Schladming-Haus: downhill skiing.

FRANCE 2002
Snow boarding at Salt Lake City.

FRANCE 2000
Jean-Claude Killy, 1968 world champion.

AUSTRIA 2004
Hermann Maier, world champion in 1998, 2000, 2001, and 2004.

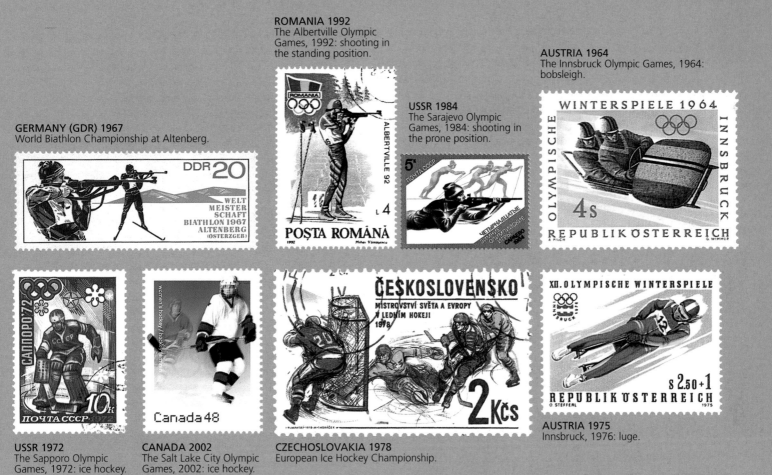

GERMANY (GDR) 1967
World Biathlon Championship at Altenberg.

ROMANIA 1992
The Albertville Olympic Games, 1992: shooting in the standing position.

USSR 1984
The Sarajevo Olympic Games, 1984: shooting in the prone position.

AUSTRIA 1964
The Innsbruck Olympic Games, 1964: bobsleigh.

USSR 1972
The Sapporo Olympic Games, 1972: ice hockey.

CANADA 2002
The Salt Lake City Olympic Games, 2002: ice hockey.

CZECHOSLOVAKIA 1978
European Ice Hockey Championship.

AUSTRIA 1975
Innsbruck, 1976: luge.

JAPAN 1977
World Artistic Skating Championship.

USSR 1984
The Sarajevo Olympic Games, 1984: ice dancing, pairs.

USSR 1980
The Lake Placid Olympic Games, 1980: speed skating.

NETHERLANDS 1982
Royal Skating Association.

ITALY 1995
World Speed Skating Championship.

HUNGARY 1984
The Sarajevo Olympic Games, 1984: pairs skating.

AUSTRIA 1964
The Innsbruck Olympic Games, 1964: female figure skater.

UNITED STATES 1984
Winter Olympics: ice dancing, pairs.

SOCCER, RUGBY, AND HANDBALL

Ball games played with the feet have existed since ancient times, but the first formal match rules were laid down in England in 1846 by the pupils of Rugby private school in Warwickshire. Two years later, in 1848, students at Cambridge University established the first rules of the game of soccer.

From the first clubs founded during the 19th century, soccer has spread all over the world. The game has been featured abundantly on the stamps of many countries in celebration not only of the World Cup, but also of many other cups and inter-club championships.

Rugby has retained more of its original sporting spirit, but is played in fewer countries. The game of rugby league arose from a split in 1890

between the English clubs, with some advocating continued amateur status while others wanted to see their players paid for their efforts. Popular tournaments such as the Six Nations (England, Ireland, Scotland, Wales, France, and now Italy) are featured on stamps issued by the nations involved, as are the world's most famous teams such as Australia, New Zealand, and South Africa.

The game of handball, which appears on stamps issued in Czechoslovakia and Germany, began in 1919 as an adaptation of the *troball* or *balle au but* game played by women during the First World War. It has since become an Olympic discipline.

PORTUGAL 2004
Portugal, organizer and finalist of Euro 2004, won by Greece.

GREAT BRITAIN 1996
Soccer legends: Billy Wright (1924–1994).

FRANCE 1938
Soccer World Cup, 1938.

MONACO 1963
Centenary of the Football Association.

ARGENTINA 2002
Argentina, world soccer champions 1978 and 1986, and flags of winners from previous years.

BRAZIL 1969
Goal scored by Pelé.

SOUTH KOREA 1983
National soccer meeting.

FRANCE 1996
Saint-Étienne soccer club and player being marked while dribbling the ball.

HUNGARY 1985
International Youth Year: women's soccer.

ITALY 2002
Juventus from Turin, Italian champions in 2001 and 2002.

FRANCE 1998
France, world champions in 1998.

GERMANY 1995
Borussia Dortmund, German soccer champions.

CENTRAL AFRICAN REPUBLIC 1987
Nola pygmies soccer team.

JAPAN 2001
Kaz and Nik, mascots of the 2002 soccer World Cup, held in South Korea and Japan.

NETHERLANDS 1979
Centenary of the introduction of soccer to the Netherlands.

SPAIN 1980
Promoting the Spanish Football World Cup, 1982.

CUBA 1985
An ancient forerunner of ball games.

ITALY 1982
Italy, 1982 world champions.

NICARAGUA 1982
Spanish Football World Cup, 1982.

BELGIUM 1998
Goalkeeper in action.

UNITED STATES 1969
Centenary of American university football: player and coach.

JAPAN 1985
Athletics meeting in Tottori: handball player (with Mount Daisen in the background).

USSR 1979
The Moscow Olympics, 1980: handball players.

ROMANIA 1975
University Handball World Championship.

AUSTRALIA 2003
Rugby World Cup, 2003.

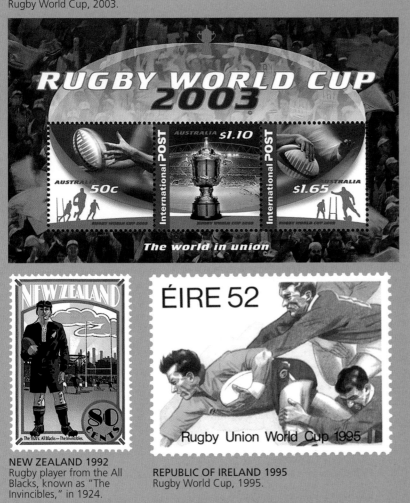

GREAT BRITAIN 1995
Centenary of Rugby League: Brian Bevan.

FRANCE 1992
Rugby players.

NEW ZEALAND 1992
Rugby player from the All Blacks, known as "The Invincibles," in 1924.

REPUBLIC OF IRELAND 1995
Rugby World Cup, 1995.

SOUTH AFRICA 1989
Rugby match between France and South Africa (Springboks), 1980.

BASKETBALL, VOLLEYBALL, TENNIS, BASEBALL, AND CRICKET

Apart from hockey, which is known to have existed in ancient Persia, the oldest of these sports are cricket and tennis — the latter being derived from the French game *jeu de paume*. Both games developed in England: the rules of cricket were laid down in 1744, and the game is now played in many parts of the Commonwealth; the first official tennis tournament took place at Wimbledon in 1877, and the game is now played all over the world. Stamps from many countries feature tennis as an Olympic sport; they also feature other great tennis tournaments such as Roland Garros (France), first held in 1891, Flushing Meadows (US), and Melbourne (Australia).

Badminton (created in England in 1893) and table tennis (Hungary 1897) — both distant relatives of tennis — have produced champions mainly in Asia and Europe, and this is reflected in the provenance of stamps showing these sports. Table tennis is a national sport in China.

Baseball is American in origin, the rules being laid down in 1845, and is played mainly in America and Asia, with stamps from these continents illustrating the sport.

However, stamps from all over the world feature basketball and volleyball, which both originated in America. Basketball was created in 1891 by a schoolteacher from Springfield, Massachusetts to replace gym exercises in the winter. Volleyball, created in 1895, has also become an Olympic sport (in 1964), as has beach volleyball (with two players per team), which emerged during the Second World War.

BRAZIL 1971
Women's Basketball World Championship.

USSR 1965
European Basketball Championship in Moscow.

VIETNAM 1980
Moscow Olympics, 1980: women's basketball.

CHINA 1981
Victory for China in the Women's Volleyball World Cup.

ITALY 1997
University Games, Sicily 1997: scoring a basket.

ST. PIERRE AND MIQUELON (FR) 1997
Volleyball player.

TAIWAN 1988
Day of Sport: volleyball.

UNITED STATES 1983
Famous baseball players: Babe Ruth.

CUBA 1969
Baseball World Championship.

CUBA 1972
World Amateur Baseball Championship: coach encouraging his team.

BELGIUM 2003
Justine Henin-Hardenne, Roland Garros women's champion, 2003.

BRAZIL 1959
Women's Tennis World Championship.

GREAT BRITAIN 1994
Wimbledon Tennis Tournament.

NETHERLANDS 1974
Sport: tennis.

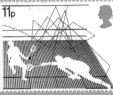

FRANCE 1978
50th anniversary of the Roland Garros stadium.

FRANCE 1977
50th anniversary of the French Table Tennis Federation.

GREAT BRITAIN 1976
Squash.

JAPAN 1981
National Athletics Meeting at Shiga: badminton.

JAPAN 1982
National Athletics Meeting at Matsue: table tennis backhand stroke.

NORTH KOREA 1976
Asian Table Tennis Championship: "smash" attack stroke.

GREAT BRITAIN 1980
A hundred years of cricket.

INDIA 1971
Indian cricket victories.

NEW CALEDONIA 1975
Cricket, a popular sport among the people of New Caledonia.

SRI LANKA 2004
Ananda–Nalanda cricket match with emblems of both clubs.

BELGIUM 1970
Hockey stick for grass play.

POLAND 1985
50th anniversary of the Hockey Sports Association.

LAOS 1966
Game of tikhy (hockey).

REPUBLIC OF IRELAND 1994
Women's Grass Hockey World Cup.

211

GOLF, POLO, AND HORSE-RIDING

The game of golf, now played in amateur and professional tournaments, emerged in Scotland as early as the 13th century, but did not spread to Europe and the United States until after 1850. Today, it is the sport that boasts the largest number of permit holders in the world.

Polo originated in ancient Persia and India, and was brought to Europe by the English during the 19th century, spreading to the United States and Argentina around 1900.

Equestrian sports date back to the 6th century BCE in central Asia in the form of races and games of skill. It was there that nomadic tribesmen first domesticated the horse. The first regulated and regularly repeated race took place in 1671 in Newmarket (England) at a race course built specially for such events. Most major horse-racing events came into being in the 19th century: the Paris Grand Prix, for example, in 1863.

Of these three sports, horse-riding is most frequently featured on stamps, for example flat racing, steeple chase, trotting races, and also dressage events and trick riding, along with show jumping. Even camel racing (dromedary and bactrian) and reindeer racing have not been forgotten.

FRENCH POLYNESIA 1974
Golf at Atimaono.

MOROCCO 1974
International golfing grand prix: the Hassan II trophy.

NEW CALEDONIA 1995
Golf (in the South Pacific Games).

ITALY 1988
Sport: golf.

ALAND (FINLAND) 1995
Tourism in the Nordic countries: woman golfer.

GREAT BRITAIN 1994
The 18th hole at Muirfield.

ARGENTINA 1987
Polo World Championship.

POLAND 1967
150th anniversary of the Podlaski stud farm: polo.

USSR 1963
Regional sports: polo.

**MONGOLIA 1987,
KAZAKHSTAN 1997**
Horse racing.

GREAT BRITAIN 1979
Horse racing at Newmarket
in 1793.

SENEGAL 1961
Horse racing.

HONG KONG 1995
International horse racing.

UNITED STATES 1974
Centenary of the Kentucky
Derby.

GERMANY (GDR) 1979
Socialist Countries Horse
Breeding Congress: racing.

GERMANY (GDR) 1979
Socialist Countries Horse
Breeding Congress:
dressage.

POLAND 1967
Dressage.

USSR 1982
Horse breeding for equestrian sports: dressage.

CHILE 1999
50th anniversary of the
World Horse Jumping
Record.

AUSTRALIA 1986
Show jumping
demonstration.

USSR 1982
Show jumping.

MOROCCO 1981
Equestrian sports: show
jumping.

FRANCE 1998
Trotting.

USSR 1963
Reindeer race.

GERMANY (GDR) 1974
Socialist Countries Horse
Breeding Congress: show
jumping.

AUSTRIA 1973
Centenary of the Viennese
Trotting Race Association.

NIGER 1972
Dromedary race.

UNITED ARAB EMIRATES 1992
Camel race.

SWIMMING AND WATER SPORTS

As a sport, swimming is as ancient as running. It has been part of the modern Olympics since their inception in 1896, as well as featuring in many other competitions. Other water sports such as diving, life-saving, and long-distance swimming have also appeared on stamps, as has water-skiing. This was invented in 1921 by French alpine infantry on Lake d'Annecy and developed to include new disciplines such as slalom, water-ski jumping, acrobatic water skiing, and barefoot water skiing. Surfing, invented by the indigenous peoples of the Pacific, spread to California and Australia around the 1920s and to the rest of the world after 1945.

Free diving has been practiced by pearl fishers since ancient times, and diving became a sport after the development of aqualungs (around 1930). The canoe (which uses one paddle) and the kayak (which uses double-ended paddles) have been used since ancient times for transport and hunting by indigenous populations from Amazonia to Greenland. The associated sports became Olympic disciplines in 1936. Traditional longboat races have always attracted a large audience. Other stamps have featured the hazards of white water rafting, a modern invention practiced in fast-flowing rivers.

ICELAND 1955
Diving.

URUGUAY 1958
South American Swimming Championship.

CHINA 1992
The Barcelona Olympic Games: diving.

CAMPIONATI MONDIALI DI NUOTO

ITALY 1994
World Swimming Championship: diving.

COLOMBIA 1981
South American Swimming Championship.

GERMANY (BERLIN) 1978
3rd World Swimming Championship, Berlin.

NORTH VIETNAM 1959
Sport: swimming in the Red River.

NORTH KOREA 1975
Diving: feet first entry.

FRENCH POLYNESIA 1975
South Pacific Games: women swimmers.

SPAIN 1974
18th World Lifesaving Championship, Barcelona.

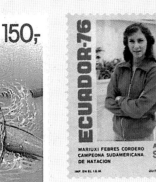

INDONESIA 1993
Jakarta Sports Week: swimming.

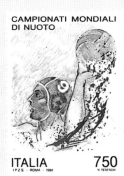

ECUADOR 1976
Mariuxi Febres Cordero, South American swimming champion.

CAMPIONATI MONDIALI DI NUOTO

ITALY 1994
World Swimming Championship: water polo.

FRENCH POLYNESIA 1971
Water Ski World Cup.

TAIWAN 1999
Surfing.

GRENADA 1977
Easter water carnival: water skiing demonstration.

NEW CALEDONIA 2001
Kite surfing.

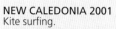

WALLIS AND FUTUNA 1975
South Pacific Games: underwater hunting.

TAIWAN 1999
Deep sea diving with aqualung.

GERMANY (GDR) 1985
World Championship in Underwater Orientation.

ITALY 2002
Canoe-Kayak World Championship: kayaking down the rapids.

TURKEY 1994
Sport tourism: white water rafting.

GRENADA 1975
Pan-American Games, rowing: eight with coxswain.

GERMANY (GFR) 1985
Sport: kayaking.

INDONESIA 1980
Adventure sports: white water rafting.

NEW CALEDONIA 1996
Pirogue Speed Racing World Championship: historical development.

POLAND 1987
Canoeing World Championship, 1986.

FINLAND 1981
Row boat racing.

HONG KONG 1995
International Dragon Boat Races.

CAMEROON 1965
Racing pirogue on the Sanaga river, Edea.

LAOS 1966
Pirogue race.

SAIL SPORTS AND AERIAL SPORTS

Deriving from races between light warships (known as "yachts" in Dutch), the first regulated sporting regatta is believed to have taken place in England in 1661. Today, competitions between all kinds of craft — from yachts, sailboards, and light dinghies, to the largest sailing ships — are celebrated on many stamps. The most famous of these events, the America's Cup, began in 1851 as a race between Great Britain and the United States around the Isle of Wight. Originally known as the One Hundred Guineas Cup, it was renamed after it was won by the schooner *America*. For 132 years the race was dominated by the United States. The cup remained in American hands until the Australian victory of 1983, followed by two victories by New

Zealand, and the Swiss victory of 2003, which made Switzerland the first European country to win this coveted prize.

Competitions very different in spirit have also been featured on stamps: round-the-world races in which sailors — solo or in teams — face the rigors of Cape Horn and the Southern Seas (known as the "roaring forties" and the "howling fifties"), as well as transatlantic and intra-pacific races. Tribute has also been paid to great sailors lost at sea.

In the field of aerial sports, there are stamps celebrating hang gliding and ultralight aircraft, as well as aerobatics and long-distance flying. Even model aircraft have been a theme.

NEW CALEDONIA 2002
Hobie Cat 16 World Catamaran Championship.

WALLIS AND FUTUNA 1983, AUSTRALIA 1989, TAIWAN 1999, HUNGARY 1985
Sail boarding.

GRENADINES 1976
Cariacou annual regatta.

ESTONIA 2004
Dragon regatta, Talinn.

USSR 1978
Pre-Olympic Soling dinghy race.

HONG KONG 1995
China Sea International Regatta.

GERMANY (GFR) 1982
Centenary of Kiel Regatta Week.

SWEDEN 1983
Norden 1983: yachting in Stockholm.

GREAT BRITAIN 1994
Sailing at Cowes.

GREAT BRITAIN 1975
Dinghy racing under spinnaker.

NEW ZEALAND 2003
Team New Zealand, winner of the America's Cup 1995 and 2000, defender in 2003.

AUSTRALIA 1987
Yachts in the America's Cup: first held in 1851, this Cup was won 28 times by America, twice by New Zealand, and once by Australia.

SWITZERLAND 2003
The Swiss yacht *Alinghi*, the first European vessel to win the America's Cup.

CANADA 2000
Tall Ships Race, Halifax.

FRANCE 1994
Alain Colas (1943–1978), winner of the 1972 Transatlantic race and first single-handed, multi-hull, round-the-world yachtsman.

FRENCH SOUTHERN AND ANTARCTIC LANDS 1992
Yacht in the Globe Challenge, a non-stop, single-handed, round-the-world race, created in 1968 by the *Sunday Times* and relaunched in 1989 by the Frenchman Philippe Jeantot.

GREAT BRITAIN 2003
Sir Francis Chichester (1901–1972), round-the-world yachtsman and winner of the first solo transatlantic race in 1960 (in *Gipsy Moth III*).

GERMANY (GDR) 1968
Aerobatics World Championship, Magdeburg.

BRAZIL 1985
40 years of military parachuting.

INDONESIA 1980
Hang glider.

POLAND 1981
Scale competition models: glider (F1 A class) and yacht (DX class).

JAPAN 1995
Model Aircraft World Championship.

NEW CALEDONIA 1980
Coral Sea air rally.

WALLIS AND FUTUNA 1991
Ultralight over the archipelago.

BRAZIL 1991
Hang Gliding World Championship.

CYCLE, MOTORBIKE, AND CAR RACING

The first velocipede race took place in Paris in 1868, and since then competitions have been held in Europe, Asia, and America. The most famous of these, the Tour de France, began in 1903 and is now run over a course of more than 900 miles (3,000km) through various European countries. Competitions of this kind, whether track or cyclo-cross events, can form the basis of a reasonably sized stamp collection.

The same is true of motorbike racing, which began with the first Paris–Dieppe race in 1897 and the first Isle of Man Trophy race in 1907. Many events are now held such as grands prix, hill climbs, speed and endurance competitions, rallies, motocross, and trials.

Car racing has diversified since the first Paris–Bordeaux race of 1895. Indeed, many stamps have been produced celebrating long-distance events and rallies such as the Monte Carlo Rally (the oldest), the Safari Rally Kenya, and the Paris–Dakar Rally. Other world championships have also featured on stamps, with images of Formula 1 drivers such as Schumacher, Fangio, Prost, and Senna. In view of the dangers, only about 50 licenses are granted worldwide allowing drivers to compete in Formula 1 events.

Some endurance races have also been featured on stamps, such as the 24-hour Le Mans and Daytona races, as well as speed records like the 714 mph (1,149 km/h) world land speed record of 1997.

FRANCE 2003
Centenary of the Tour de France showing some of the great winners.

Jacques Anquetil
(1957, 1961, 1962, 1963, 1964)

Eddy Merckx
(1969, 1970, 1971, 1972, 1974)

1903 2003
le Tour de France
0.50 € RF

Miguel Indurain
(1991, 1992, 1993, 1994, 1995)

Lance Armstrong
(1999, 2000, 2001, 2002)

Baanwielrennen
Cyclisme sur piste

BELGIUM 2001
Cycle track racing.

CYCLING USA 50

UNITED STATES 1996
Cycling.

8分
中国人民邮政

CHINA 1985
National Workers' Games: cycling.

日本郵便 平成7年 1995
50 NIPPON
第50回国民体育大会記念

JAPAN 1995
National Athletics Meeting: cycle track racing.

€ 0,41
ITALIA CAMPIONATI MONDIALI DI CICLOCROSS

ITALY 2003
World Cyclo-Cross Championship.

VIETNAM 1992
Motocross: Suzuki 250.

CZECHOSLOVAKIA 1957
International six-day motorcycle race.

BELGIUM 1999
Trials.

SENEGAL 1989
Thierry Sabine, co-founder of the Paris–Dakar Rally (cars, motorbikes, and trucks), killed in an accident.

ISLE OF MAN 1973
50th anniversary of the Isle of Man Motorcycle Grand Prix.

BELGIUM 1999
Speed racing.

VIỆT NAM
4000đ
BƯU CHÍNH
SUZUKI RM 250 F 1992

XXXII. MEZINÁRODNÍ ŠESTIDENNÍ MOTOCYKLOVÁ SOUTĚŽ
60h
127
ČESKOSLOVENSKO

BELGIË-BELGIQUE
17+4
Trial 1999 (fr) CLOVIS

1ᵉ RALLYE PARIS-DAKAR 220F
Thierry Sabine
POSTES 1989
SENEGAL

Manx Grand Prix Golden Jubilee 1923 1973
ISLE OF MAN 3P

BELGIQUE-BELGIË 17+4
7
Vitesse/Snelheid 1999 (fr) CLOVIS

AUSTRALIA
50c
Australian Heroes of Grand Prix Racing

AUSTRALIA 2004
Australian Motorcycle Grand Prix.

SENEGAL 1989
11th Paris–Dakar Rally.

NIGER 1969
The Citroën "Croisière Noire" race (1924–1925): run with six-wheel-track vehicles between Colomb and Bechar (Sahara) and Cape Town.

KENYA 1977
25th anniversary of the Safari Rally, Kenya.

BRAZIL 2000
Ayrton Senna, three-time world champion with McLaren, died during the San Marino Grand Prix in 1994.

ITALY 2001
Ferrari, constructor world champion, 2000.

MONACO 1967
1931 Bugatti.

MONACO 1967
1958 Cooper-Climax.

BELGIUM 1996
Centenary of the Spa Grand Prix: 1939 Mercedes.

FRANCE 1973
50th anniversary of the Le Mans 24-hour race.

GREAT BRITAIN 1998
1964 World Speed Record: Donald Campbell at 403 mph (648 km/h).

COMBAT SPORTS

Although many forms of combat have existed all over the world since ancient times, martial arts skills, involving self-control, are essentially Asian in origin. Judo (meaning "way to suppleness"), the most widely known of these arts, is today featured on stamps from every part of the globe. It was invented by Japanese Samurai warriors in the 13th century to hone their bare-hand fighting skills should they find themselves without weapons. The first modern judo school opened in Tokyo in 1882. It developed this form of combat into a way of life that reached the West in the 20th century and became an Olympic discipline in 1992. Asian stamps also show other martial arts such as karate (created in China by a Buddhist monk in the 6th century),

kung fu (also Chinese in origin), kendo (16th-century Japanese sword fighting), taekwondo (Korean in origin), and sumo wrestling (a form of Japanese court entertainment, regulated in the 14th century and promoted to a national art form). Women's sumo wrestling was originally restricted to courtesans and prohibited in the 19th century but reappeared in 1996. Other world sports featured on stamps include boxing (regulated in 1867 by the Marquess of Queensbury), fencing (which became a sport in Spain in the 15th century and was made an Olympic discipline at the first modern games in 1896), and archery and shooting (the first shooting society was formed in Switzerland in 1466).

CONGO 1977
Bonojo fighters.

JAPAN 1995
World Judo Championship.

ICELAND 1955, USSR 1963
Wrestlers.

JAPAN 1979
Sumo wrestlers.

NORTH KOREA 1995
Taekwondo: hand and foot combat.

FRANCE 1979
World Judo Championship.

SENEGAL 1961
African wrestling.

KAZAKHSTAN 1997
Wrestlers.

CUBA 1970
Central American and Caribbean Games: boxing.

UNITED STATES 1993
Joe Louis (1914–1981), undefeated world heavyweight champion from 1935 to 1946.

KENYA 1978
The Commonwealth Games: boxing.

FRANCE 1991
Marcel Cerdan, middleweight champion from 1933 to 1949: 119 victories out of 123 fights.

LAOS 1982
Lao boxing, known as "tiger fighting": dodging a kick.

NORTH VIETNAM 1967
Women's sword fighting.

MACAO (PORTUGAL) 1997
Martial arts: kung fu, judo, karate.

JAPAN 1972
National Athletics
Meetings: kendo (Japanese
sword fighting).

GREAT BRITAIN 1991
World University Games: fencing.

AUSTRIA 1974
Saber fencing.

BELGIUM 1963
350 years of the Saint-Michel Brotherhood of Fencers
(Ghent).

HUNGARY 1970
75th anniversary of the
Hungarian Olympic
Committee: fencing.

USSR 1963
Regional sports: archery.

MONGOLIA 1968
Archer.

JAPAN 1980
Archer with Mount Nantai
in the background.

**REPUBLIC OF SERBIAN
KRAJINA (CROATIA) 1996**
Jasna Sekaric, Olympic
pistol shooting gold
medallist.

POLAND 1987
Polish winner at the World
Championship: free pistol
shooting.

NORTH VIETNAM 1965
National sports: jousting.

FRANCE 1958
Water jousting.

NORTH VIETNAM 1959
Sports: rifle shooting.

TRADITIONAL SPORTS

Stamps provide a medium for many countries to publicize their traditional sports, which have often remained confined within their national borders or those of their neighbors. This is true of bullfighting, which is widespread only in the Iberian Peninsula, Latin America, and France. Bullfights have been in existence in Spain since the Middle Ages. Initially practiced on horseback by noblemen, bullfighting grew in popularity after the 17th century with bullfighters from among the common people fighting on foot. Horseback bullfights are still held in Portugal.

The Basque sport of pelota, which dates back to the 12th century, is related to tennis and very similar to the French game *jeu de paume*. It has spread to various parts of the world, following Basque emigration to the colonies. Bungee jumping, rediscovered in the 1970s, had already been practiced at traditional celebrations on Pentecost Island (Vanuatu).

Other traditional sports represented here include *pétanque* (French bowls), various Highland sports, stone-lifting, and fruit-carrying in the Pacific region and Asiatic games.

MONGOLIA 1976
Riding skills.

JAPAN 1964
Soma equestrian festival: warriors on horseback.

MONGOLIA 1987
Mounted archer.

KAZAKHSTAN 1997
The goatskin game (koknar).

ALGERIA 1977
"Fantasia" display by armed horsemen.

SPAIN 1997
The bullfighter Manolete (1917–1947), killed by a bull in the Linares bullring.

PORTUGAL 1992
Centenary of the Campo Pequeno bullring: horseback bullfight.

SPAIN 1960
Bullfighting: passes with the *muleta* (the red cape used by the matador).

ST. PIERRE AND MIQUELON (FR) 1991
Basque pelota, brought to Canada many years ago by Basque colonists.

SPAIN 1986
World Pelota Championships.

BELGIUM 1998
The game of *balle pelote*.

ST. PIERRE AND MIQUELON (FR) 1994
French Overseas Departments Pétanque Championship.

FRANCE 1958, BELGIUM 2003
The game of boules: preparing and throwing.

FRENCH POLYNESIA 1989
Stone-carriers' competition.

FRENCH POLYNESIA 2000
Fruit-carriers' competition.

GREAT BRITAIN 1994
The Highland Games at Braemar.

CANADA 1997
The Highland Games: caber turning, bagpiper, drum, and dancer.

CONDOMINIUM OF THE NEW HEBRIDES 1969
The Saut du Gaul (ancestor of bungee jumping) on Pentecost Island.

NEW ZEALAND 2003
Modern bungee jumping from a viaduct.

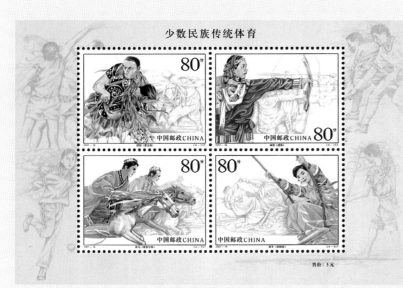

CHINA 2003
Traditional sports: wrestling, archery, horse racing, swing.

NORTH KOREA 1960
Traditional sports.

English Sundew   Venus Flytrap

NATURE

LANDSCAPES OF THE WORLD

All countries like to feature their sites of natural beauty on their stamps: this serves to publicize their tourist attractions, and also allows philatelists to collect images of the geographical features of our planet, country by country. A collection of this type can also serve an educational purpose, providing an attractive aid to the teaching of geography. The selection below highlights themes that include the world's highest mountains, caves and rock formations, outstanding waterfalls and cascades, and desert, river, and coastal landscapes.

NEPAL 1982
The Everest Mountain chain.

JAPAN 1967
Mount Fuji Yama (after a painting by T. Yokoyama).

KENYA, UGANDA, TANGANYIKA (TANZANIA) 1968
Mount Kilimanjaro.

FRANCE 2003
Mont Blanc.

SWITZERLAND 1971
Les Diablerets.

AUSTRALIA 1993
Uluru (Ayers Rock): national park.

CHINA 1989
The five peaks of Mount Huashan.

ARGENTINA 1977
Sierra de la Ventana (Buenos Aires).

Mountains

Rocks and caves

TURKEY 1977
Pamukkale (dubbed "the cotton castle"), formed by petrified waterfalls.

CHINA 1981
Stone forest.

CZECH REPUBLIC 1995
Panska Skala basalt organs.

GUINEA 1966
The Vonkou stone at Télimélé.

ITALY 1977
The Castellana Caves.

Waterfalls

BRAZIL 1978
The Iguaçu Falls.

UNITED STATES 1999
Niagara Falls.

ZIMBABWE 1986
The Zambezi (or Victoria) Falls.

MEXICO 1982
The Basaseachic Falls,
1,020 ft (311m) high.

ALGERIA 1980
Valley in the Aurès Mountains.

MOROCCO 1983
The Ouzoud Falls.

AUSTRIA 1970
The Krimmler–Salzburg Falls.

LAOS 1991
The Champassak Falls.

SOUTH WEST AFRICA
(NAMIBIA) 1988
Oasis in the Namibian Desert.

VIETNAM 1984
Along Bay.

NORWAY 1976
The "Prekestolen" (preacher's
pulpit), rising 1,968 ft (600m)
vertically over the fjord.

JAPAN 1973
Yoshino River, Tsurugi-San Park.

TRISTAN DA CUNHA
(GREAT BRITAIN)
Coastal landscape of
Stoltenhoff Island:
"Ridge where the
goat jump off."

COMOROS ISLANDS (FR) 1973
Prophet Hole at Mitsamiouli
(Grand Comoros).

Coastal landscapes

TUNISIA 2000
Mediterranean landscape
(painting by A. Berraies).

GABON 1974
Cape Esterias beach.

NEW CALEDONIA 1991
Fayawa-Ouvea Bay.

FORESTS, TREES, AND FRUIT

Stamps from every part of the world have featured the various forests and jungles of our planet, from those in the far north to the rich, natural environments of mangrove swamps, protected by their tangled tree roots. Characteristically, stamps feature trees that are emblematic of their country, for example the cedar of Lebanon and the ipé tree of Venezuela.

The stamps representing fruit, whether ordinary or "exotic" (to western eyes), are beautifully illustrated and informative.
Mushrooms and fungi are another traditional theme of philately, making it possible to build up a comparative specimen collection – edible and poisonous mushrooms, for example.

GERMANY 2000
Forest in Hainich national park.

JAPAN 1973
Forest on Mount Tsurugi.

SLOVAKIA 2004
Dobroc primal forest and forest warden.

CHINA 1998
Primitive forest of Shennongjia.

AUSTRALIA 1993
Virgin forest, Fraser Island.

MADAGASCAR (FR) 1954
Forest of pachypodes.

FRANCE 2002
Heart in Voh mangrove, New Caledonia (aerial photo by Y. Arthus-Bertrand).

NEW CALEDONIA 1974
Mangrove swamp.

NORTH KOREA 1974
River in the morning (modern painting).

GREAT BRITAIN 1973
Oak tree.

FRENCH WEST AFRICA 1954
The multi-purpose baobab tree.

Forests

CHINA 1985
May blossom: japonica flowers.

SINGAPORE 2002
Flame tree (scarlet-red flowers, 60 ft/18m tall).

ITALY 1968
Cypresses in the Tuscany landscape.

NEW CALEDONIA 1984
Pritchardiopsis palm; very rare species.

BRAZIL 1978
Ipé tree (yellow flowers, 130 ft/40m tall).

228   NATURE

CONGO 1975
Papaya.

SINGAPORE 2004
Tropical nutmeg, grows by the sea.

WALLIS AND FUTUNA 1994
Coconut, has many uses: milk, nutritious flesh, butter, container.

ST. PIERRE AND MIQUELON (FR) 2003
Blueberry, type of berry specific to North America.

Fungi

USSR 1986
Fly agaric (poisonous).

ANGOLA 1993
Parasol mushroom (edible and delicious).

NEW ZEALAND 1982
Nectarines, cross between the plum and yellow peach.

GREAT BRITAIN 1993
Blackberries.

Fruit

CANADA 1989
Spindle-shaped yellow coral (edible).

SPAIN 1994
Boletus edulis (edible).

RWANDA 1980
Geaster, or earthstar (decorative, of no culinary interest).

Trees

LEBANON 1965
Cedar tree, national emblem of Lebanon.

CHINA 1993
Bamboo stems.

USSR 1987
Ferns.

VIETNAM 1986
Decorative bonsai: dwarf fig.

229

FLOWERS

From the tropical to the temperate, from the aquatic to the carnivorous, the abundance of stamps celebrating the rich variety of plants and flowers on our planet, issued by so many different countries, creates a vast bouquet representing every latitude and forming an inexhaustible collection.

Cactus flowers

ANGOLA 1993

POLAND 1981

TROPICAL FLOWERS

Other tropical flowers

FRENCH POLYNESIA 2001
The tiare, a scented flower used in the production of the cosmetic oil "monoi de Tahiti."

ZAIRE 1984
The hypericum, with its attractive yellow flowers.

SIERRA LEONE 1963
Crinum (white lily).

Orchids

CAYMAN ISLANDS 1971

NEW HEBRIDES 1973

NICARAGUA 1984
Hairy beggarticks (*Bidens pilosa*), a medicinal plant with beneficial properties for diabetics.

INDONESIA 1966
Hibiscus.

SRI LANKA 1976
Rhododendron zelanicum; grows in the mountains.

WALLIS AND FUTUNA 1998

NEW CALEDONIA 1993

FRENCH POLYNESIA 1994
"Belle de Nuit": all the flowers in a particular area bloom together on a single night.

MALAYSIA 1979
Rafflesia, parasitic plant of the virgin forest.

MONSERRAT 1976
Scented blossom of the cannonball tree.

MAYOTTE (FR) 2001
Porcelain rose, member of the ginger family.

Aquatic flowers

BRAZIL 1979
Amazonian water lily.

USSR 1984
Yellow water lily.

Carnivorous plants

GUYANA 1971
Carnivorous pitcher plant
from Mount Roraima
(9,000 ft/2,730m).

UNITED STATES 2001
English sundew and Venus flytrap, both carnivorous.

English Sundew *Venus Flytrap*

TEMPERATE PLANTS

CHINA 1960
Chrysanthemums.

FRANCE 2000, TURKEY 1998
Tulips.

GREAT BRITAIN 1997
Flower painting: passion flower.

USSR 1976
Crocus from the Caucasus.

ITALY 1981
Anemones.

GERMANY 1991
Androsace (rock jasmine) in the
Oberhof botanical gardens.

ESTONIA 2003
Tulips, hellebores, narcissi,
crocuses.

CANADA 2001, FRANCE 1999, GREAT BRITAIN 1976
Roses.

GREAT BRITAIN 1987
Echinops.

MINERALS, FOSSILS, AND PREHISTORIC ANIMALS

The selection of stamps on these pages represents two different themes of philately: minerals, and prehistoric animals. Stamps on minerals are often issued by countries rich in mineral resources, which naturally enjoy publicizing the fact.

Prehistoric animals, on the other hand, have captured the imagination of people all over the world because of the enormous size of the ancient dinosaurs and their mysterious disappearance. With a few rare exceptions,

these extinct creatures have only been found in the form of fossils and bones, and to reconstruct how they looked has required painstaking scientific work.

Many series of stamps and illustrated blocks on this theme have been issued for purely commercial reasons, taking advantage of the attraction the subject has for collectors. The prehistoric animals depicted are often spectacular but not always scientifically accurate.

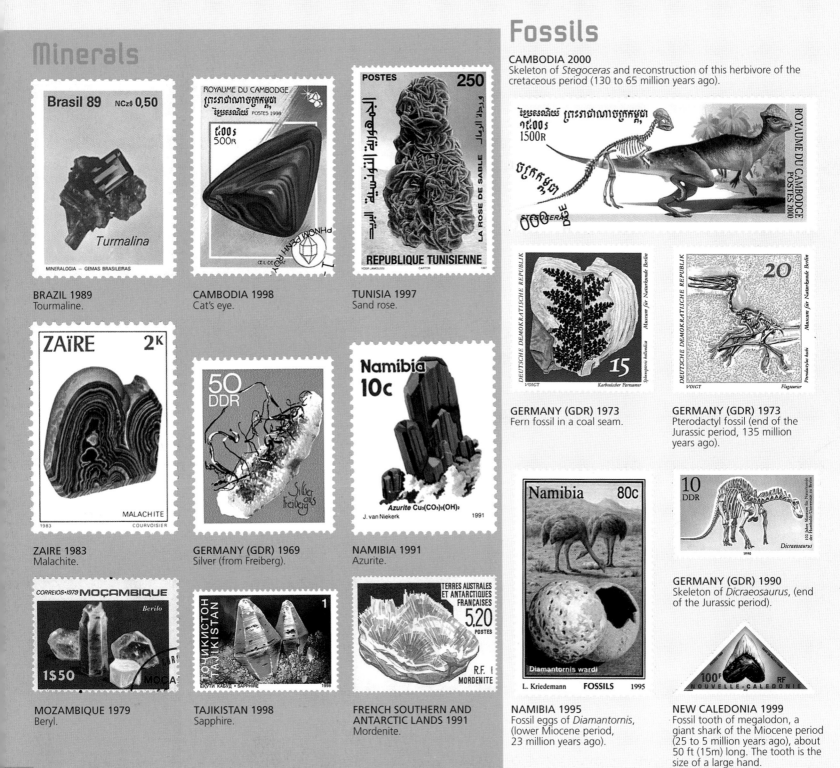

Minerals

BRAZIL 1989
Tourmaline.

CAMBODIA 1998
Cat's eye.

TUNISIA 1997
Sand rose.

ZAIRE 1983
Malachite.

GERMANY (GDR) 1969
Silver (from Freiberg).

NAMIBIA 1991
Azurite.

MOZAMBIQUE 1979
Beryl.

TAJIKISTAN 1998
Sapphire.

FRENCH SOUTHERN AND ANTARCTIC LANDS 1991
Mordenite.

Fossils

CAMBODIA 2000
Skeleton of *Stegoceras* and reconstruction of this herbivore of the cretaceous period (130 to 65 million years ago).

GERMANY (GDR) 1973
Fern fossil in a coal seam.

GERMANY (GDR) 1973
Pterodactyl fossil (end of the Jurassic period, 135 million years ago).

GERMANY (GDR) 1990
Skeleton of *Dicraeosaurus*, (end of the Jurassic period).

NAMIBIA 1995
Fossil eggs of *Diamantornis*, (lower Miocene period, 23 million years ago).

NEW CALEDONIA 1999
Fossil tooth of megalodon, a giant shark of the Miocene period (25 to 5 million years ago), about 50 ft (15m) long. The tooth is the size of a large hand.

Saber-tooth cat

32 USA

Eohippus

32 USA

UNITED STATES 1996
Saber-toothed tiger: cat weighing 1,000 to 1,350 lb (500–600kg), with giant teeth (600,000 years ago). *Eohippus*: horse the size of a fox terrier (50 million years ago).

USSR 1990
Saurolophus, 30 to 40 ft (9–12m) long, with a bony spine (70 million years ago).

USSR 1990
Indricotherium (25 to 30 million years ago), the largest known mammal: 16 ft (4.7m) tall, weighing 11–20 tons. The stamp caption incorrectly reads "chalicotherium."

MOZAMBIQUE 1999
Diamonds were formed over 3,000 million years ago, at high temperature and under extreme pressure. The *velociraptor* (speedy thief), an intelligent carnivore almost 6 ft (1.8m) in length is more recent (85 million years ago).

Prehistoric animals

USSR 1990
Sordes, from the pterosaur family of the Jurassic period (195–135 million years ago).

USSR 1990
Thyestes, small, jawless fish of the Silurian period (435–410 million years ago).

UNITED STATES 1997
Detail of a scene in Montana 75 million years ago (toward the end of the Cretaceous period).

CHAD 1996
Evocation of geological periods: formation of zoisite (variety of epidote silicate), and *Corythosaurus* ("helmet lizard"), a 4-ton herbivore of the late Cretaceous period (70 million years ago).

TANZANIA 1991
Phiomia and *Gomphotherium*, ancestors of the mammoth (36 million years ago), and deinothere (giant mammoth with shoulder height of 16 ft/4.7m).

WILD ANIMALS OF THE SAVANNAH AND VIRGIN FOREST

The first of these two spreads devoted to wild animals focuses on those in tropical countries, living in the desert, on the dry grasslands, and in virgin forest. This is a topic that allows many countries in Africa, Asia, and South America to celebrate their unusual fauna, and is an interesting and beautiful theme for philatelists.

Countries in the north have also issued stamps on this theme and taken part in internationally coordinated issues that are intended to raise public awareness of the plight of endangered species. Issues like those bearing the panda logo of the WWF (World Wide Fund for Nature) are particularly sought after by collectors.

Even to the untrained eye it is clear that certain species have adapted to live in very different environments, for example the leopard of the African savannah and the snow leopard. Conversely, other species, like the lemurs of Madagascar and the orangutans of south-east Asia, have remained confined to very precise areas.

SOUTH AFRICA 1995
Warthogs.

SPANISH SAHARA 1957
Striated hyena.

MOROCCO 1984
Jerboa.

GUINEA 1977
Hippopotamus.

UPPER VOLTA (BURKINA) 1962
The Defassa waterbuck (375 lb/170kg), a big game antelope.

BURUNDI 1975
The slender-necked Dama gazelle (165 lb/75kg), a species disturbingly on the decline.

LESOTHO
Young black-backed jackals.

MAURITIUS 1994
Indian mongoose, kills snakes.

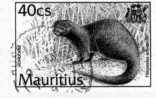

CENTRAL AFRICAN REPUBLIC 1983
Black rhinoceros, endangered species.

RWANDA-URUNDI 1959
Impalas.

CHAD 1965
Oryx, endangered species.

GUINEA-BISSAU 1988
Zebra, the only wild horse living in large numbers in the wild.

FRENCH SOMALI COAST 1962
Fennec fox (*Vulpes zerda*), a small desert canine.

BRAZIL 1984
Water buffalo, island of Marajo.

TANZANIA 1980
Giraffe.

ZAIRE 1984
Lord Derby elands, the largest of the antelopes (weighing up to 1,100 lb/500kg).

FELIS CARACAL
REPUBLIQUE DE HAUTE·VOLTA 60F

UPPER VOLTA 1979
Lynx *Felis caracal*.

из Красной книги СССР
Ирбис
15·
ПОЧТА СССР 1987

USSR 1987
Snow leopard
(*Panthera uncia*).

REPUBLIQUE DE
10F
POSTES
CÔTE D'IVOIRE

IVORY COAST 1959
African elephant, bigger
than its Asian cousin, with
larger ears.

RWANDA-URUNDI 1959
Gorilla, the largest living
primate.

RUANDA
GORILLA 10c
URUNDI
J. VAN NOTEN   COURVOISIER S.A.

ANGOLA 1500 Nkz
DIA DE ÁFRICA

ANGOLA 1993
Savannah leopard (*Panthera pardus*), more robust than the African lion and Asian tiger.

REPUBLIQUE du BENIN 200f
Lions Africains   Postes 2001

BENIN 2001
African lions (*Panthera leo*), hunters of zebras and giraffes. Their roar can be heard for
over 6 miles (9 km).

1995-11   (2-1)J   1995-11   (2-2)J

CHINA 1995
Asian elephants: the herd is led by a female matriarch.

BRAZIL 1976
Golden lion tamarind
(*Leontopithecus rosalia*),
with magnificent silky fur,
endangered species.

GUINEA-BISSAU 1983
Mandrill (*Mandrillus
sphinx*), one of the most
colorful mammals.

ALVARO ALVES MARTINS CASA DA MOEDA DO BRASIL
Brasil 76 1,00
MICO LEÃO · LEONTOPITHECUS ROSALIA CHRYSOMELAS

República de Guiné-Bissau 5p00
Macacos Africanos
Republique du Guinée-Bissau
1983

180F
POSTES 1998
République du Niger

NIGER 1998
Lioness and cub. Lions sleep 20 hours a day.

30¢
Panthera tigris   Malaysia

MALAYSIA 1979
Asian tiger (*Panthera tigris*), one of the greatest of all
cats, endangered species.

PARAGUAY
Great anteater (*Tamanoir*),
gentle and harmless, feeds
on ants.

CONGO 1991
Baboon (*Papio hamadryas*).

VIETNAM 1981
Orang-utan
(*Pongo pymaeus*).

MADAGASCAR (FR) 1954
Ring-tailed lemur (*Lemur catta*), native to Madagascar.

CORREO DEL PARAGUAY
₲0.75

Việt nam
30

CONGO 1991

Papio hamadryas   Postes 1991
Republique
du Congo   75F

MADAGASCAR
POSTE AÉRIENNE
200F
RF   LEMUR CATTA

235

WILD ANIMALS OF THE WOODS, PRAIRIES, AND MOUNTAINS

The second selection of stamps on the wild animal theme features fauna from the mountainous and temperate regions of countries in Europe, Asia, and North America.

Many of these animals, such as the wolf and fox, are part of the culture of northern countries, often appearing in popular children's stories. Additionally, the bear has given its name to major European cities such as Berlin and Bern. It is interesting to note the widespread dispersal of some of these mammals. The hare, for example, lives both on arctic ice floes and in the tropics, and is also the hero of numerous African and Korean folk tales and European fables.

A number of these animals (like the mountain ibex) are endangered and have been placed under protection; others have been reintroduced into the wild in certain areas, like the wolf in national parks in Italy and the European bison in Poland.

Series of stamps with the WWF logo featuring these animals and those of the tropics are highly sought after by collectors.

AUSTRALIA 1995
Koala (*Phascolarctos cinereus*) and cub on a eucalyptus branch.

CHINA 1963
Giant panda (*Ailuropoda melanoleuca*), an attractive herbivore.

ITALY 1967
Brown bear (*Ursus arctos*) in the Abruzzi national park.

USSR 1961
Brown bear looking for food in a tree.

GERMANY (BERLIN) 1989
Bear, depicted on the Berlin coat of arms and origin of the city's name.

USSR 1987
Marmot (*Marmota marmota*); like the bear, the marmot hibernates.

FRANCE 1996
Ibex (*Capra ibex*) and gentian flower in the Vanoise national park.

FRENCH SOUTHERN AND ANTARCTIC LANDS 1985
Mouflon (*Ovis amon*), ancestor of the sheep.

ETHIOPIA 1990
Ibex (*Walia ibex*), exists only in the mountains of Ethiopia, critically endangered species.

NEW CALEDONIA 1994
Deer farming (*Cervus elaphus*): Bourail Fair.

NORTH KOREA 1979
Fallow deer drinking (*Dama dama*).

BELGIUM 1997
Roe deer (*Capreolus capreolus*), in the eastern cantons.

CANADA 2003
Canadian elk (*Alces alces*), the largest of the cervidae.

Canis lupus Hunt

EESTI 4,40

S.STERN 2004

ESTONIA 2004
Head of a gray wolf (*Canis lupus*).

PARCO NAZIONALE DELLA CALABRIA - LA SILA

800 € 0,41 ITALIA

I.P.Z.S. - ROMA - 1999 A.M. MARESCA

ITALY 1999
Wolf in Calabria national park. Two centuries ago the wolf was the most widespread of western mammals, but is now endangered.

6 50 POLSKA • POLSKA 6 50 •

KARAT-2000 Bison Bonasus L. • PWPW'II • Bison Bonasus L. • PWPW'II

POLAND 2000
European bison (*Bison bonassus*), smaller than its American cousin: the remaining specimens are being reintroduced into the forests of Poland.

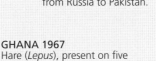

1980

2к Почта СССР

USSR 1980
Black fox (*Vulpes cana*), present from Russia to Pakistan.

ANIMAIS DO ZOO DE LISBOA
RAPOSA
VULPES VULPES

PORTUGAL 16.00

PORTUGAL 1980
Common red fox (*Vulpes vulpes*).

USA 34

UNITED STATES 2001
American bison (*Bison bison*): 6 ft tall (1.82m) to the withers, it weighs 3,300 lb (1.5 metric tons).

USSR 1988
Boar (*Sus scrofa*): shy, omnivorous animal living in deciduous woodland.

20к ПОЧТА СССР 1988

GHANA 1967
Hare (*Lepus*), present on five continents.

Ø1
HARE
GHANA
HARRISON AND SONS LTD

FRANCE 2001
Ermine (*Mustela herminea*): small but bold carnivore; lives in woods.

0,69€ 4,50F RF
LA POSTE 2001
l'hermine

SWEDEN 1992
Red squirrel (*Sciurus vulgaris*).

SVERIGE
Ekorre *Sciurus vulgaris*
6 KR
S.ULLSTRÖM 1992 L.SJÖÖBLOM SC

JAPAN (NO DATE GIVEN)
Korean squirrels (*Eutamia sibericus*).

NIPPON 80
日本郵便

GERMANY (GDR) 1982
Polecat (*Mustela putorius*); strictly nocturnal, this animal is unharmed by adder venom.

Internationale Leipziger Rauchwarenauktion
DDR 20
ILTIS 1982

USSR 1987
Badger (*Meles meles*).

ПОЧТА СССР
10к

FRANCE 1997
Raccoon (*Procyon lotor*) in the Guadeloupe national park; lives near watercourses.

3,00
REPUBLIQUE FRANÇAISE
LA POSTE 1997
Parc de la Guadeloupe

PARAGUAY 1964
Hedgehog.

CORREO DEL PARAGUAY
₲ 0.10

GREAT BRITAIN 1992
Fox in winter.

HORSES AND FARM ANIMALS

The horse is the most highly regarded of the animals domesticated by man. It is more than a simple mount or means of transport; in every civilization the horse confers a certain nobility on its rider, while different breeds are used for plowing and traction.

Naturally enough, the horse is a very popular theme for stamp collectors. Most countries have produced stamps on this subject — notably central Asia, Europe, and the Arab states. Some of these form part of themes already included here, such as equestrian sports and transport, but the horse also features in its own right, as seen in the selection below, in its role in battle (in the Turkish miniature) or, on a more peaceful note, being ridden side-saddle by a Russian woman.

Other domestic animals, including farm and ranch animals, are also shown.

RAS AL KHAIMAH 1972, POLAND 1989
Arabian thoroughbred.

Horses

AUSTRALIA 1986, ST. PIERRE AND MIQUELON (FR) 1998
Wild horses.

FRANCE 1998
Camargue horse.

GREAT BRITAIN 1978
Thoroughbred.

NEW CALEDONIA 1977
Mare and foal (Society for the Encouragement of Horse Breeding).

HUNGARY 1974
Foal.

GERMANY (GDR) 1974
Haflinger pure-breds.

MONGOLIA
Breaking in a herd of horses.

TURKEY 1968
Horse with mounted archer (Turkish miniature).

BELGIUM 1976
Draft horses from the Ardennes.

SPAIN 1987
The Jerez Horse Fair.

RUSSIA 2004
Woman riding side-saddle.

CHINA 1993
Bactrian (two-humped) camel.

UNITED ARAB EMIRATES 1992
Dromedaries (one hump).

BOLIVIA 1995
Andean llamas.

HUNGARY 1974
Lamb.

ROMANIA 1994
Kid goat.

FRENCH SOUTHERN AND
ANTARCTIC LANDS 1989
Kerguelen ram and sheep.

GREAT BRITAIN
1984
Highland cow.

GREAT BRITAIN 1992
Sheep in winter.

BARBADOS 1982
Black belly sheep.

SWITZERLAND 2004
Production animal: the pig (Swiss
animal protection league).

UNITED STATES 1973
Herd of Angus and Longhorn
cattle.

MADAGASCAR (FR) 1946
Zebu cattle.

Farm animals

UPPER VOLTA (BURKINA)
1972
Goat.

ARGENTINA 2003
Cattle.

DOGS, CATS, AND OTHER PETS

Along with horses, cats and dogs are the animals most frequently featured on stamps. Found in every region of the world and in countless homes, most countries have devoted several series of stamps to dogs and cats, either illustrating the different breeds, or showing them at leisure or working alongside man.

As a working animal, the dog is shown far more often than the cat, seen in a variety of tasks such as hunting, guiding the blind, pulling sledges, and guarding sheep. Cats, altogether more independent in nature, were considered by the Egyptians to be sacred animals. They are shown at play or at leisure, but, unlike dogs, they are rarely shown at work!

Other pets such as rabbits, hamsters, goldfish, and other animals also occasionally feature on stamps, obeying the whims of fashion and appeal. Additionally, stamps have been used to pay tribute to societies for the protection of animals in various countries. In the two examples below it is interesting to note that it is the dog that has been chosen to represent these societies.

KAMPUCHEA (CAMBODIA) 1984
Wild dog.

BHUTAN
Dhole (*Cuon alpinus*): canine from Asia with very thick fur.

REPUBLIC OF IRELAND 1983
Irish setter (hunting dog).

SPAIN 1983
Burgos pointing dog (hunting dog).

USSR 1988
Husky and bear-hunting.

POLAND 1989
Czech pointer.

UNITED STATES 1984
Collie and Alaskan Malamute.

GREAT BRITAIN 1979
Highland terrier.

CANADA 1988
Newfoundland (used in sea rescues).

SWITZERLAND 1989
St. Bernard (used in mountain rescue).

FRANCE 1999
Pyrenean mountain dog.

RUSSIA 2000
Pet dog: French bulldog.

AUSTRIA 1966
120th anniversary of the Viennese animal protection league.

CUBA 2001
Police dog sniffing for drugs.

FRENCH POLYNESIA 1974
Animal protection league.

PERU 1988
World dog championship in Lima.

Dogs

GREENLAND (DENMARK) 2003
Sled dog.

NETHERLANDS 1985
Dogs for the blind.

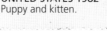

MONACO 1989
Dog show: Yorkshire Terrier.

UNITED STATES 1982
Puppy and kitten.

PERU 1988

CYPRUS 2002
White and tortoiseshell cat, and European gray.

NORWAY 2001
Kittens.

ALDERNEY (GUERNSEY, GREAT BRITAIN) 1996
Kitten playing with a butterfly.

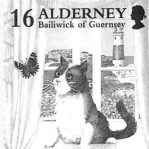

FRENCH SOUTHERN AND ANTARCTIC LANDS 1994
Black cat (*Felix catus*), imported to the Kerguelen Islands.

GREAT BRITAIN 2001
Humorous photograph: cat sitting on a sign written in French saying "Beware of the dog."

Cats

AUSTRIA 2001
The cat as "king."

EGYPT 1980
Cat in ancient times (sacred animal).

COLOMBIA 1980
The cat's seven lives (Rafael Pombo, 1833–1912).

SLOVAKIA 2003
Wildcat (*Felix sylvestris*).

CANADA 2004
Pets: goldfish, cats, rabbit, dog.

VIETNAM 1979
Cat.

SWEDEN 1994
Cats: Siamese, Persian, European, Abyssinian.

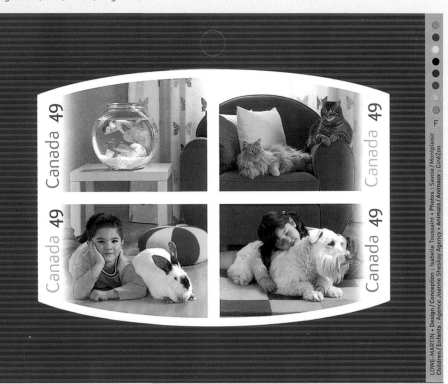

LOWE-MARTIN • Design/Conception • Isabelle Toussaint • Photos : Savoie / Montplaisir Children / Enfants • Agence Joanne Sheskay Agency • Animaux • CinéZoo

FAUNA OF THE COASTS AND TROPICAL LAGOONS

Marine life, like land-dwelling animals, is also a very popular subject in philately. The colorful appearance of aquatic creatures and the distant oceans they evoke make them very appealing. The universal nature of the Latin names that appear on most stamps devoted to exotic fauna and flora are useful to the collector, making it easy to identify them and avoid the confusion inherent in the numerous common and popular names used in the various languages and dialects.

The first of these two selections on marine fauna looks at the corals, fish, and shellfish of tropical coasts and lagoons. Most of these stamps have been issued by countries in tropical latitudes.

Corals and tropical fish

FRENCH SOMALI COAST 1966
Crinoid (echinoderm with a five-branch body) on fire coral.

NEW CALEDONIA 1988, FRENCH POLYNESIA 1991, FRENCH SOMALI COAST 1963
Corals.

SENEGAL 1973
Radiolarian: single-cell plankton whose skeleton is made of silica, not calcium.

PANAMA 1965
Seahorses.

NEW HEBRIDES, MAYOTTE (FR) 1999
Lion fish *Pterois volitans*, with spectacular, long, and very photogenic fins that are poisonous in some species.

COMOROS ISLANDS (FR) 1977
Raccoon butterfly fish (*Chaetodon lunula*).

SINGAPORE 1995
Harlequin sweetlips (*Plectorhinchus chaetodonoides*).

WALLIS AND FUTUNA 1992
Surgeon fish (*Acanthurus*).

BRAZIL 1969
Scalare angel fish (*Pterophyllum scalare*), lives in tropical rivers.

MICRONESIA 1995
Divers and tropical fish among the corals of Chuuk lagoon.

COMOROS ISLANDS (FR) 1966
Grouper. If there is a shortage of males during the mating season, older females can change sex.

NEW CALEDONIA 1984
Clown fish (*Amphiprion clarkii*), lives in symbiosis with sea anemones, unaffected by their poison.

NEW CALEDONIA 1965
Juvenile coris. These wrasse are all female as juveniles and change color when they reach adulthood; some change sex and become male.

UNITED STATES 1999
Tropical aquarium fish.

Warm-water fauna

MEXICO 1982
Carey turtle.

CAPE VERDE 1980
Moray eel (*Muraena helena*): nocturnal hunter; hides in holes in rocks during the day. The toxic glands in its mouth give it a dangerous bite.

BRAZIL 1979
Amazonian manatee (*Trichechus inunguis*).

ANGOLA 1993
Turtles.

FRENCH TERRITORY OF THE AFARS AND ISSAS 1971
Manta ray, or "devilfish" (*Manta birostris*). Can weigh as much as a ton and measure 23 ft/7m in width. It is capable of capsizing a boat.

NEW CALEDONIA 2003
Dugong grazing on seaweed (*Dugon dugon*).

Shellfish

BRAZIL 1989
Hebrew volute (*Voluta ebraea*).

FRENCH TERRITORY OF THE AFARS AND ISSAS 1975
Murex (*Murex scholopax*). In ancient times a purple dye was extracted from murex and used to color the clothing worn by dignitaries.

NEW HEBRIDES 1972
Green snail (*Turbo marmoratus*): this large, thick shellfish (weighing over 2 lb/1kg) is capable of stripping bare a seaweed-covered rock when grazing.

FRENCH POLYNESIA 2002
Purple pencil-urchin (*Heterocentrotus trigonarius*).

WALLIS AND FUTUNA 1979
Blue starfish (*Linckia laevigata*).

NEW CALEDONIA 1985
Cone shell (*Conus lamberti*): these colorful shellfish are dangerous, as they have a poisonous tooth at the end of a filament and strike anything that moves.

MAYOTTE (FR) 2000
Two large shellfish (almost 20 in/50 cm): horned helmet shell (*Cassis cornuta*) and triton's trumpet shell (*Charonia tritonis*).

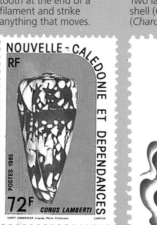

USSR 1975
Veined rapa whelk *Rapana venosa*, a voracious predator that can become invasive because of its reproductive capabilities.

WALLIS AND FUTUNA 1979
Squamosa clam (*Tridacna squamosa*). The largest can reach over 3 ft (1m) in diameter. Portuguese navigators used these shells as holy water fonts at the entrance to churches.

FAUNA OF THE OPEN SEA AND POLES

The stamps in this second selection on marine life provide examples of life in the ocean depths, the migration of tuna and whales across the seas, life on polar ice floes, and sharks — fascinating both for the danger certain species pose and for their extraordinary sensory abilities in locating prey. These stamps originate from a wide variety of countries: the open sea, which begins 200 miles (300km) offshore, is not the territory of any particular country. Moreover, migratory fish and mammals can be found near the coasts of countries in very different latitudes depending on the season; for example, whales reproduce in tropical waters but feed in the cold waters of the great northern and southern oceans, which are richer in plankton.

CISKEI 1983
Scalloped hammerhead shark (*Sphyrna lewini*): its hammer-shaped head increases its sensory perception, helping it to locate prey.

COMOROS ISLANDS (FR) 1954
Coelacanth, a veritable living fossil and prehistoric ancestor of most present-day vertebrates.

CONGO 1961
Lophius or Angler fish, lives in the dark ocean depths. It moves a luminous filament above its mouth to attract prey.

ALGERIA 1985
Mediterranean red tuna: a tireless migrator capable of crossing the sea at the speed of an ocean liner.

WALLIS AND FUTUNA 2000
Pacific yellow tuna: can weigh as much as 1,300 lb (600kg).

FRENCH SOUTHERN AND ANTARCTIC LANDS 2001
Squid. Depending on the species, squid range from 1 inch to 50 ft (2cm to 15m) in length. Large specimens have been known to attack sperm whales.

FRENCH TERRITORY OF THE ARARS AND ISSAS 1973
Pink octopus; has tentacles over 3 ft (1m) long.

ASCENSION ISLAND 2004
Blue marlin: much sought after by big game fishermen, it can weigh over 1,700 lb (800kg).

MAYOTTE (FR) 2003
Sailfish: when it opens its dorsal fin on the surface of the water it is driven by the wind like a sailboat.

VIETNAM 1991
Bull shark (*Carcharinus leucas*), one of the few sharks to live in both salt and fresh water. Presents a danger to swimmers from the Amazon to the Mississippi, hundreds of miles from the sea.

PORTUGAL, AZORES 2004
White swordfish.

Ocean depths and high seas

MADAGASCAR 1993
White tip shark (*Carcharinus longimanus*), 13 ft (4m) long: the most dangerous of the sharks, driven to a frenzy by the smell of blood, hunt their quarry in packs.

PANAMA 1965
Dorado, much prized for its flavor; its magnificent iridescent colors disappear when it dies after being caught.

FRENCH TERRITORY OF THE AFARS AND ISSAS 1973
Sawfish (*Pristis pectinatus*): member of the ray family; harmless despite its length (26 ft/8m) and its saw-like extremity.

TANZANIA 1995
Short-fin Mako shark (*Isurus oxyrhinchus*), one of the fastest sharks in the ocean.

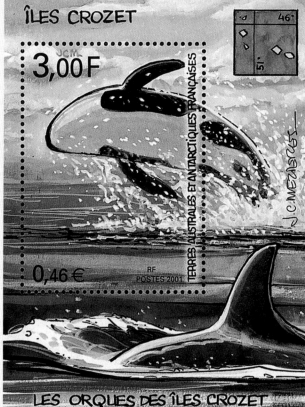

3,00 F

0,46 € RF POSTES 2001

LES ORQUES DES ÎLES CROZET

CANADA 2000
- Narwhal (*Monodon monoceros*): small whale characterized by its long unicorn-like rostrum.
- Blue whale (*Balaenoptera musculus*): migratory, the largest creature ever to have inhabited the earth – up to 100 ft (32m) long and weighing 145 tons. The mother whale feeds her 2-ton calf 44 gallons (200 liters) of milk per day, forcefully expelled underwater.
- Bowhead whale (*Balaena mysticetus*): playful and a slow swimmer; its baleen can be as much as 16 ft (5m) long.
- Beluga or white whale (*Delphinapterus leucas*): has a vast repertoire of sounds with which it communicates.

GHANA 1983
Short-fin pilot whale (*Globicephala macrorhynchus*): small, toothed whale, sedentary.

FRANCE 2002
Bottle-nosed dolphin: common in all temperate oceans. An intelligent mammal, it is popular with the public.

FRENCH SOUTHERN AND ANTARCTIC LANDS 1977
Blue whale.

FRENCH SOUTHERN AND ANTARCTIC LANDS 2001
Orca or killer whale. Despite its attractive appearance it is a deadly predator, feeding on penguins and seals.

MEXICO 4.00 FAUNA de MEXICO

ballena gris (*Eschrichtius robustus*)

JOANA BIELSCHOWSKY T.I.E.V. 1982

MEXICO 1982
Gray whale: 40 to 50 ft (12–15m) in length and weighing 25 to 30 tons, migratory, lives in groups.

JAPAN 1993
Seal and cub on the ice field.

UNITED STATES 1999
Arctic fox (North Pole): its fur remains white all year round.

FRENCH SOUTHERN AND ANTARCTIC LANDS 1978
Sea elephant (weighs over 4 tons). Its nasal appendage acts as an amplifier, making its roar audible for miles around.

ST. PIERRE AND MIQUELON (FR) 2002
Common seal.

FRENCH SOUTHERN AND ANTARCTIC LANDS 1971
Ice fish, member of the weaver family. It has colorless blood that remains liquid even when caught in the ice.

USSR 1987
Polar bear (North Pole).

FRENCH SOUTHERN AND ANTARCTIC LANDS 2003
Colony of emperor penguins (South Pole) with their young.

North and South Poles

245

BIRDS OF THE WORLD

The presence of birds in every part of the world and their fascinating ability to fly has made them the subject of stamps issued by every country on the planet, without exception. It is interesting to note that certain species are found in very different countries, either because they exist universally (for example, roosters and falcons), or because they are migratory (like ducks, geese, swallows, and storks).

The migration record belongs to the Arctic tern: this bird, related to the swallow, covers 25,000 miles (40,000 km) each year, traveling from one Pole to the other following a route mainly over the ocean, and therefore has little opportunity to land and rest! The mystery surrounding the ability of migratory birds to find their way has been the subject of much research.

CHINA 2004
Peacocks.

CHINA 1983
"Birds of good omen."

GREAT BRITAIN 1993
Family of swans.

LIECHTENSTEIN 1986
Migratory swallows (promoting the protection of nature).

ICELAND 1972
Arctic tern (record migratory bird).

CENTRAL AFRICAN REPUBLIC 1981
Guinea fowl.

CHINA 1994
Black-necked crane.

GREAT BRITAIN 1995
Robin.

LUXEMBOURG 1970
Goldcrest (promoting the protection of birds).

GUINEA 1962
Crested crane.

CEYLON 1964
Jungle cock.

MEXICO 1984
Black-bellied duck.

FRANCE 1973
Alsace stork, migrates each year between Europe and Africa.

CHINA 1984
Japanese ibis in flight.

SENEGAL 1978
Gray pelican in the Saloum river delta national park.

GREAT BRITAIN 2000
Gannet colony.

MAURITANIA 1981
Flight of pink flamingos in the Banc d'Arguin national park.

PARAGUAY
The majestic hawk eagle: attacks prey larger than itself.

ST. PIERRE AND MIQUELON (FR) 1998
White-headed eagle: a scavenger more than a predator; migrates long distances.

FRENCH POLYNESIA 1980
Frigate bird: the fastest predator bird on the tropical coast; has a red crop during the mating season.

URUGUAY 1962
Yellow cardinal.

UPPER VOLTA 1965
Long-tailed sunbird.

BRAZIL 1991
Glittering bellied emerald humming bird (*Chlorostilbon aureoventris*): smallest of the birds.

SINGAPORE 2004
Hornbill, with a bony crest on its head.

PORTUGAL 1980
Owl in the moonlight.

BOLIVIA 1995
Andean condor.

MOROCCO 1973
Eleanora's falcon, a slow-flying migratory bird and graceful hunter that dives at extraordinary speed.

TOGO 1972
Paradise Whydah: lays its eggs in other birds' nests, like the cuckoo.

PHILIPPINES 1984
Philippine hanging parrot.

CZECH REPUBLIC 2004
Green-winged macaw *Ara chloroptera*: in the wild it emits a strident shriek; in captivity it can learn to imitate the human voice.

REPTILES, INSECTS, AND BUTTERFLIES

There are more species of insects than of any other living creature, yet insects and reptiles appear far less often on stamps than mammals and birds. Perhaps this is because of the sense of revulsion they induce in many people.

Most stamps featuring insects concentrate either on the possible danger they represent or, by complete contrast, on the beauty of their coloring.

This is certainly true of butterflies, whose colorful wings have inspired stamp issues from nearly every country in the world, making them almost as popular as horses, dogs, and cats. Butterflies have also been the subject of stamps issued by certain countries expressly for collectors and not for postal use; some examples of these issues, described as "unnecessary" by the Universal Postal Union, can be found below.

POLAND 1988
Dragonfly.

Insects

CONGO 1971
Stag beetle: lives in old wood.

SPAIN 1979
Southern European scorpion (now also found in southern England): has a sting that is painful but not deadly.

UNITED STATES 1999
• The scorpionfly is an ancient insect with a long head and is harmless despite its resemblance to a scorpion.
• The jumping spider (which can jump 40 times its body length) has four pairs of eyes, giving it excellent vision. It hunts insects.

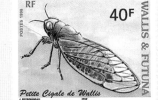

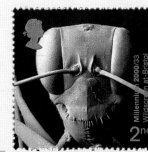

MALI 1977
Praying mantis.

WALLIS AND FUTUNA 1998
The small Wallis cricket.

BELGIUM 1971
Common gadfly.

GREAT BRITAIN 2000
Ant.

JAPAN
Ladybirds.

Amphibians and reptiles

UNITED STATES 2001, GREAT BRITAIN 2001
Frogs.

UNITED STATES 2001
Blue-spotted salamander (has blue markings instead of the usual yellow ones).

INDONESIA 2000
Komodo dragon.

TANZANIA 1993
Mississippi alligator.

GUINEA 1967
African rock python.

FRENCH TERRITORY OF THE AFARS AND ISSAS 1976
Black-necked cobra, whose venom is deadly at full strength.

USSR 1989
Bees.

VIETNAM 1991

NORTH KOREA 1987

Butterflies

CUBA 1982

NICARAGUA 1982

CENTRAL AFRICAN REPUBLIC, ECUADOR 1993
Caterpillar.

UNION ISLAND (ST. VINCENT AND THE GRENADINES)
1985 ("UNNECESSARY" ISSUE)

EQUATORIAL GUINEA
1977
("UNNECESSARY" ISSUE)

NAMIBIA 1993

KAMPUCHEA
(CAMBODIA) 1983

MALAYSIA 1970

TAIWAN 1990

LESOTHO 1984

UNITED STATES 1977

USSR 1991

GREAT BRITAIN 1981

POLAND 1991

BULGARIA 1990
Sphinx moth.

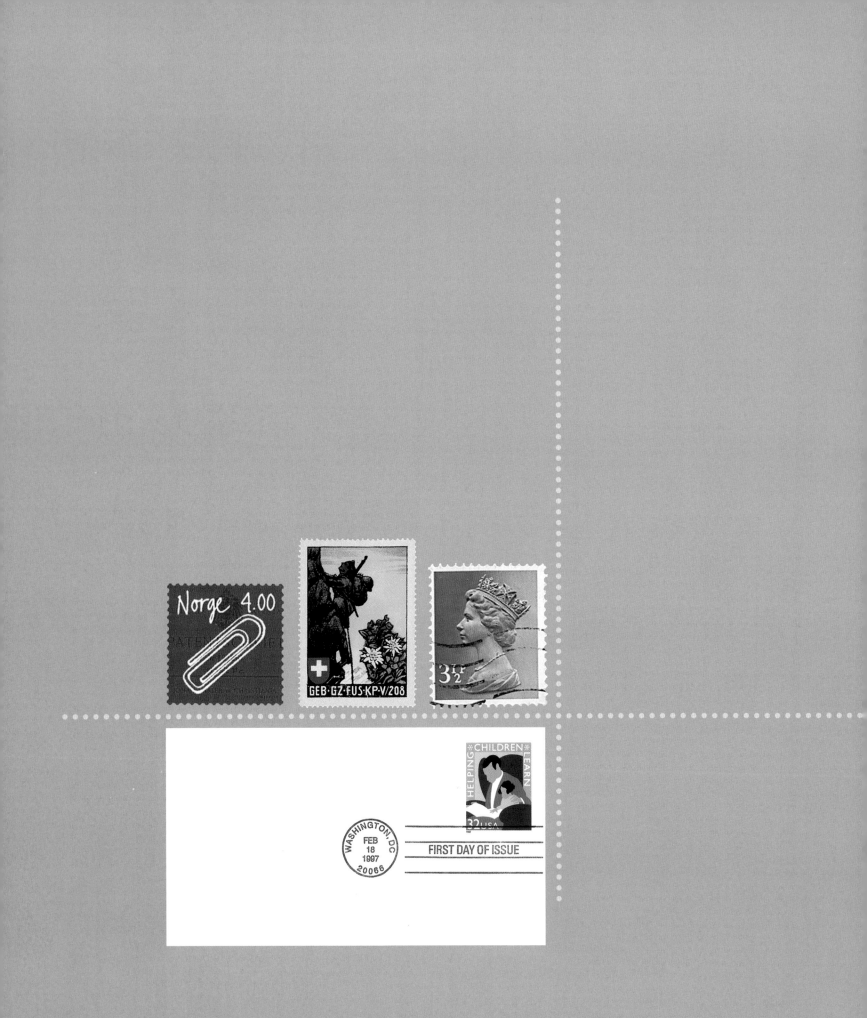

APPENDIX

REMARKABLE STAMPS

THE FATE OF THE "ONE CENT GUYANA"

In 1856, the governor of British Guyana, realizing that the boat bringing stamps from Britain would arrive late, decided to have some provisional stamps of between 1 and 4 cents in value printed locally. Each of these mediocre quality stamps was certified by being signed by an employee at the local post office.

In 1873, a Scottish schoolboy found among his family papers what would prove to be a unique specimen of one of these stamps — a one cent black on magenta — and sold it for 6 shillings (less than US$1) to a dealer. The stamp was sold on for £120, then purchased for £150 in 1900 by a famous French–Austrian collector, Count Philippe von Ferrari. When he died in 1917, the count bequeathed his collection to the Berlin Museum. However, it was confiscated by France as war damages and sold at auction between 1921 and 1925. The one cent Guyana fetched £7,300 in 1922 and was sold on for US$40,000 in 1940, US$240,000 in 1970 and US$935,000 in 1980!

THE WORLD'S MOST EXPENSIVE STAMPS

The series of 1 penny Victoria stamps produced in the 1840s — the world's first stamps — includes many different versions with considerable differences in value.

For example, the stamp shown on the left is from the author's private collection and is worth "only" £40, whereas the most expensive penny black (on an envelope) was sold for US$2.5 million in 1991.

The most expensive American stamp, the Alexandria Blue Boy (Virginia 1846), is a unique black on blue specimen found on a secret love letter. It was sold for US$1 million in Geneva in 1982.

The Swedish 3 skilling banco stamp of 1855, which is yellow instead of green, was sold for US$1,357,000 in 1990.

The 1849 block of four Cérès 1 franc vermilion stamps, one of which is upside down, was sold for €918,000 (over US$1 million) in Paris in 2003 to a purchaser whose identity has remained secret.

The 1847 1 penny vermilion and 2 pence blue from Mauritius, of which only two examples are known to survive, are valued respectively at almost US$1 million and over US$1.3 million. The only known example of a letter stamped with these two stamps, sent from Mauritius to Bordeaux in 1847, was sold for US$4.5 million in Zurich in 1993 — the highest price paid in a stamp auction to this day.

So, in terms of weight, the stamp may well be the world's most expensive commodity.

FORGERIES AND FORGERS

During the 19th century, fraud became a problem mainly for postal authorities with the counterfeiting of ordinary stamps used in the post. Although this produced only a limited amount of profit, it nevertheless required genuine skill on the part of the forger. However, the real profit came from the forging of rare stamps. The principle is as follows: where the difference in value between two similar stamps is substantial, the forger modifies the stamp of lesser value to create one of the rarer examples (by changing color through the use of chemicals, removing the postmark and re-gluing the reverse, adding a surcharge, removing the word "copy" on a legal reproduction of a rare stamp, etc.).

Paradoxically, some "authenticated" forgeries, such as those produced by the famous stamp forger Jean de Spérati at the end of the 19th century, have themselves become highly valued (in this illustration the genuine stamp is on the left, the forgery on the right).

In new condition, the 1.50 franc stamp showing the liner *Normandie* (France 1935) is usually valued at €30. The pale blue version issued as a limited edition when the *Normandie* won the Blue Riband is worth €155; and the rare, greenish-blue version is valued at €25,000. Both these stamps have been the subject of forgery.

Unusual "varieties" of a stamp are also very tempting to the forger. These are stamps put into circulation without the postal authority noticing an anomaly (for example, uneven perforations, a missing color, stamp upside down, etc.), which increases their value; some forgers go so far as to "create" such rare varieties themselves.

Another trap, this time for ordinary collectors, are vignettes intended to deceive: printed with an original design, these appear to be genuine stamps with a face value and a country name, but the country is completely imaginary (Bukhara, Nagaland, etc.) and they have no philatelic value. The stamp above was issued by "Sealand" — a defensive platform constructed during the Second World War in international waters off England, which later became home to offshore radio stations and then Internet sites — but it has no legal value.

Like Philippe von Ferrari, whom we have already mentioned, other well-known 20th-century figures have also been great stamp collectors. They include Prince Rainier III of Monaco, and knowledgeable philatelists like President Roosevelt (seen here on a stamp from Monaco). The Queen of Great Britain has one of the finest stamp collections in the world.

What do philatelists collect? In the first place, stamps, preferably unused (their value is, with some exceptions, higher). However, the number of stamps in the world today is so high (500,000 different stamps and 10,000 new stamps issued each year) that it is impossible to collect them all. So collectors have to limit themselves to a particular country, year, or a very specific theme (for example, not "animals" but "dogs" or even "working dogs"). Among the 120 themes presented in this volume, a would-be collector may perhaps find a suitable subject. Catalogs arranged by country or thematically are an essential tool for identifying which stamps to purchase and knowing what price to offer.

In addition to the stamps themselves and the subject represented, another area of interest to philatelists is the postmark on the stamp or envelope. Rare postmarks can be collected (such as those used by temporary post offices operating during the First World War) or postmarks indicating the adventures that may have befallen an envelope in transit (for example, "envelope recovered from a damaged mail plane," "envelope has been fumigated" – when coming from a country experiencing an epidemic, etc.).

The envelope shown here, addressed to St. Petersburg in Russia, was transported by piloted balloon from Paris in October 1870 in order to get across enemy lines while the city was under siege, but was intercepted by the Germans when the balloon landed in Alsace.

The envelope opposite was part of the first mailbag transported by plane over the Atlantic: when the plane ditched at the end of the crossing, 650 ft (200 m) from the Normandy coast, Captain Byrd rescued the bag, signed each of the envelopes and had them stamped with the Ver-sur-Mer postmark (July 2, 1927). This envelope sold for €3,300 in 2004.

Postal logos attached to postmarks are also collectors' items in their own right. Anything that retraces the life of an envelope that has traveled has a value in philately.

However, the "First Day Cover" postmarks printed on an envelope on the day a new stamp is issued are of limited value to collectors, as the envelope has not really traveled.

Postcards bearing stamps showing the same subject as the card itself are also collectable, providing the stamp is canceled with a postmark to match: these are known as "maximum cards." The postcard here is of the Lourdes basilica in France with a matching stamp canceled with the town postmark.

Great Britain 2000. This image of Queen Elizabeth II, engraved after a bust by Machin, is a classic among young English collectors: over 100 different examples have been issued since 1970, with variations in color and face values to cover all items posted.

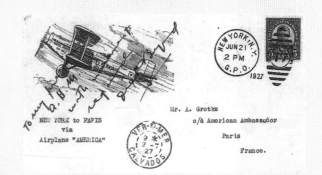

The perforations that give the stamp its characteristic form is an Irish invention dating from 1847, and was adopted within a matter of years by every country in the world. In the block of stamps above (Great Britain 2000), the perforation is missing in two places on each stamp: this is not a fault but a deliberate device used nowadays by some countries to frustrate the work of forgers.

UNUSUAL COLLECTIONS

FRANCE 1999
Heart-shaped stamp issued for St. Valentine's Day.

MALTA 1968
Polygonal stamp.

COLOMBIA 1952
Fiscal stamp, one of the smallest stamps in the world (actual size).

USSR 1988
1918 stamps featured on a 1988 stamp.

Many different themes can form the basis of collections. It is really a matter of individual taste and imagination, but possibilities include stamps in unusual shapes (round, polygonal, heart-shaped, etc.), "stamps on stamps" (issues featuring a famous stamp of the past), stamps in gold or silver (note, these can be difficult to re-sell), and stamps on unusual subjects.

One can also collect the so-called "Cinderella stamps": these are images made to resemble stamps in their format and perforations, but which do not carry the name of a country or a face value. Some are valued in specialist catalogs. They are not normally canceled, except in special cases such as the "stamps" issued by hotels in the Swiss and Austrian Alps during the last century for the transport of their clients' mail to the post office in the valley.

SWITZERLAND
A so-called "regimental" stamp, sold between 1920 and 1940 to raise funds for Swiss military households.

STAMPS ON UNUSUAL SUBJECTS

ARGENTINA 1973
A rather prudent Argentinian postal authority issued this stamp for the presidential election. It shows an empty chair.

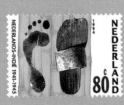

NETHERLANDS 1994
The meaning of this illustration commemorating the Second World War in the Dutch Indies remains cryptic.

NORWAY 1999
Paper clip: one in a series of stamps on Norwegian inventions.

SWITZERLAND 2004
"Ding dong Helvetia": stamp designed by the humorist Emil Steinberger.

AJMAN 1971
Nudes by Baldung and Bronzino (16th century). Issued by Muslim countries, these stamps were intended only for "foreign" collectors.

POSTAL HISTORY

Many stamps from different countries feature the history of postal delivery prior to the invention of the stamp. For many years, the post remained the exclusive privilege of royalty and the Church. The first private message transport services were introduced in the 16th century by Thurn and Taxis in Germany and the Netherlands. Local post services then developed within towns, while a complex tariff system governed the exchange of mail between towns and between countries.

BELGIUM 1959
Charles V receives the oath from J.-B. Taxis, the postmaster general.

AUSTRIA 1972
Messenger of the Vienna local post service (18th century).

MADAGASCAR 1973
Man carrying the post.

PERU 1936
Inca messenger.

FRANCE 1962
Royal messenger in the late Middle Ages.

SPAIN 1985
Monk carrying post between abbeys.

AUSTRALIA 1959
Postmaster on board the brig *Experiment*.

SOUTH VIETNAM 1971
Postilion galloping.

UNITED STATES 1960
Pony Express rider between Sacramento and St. Joseph (1860).

At the change of the millennium, many countries chose to commemorate the great events of the 20th century in their stamps. The United States, for example, issued ten blocks, each featuring events from the ten previous decades. Russia and France issued blocks on specific subjects (culture, society, the sciences, etc.). China and Great Britain issued series on a wide range of subjects, as did Japan with 17 different blocks. Germany was among the countries who abstained from these commemorations.

GREAT BRITAIN 2000
Partial series: expression through movement; Norfolk and Norwich project; cycle lane network; Doncaster Earth Centre.

CHINA 1999
Stamps illustrating the period: Mao Zedong and 1959 stamp; Second World War against Japan (1995); Deng Xiaoping and 1997 stamp; and National Defense (1989).

FRANCE 2000
"The century in stamps": block featuring important moments in the life of society.

JAPAN 2000
The 20th century (eighth series): baseball player; Helen Keller's visit to Japan; planes and clothing of 1937–1940; the writer Yamamoto Yuzo, etc.

RUSSIA 2000
The writer Maxim Gorky and the ballerina Galina Ulanova (stamps from the "Culture" block).

Space Shuttle Launched, Berlin Wall Falls

The space shuttle Columbia, the first reusable spacecraft, was originally launched April 12, 1981. Sandra Day O'Connor became the first female justice on the U.S. Supreme Court, and Sally Ride became the first American woman in space. The Iran-Contra hearings made headlines. Several events signaled the easing of international tensions. In December 1987 President Ronald Reagan and Soviet leader Mikhail Gorbachev signed a nuclear arms reduction treaty. The fall of the Berlin Wall in November 1989 presaged the end of the Cold War. The Vietnam Veterans Memorial was dedicated November 13, 1982. A new national holiday, Martin Luther King Day, was first celebrated in January 1986.

The growth of cable television, video games, and compact discs had a major impact on home entertainment. Dallas and The Cosby Show topped TV ratings. Hip-hop culture and music videos gained popularity.

New Words: yuppie, infomercial, biodiversity.

UNITED STATES 2000
The 1980s: launch of the space shuttle; fall of the Berlin Wall.

Original design: Hokus Pokus Créations (Rennes)

Project Manager, English-language edition: Catherine Burch
Copyeditor, English-language edition: Sandra Stafford
Design Coordinator, English-language edition: Cambridge Publishing Management Limited

Library of Congress Cataloging-in-Publication Data

Lemerle, Laurent.
The world in stamps / Laurent Lemerle.
p. cm.
ISBN 0–8109–5519–9 (hardcover)
1. Postage stamps—Catalogs. I. Title.

HE6224.L46 2006
769.56'4—dc22

2005035231

Printed and bound in France
10 9 8 7 6 5 4 3 2 1

HNA
harry n. abrams, inc.
a subsidiary of La Martinière Groupe

115 West 18th Street
New York, NY 10011
www.hnabooks.com